THE MARVELS OF THE HEART

Kitāb sharḥ ʿajāʾib al-qalb

Book 21 of

The Revival of the Religious Sciences

Iḥyāʾ ʿulūm al-dīn

أَلَا بِذِكْرِ ٱللَّهِ تَطْمَئِنُّ ٱلْقُلُوبُ

Verily in the remembrance of God
do hearts find tranquility

Qurʾān 13:28

AL-GHAZĀLĪ

Kitāb sharḥ ʿajāʾib al-qalb

THE MARVELS OF THE HEART

BOOK 21 of the *Iḥyāʾ ʿulūm al-dīn*

THE REVIVAL OF THE RELIGIOUS SCIENCES

TRANSLATED *from the* ARABIC
with an INTRODUCTION *and* NOTES
by WALTER JAMES SKELLIE
with a FOREWORD *by* T. J. WINTER

FONS VITAE
2010

First published in 2010 by

Fons Vitae
49 Mockingbird Valley Drive
Louisville, KY 40207 USA

www.fonsvitae.com

Library of Congress Control Number: 2010922187

ISBN 978-1-887752-31-2

Editors: Muhammad I. Hozien and Valerie J. Turner
Typesetting: Neville Blakemore, Jr. and Muhammad I. Hozien
Index: Valerie J. Turner
Printer: Friesens Corporation, Canada
Typeface: Adobe Minion Pro, 11/13.5

Printed in Canada

Contents

Foreword

That the "heart" is the center of all our deeper forms of knowing appears to be a truism in the major world religions. In the Islamic universe, the principle that the Qurʾān itself was revealed not to the Prophet's mind but to his heart (2:97; 26:194) led to a permanent division between merely ratiocinative and inspirational forms of religious knowledge. Islamic civilization came to be characterized by the concurrent flow of two rivers, of rationalist and mystical disciplines of knowledge, and most of the time this coexistence was a peaceful one. Formal systematic theologians (*mutakallimūn*) cultivated their sciences in the world of the exoteric *madrasa*, speculating about a God of supreme otherness (*tanzīh*); while the Sufis met in separate lodges (*khanqāh, tekke, zāwiya, daotang*), encountering, in love, the God who may, in a mysterious way, be likened (*tashbīh*) to what we know.

The greatest thinkers of the civilization were often those who theorized about this tension, and sought to produce a universal theology of Islam that could reconcile *tanzīh* with *tashbīh*. This required mastery of all the relevant disciplines, including the legacy of the Greeks as it had been selectively integrated into Islamic thought. The Greeks had themselves faced an analogous tension, which was to some extent reflected by the Aristotelian and Platonic traditions. By the time their culture was assimilated by the Muslims, complex Neoplatonic schemes had attempted, and in some measure achieved, a concord; but it fell to the Muslims to reconcile this late Hellenistic system with the givens of revealed monotheism. With its focus on the undifferentiated One, Islam was, in an important way, more hospitable to the Greek legacy than was trinitarian Christianity, and its rapid and permanent assimilation, visible in the great texts of medieval theology, including those of Ghazālī, is not surprising.

Surveying the *madrasa* texts, one might think that Islam was an entirely rationalizing tradition, with logic at the heart of the core disciplines of theology and law. This impression would be confirmed even by a careful reading of Ghazālī's formal metaphysical works: the *Incoherence of the Philosophers*, the *Jerusalem Epistle*, and the *Just Mean in Belief*. To the end of his life he continued to recognize the community's urgent need for a formal theology that could refute the myriad errors that appeared in the diverse intellectual and cultural landscape of the central Islamic lands. However, Ghazālī's greatness and his impact do not lie primarily in these texts, in spite of their brilliance. Instead, the Muslim world found itself convinced by Ghazālī's claim that the inspired or revealed knowledge, which, as he says in Chapter 8 of this book, is acknowledged as a possibility even by the formal philosophers and theologians, is not as unlikely and as inaccessible an event as the exoterists believe. Ghazālī proposed a model of theology that put discussions of *tanzīh* and *tashbīh* in their due relation, and showed how religion alone, and not Greek philosophy, could define this.

Avicenna (Ibn Sīnā), and the fashionable philosophical stream that followed him, preferred a path to the higher intelligibles that lay through the correction of intellectual understanding, combined, as he suggests in some of his later works, with some form of spiritual discipline. Avicenna's actual form of spiritual liberation, however, seemed problematic to many: the "best friend of the wise," according to him, was wine, with its power to free the mind; and some sources record that his wine drinking played a part in his final demise. For Ghazālī, there was certainly immense richness in Avicenna's theory of the soul, but his spiritual method seemed inadequate. What the community needed, he concluded, was a highly intellectual conception of the soul, which could be shown to be compatible with revelation, driven by a method of spiritual growth rooted entirely in Sufism.

In the Sufi literature, and in the teaching of his own spiritual instructors, Ghazālī had discovered a vast body of information and counsel about the "heart." The Qur᾽ān and *ḥadīth* had not defined the heart, and instead merely took it for granted as part of a human being's first-order knowledge about himself. The *nuẓẓār*, the Hellenized theologians and philosophers, could elaborate on the "heart," and their analysis might well be helpful to those who were curious about the arrangement and nature of its faculties. Its "wonders," however, were to be detected in the course of a process of spiritual purgation. The heart contains signs of God that are no less astonishing, and no less indicative of the divine creative nature than are God's signs in nature (Qurʾān 41:53).

This helps to explain the tenor of this work. Ghazālī is not only explaining the geography of this inner kingdom, to help his readers better assimilate the later sections of his *Revival*, which will deal with the specific threats that can subvert it, but also, throughout, he is inviting us to consider the faculties of the human self as intrinsically extraordinary. Thus he motivates us not only to read further, but to reflect on God's creative power and His purposes for us. If the Qurʾān tells us that the heart is the essence of man, so that the Prophet on his Ascension saw the highest perfection *with his heart* (53:11), and if revelation itself descended 'on his heart', then the heart is the unique interface of the eternal and the finite realms, where the "event horizon," to borrow a term from modern physics, exists in the world while breaking all the rules, to produce miracles and "signs." The heart, therefore, is like the Kaʿba itself, whose Black Stone "fell from Heaven," and which represents, in its aporetic mystery, the eternity of God, approachable only through rituals of self-purification, not logic and formal analysis.

As elsewhere in the *Revival of the Religious Sciences*, one receives the impression that Ghazālī's account is motivational, and that he does not propose this account of an essentially mysterious fact as quite factual. His psychological doctrines, as most recently and lucidly explained by Timothy Gianotti in *Al-Ghazālī's Unspeakable Doctrine of the Soul* [Leiden: Brill, 2001], form part of a complex hierarchy of knowledges, and are to be understood as props to the beginner's understanding, laced with coded clues to something deeper. His deeper system is to be disclosed only to the elect, who have already made substantial progress in their inward journeys. Because of the danger of misunderstanding by those who understand only outward words (*ʿibāra*) and whose hearts are still unreceptive to mystical allusions (*ishāra*), the full doctrine of the soul must remain veiled, to be spoken of only in the closed circles of those who will be sure to understand it in ways that cannot clash with formal theology.

It is fortunate that this translation, so long available only in photocopy to academic cognoscenti, is now entering the world of print, and Fons Vitae, now emerging as America's principal sponsor of translations of Islamic texts, is to be warmly congratulated on making this important book available.

T. J. Winter
University of Cambridge

Editor's Note

This translation of *Kitāb sharḥ ajāʾib al-qalb*, book 21 of the *Iḥyāʾ ʿulūm al-dīn* of Ḥujjat al-Islam, Abū Ḥāmid al-Ghazālī, was originally presented in April 1938 by Walter James Skellie as a PhD dissertation at the Kennedy School of Missions, Hartford Seminary. The title was "The Religious Psychology of al-Ghazzālī: A Translation of his Book of the *Iḥyāʾ* on the Explanation of the Wonders of the Heart, with Introduction and Notes." Given its specific purpose, as a dissertation at a theological seminary (and the time in which it was written—seventy-two years ago), certain changes were necessary to make the work more accessible to modern readers and appropriate for a broader audience familiar with Islam and its texts.

Skellie's introduction is included here, without pages liv–lxxi, which are a summary of Imam al-Ghazālī's book. This has been omitted as being an unnecessary and cursory restatement of Imam al-Ghazālī's definitions, metaphors, and parables that is repetitious when it appears before the translation itself; ultimately it detracts from the readers' discovery of Imam al-Ghazālī's own more eloquent style. While Skellie naturally used the Qurʾān translations available to him at the time (Rodwell, 1924 and Palmer, 1928), we have made use of modern translations by A. J. Arberry, Marmaduke Pickthall, A. Yusuf Ali, and the Saheeh International edition (listed in full in the bibliography). Qurʾānic verse numbers have been adjusted to follow the standard Cairo edition, rather than that of Flügel. In the text, where Imam al-Ghazālī has written the beginning of a verse and noted "to the end of the verse," in accord with contemporary practices, the editors have completed these verses in hard brackets for the benefit of the reader.

With regard to blessings on prophets and others, Skellie states in a footnote: "The eulogistic phrases are translated at their first occurance and then generally omitted." The editors have returned these blessings to accord with the outlook and intention of Imam al-Ghazālī, who, in keeping with his faith, referred to God, the Exalted (*subḥānahu wa-taʿāla*) and after mentioning any of the prophets or their companions, added the invocations, as outlined in the following table with the appropriate Arabic glyphs (where available).

Arabic glyph	English meaning	Usage
عزّ وجلّ	Mighty and majestic is He	on mention of God
عليه السلام	Peace be upon him	on mention of a prophet
عليهم السلام	Peace be upon them	on mention of more than one prophet
صلى الله عليه وسلم	May the peace and blessings of God be upon him	on mention of the Prophet Muḥammad, and on occasion following the mention of other prophets
رضي الله عنه	May God be pleased with him	on mention of a companion of the Prophet Muḥammad
رضي الله عنها	May God be pleased with her	on mention of a female companion of the Prophet Muḥammad
رضي الله عنهم	May God be pleased with them	on mention of several companions of the Prophet Muḥammad

In addition, Arabic terms have been adjusted to adhere to the transliteration system utilized by the *International Journal of Middle East Studies*; Greek terms are transliterated. Common Era (CE) dates have been added. Wherever the translator has referred to a citation in the first edition of the *Encyclopaedia of Islam*, the editors have added citations to the *Encyclopaedia of Islam*, second edition (EI^2), which is more readily available. Additional modern sources added by the editors are noted as such in the footnotes and also appear in the bibliography, which has been included in full and reorganized. Finally, an index has been compiled for the benefit of the reader. Further, *ḥadīth* terminology has been standardized and made consistent throughout the work, to reflect common usage in Islamic scholarly texts.

With regard to the texts used, Skellie notes that the translation was made from the text in *Itḥāf al-sāda al-muttaqīn*, which is the commentary on the *Iḥyāʾ* by Murtaḍā al-Zabīdī. He notes that references were also made to other texts, as follows:

1. *Iḥyāʾ ʿulūm al-dīn*, published by Muṣṭafā al-Bābī al-Ḥalabī (Cairo, 1346/1927), hereafter referred to as Cairo text.
2. The text of the *Iḥyāʾ* in the margin of the *Itḥāf*.
3. A manuscript in the Princeton University Library, probably from the fifteenth century. It is no. 1481, and is described in *A Descriptive Catalog of the Garrett Manuscripts Deposited in the Princeton University Library* (Princeton University Press, 1938), p. 448. It is referred to as Princeton MS.
4. A recently acquired manuscript called *Maḥajjat al-bayḍāʾ fī iḥyāʾ al-iḥyāʾ* (dated 1047/1647), which is a text with occasional comment. It is referred to as *Maḥajjat* MS. Where both manuscripts agree they are indicated by MSS.

We believe that the Cairo text is the closest to the completed work of Imam al-Ghazālī; as such it is the text used by the vast majority of translators of the *Iḥyāʾ*. Zabīdī's commentary did not include the complete text of the *Iḥyāʾ*, as stated on the cover page, rather this was added to the margins. Skellie's translation does include the missing portion in the notes; these portions have now been restored to the main text, with only the differences between the manuscripts indicated in the footnotes. Thus this work is a complete translation of *Kitāb sharḥ ajāʾib al-qalb* of the *Iḥyāʾ* as published in the Cairo edition.

Translator's Introduction

A Biographical Sketch of Ghazālī

Abū Ḥāmid Muḥammad b. Muḥammad b. Aḥmad al-Ghazālī al-Ṭūsī was born in Ṭūs, Persia, in the year 450/1058–9 and died in 505/1111. His biography has been thoroughly studied and sympathetically written by competent authorities,[1] and an understanding of his life is indispensable for any adequate understanding of his principles of religious psychology as found in this book from his great work, *Iḥyāʾ ʿulūm al-dīn*. Only a brief summary of the principal events of his life can be given here.

Ghazālī's father died when his son, who was to achieve such fame, was but a small boy. Before his death, the father gave his two sons into the charge of a Sufi friend who faithfully cared for them and began their training. Ghazālī studied in a *madrasa* in Ṭūs and later in Jurjān and Nīshāpūr. In this last place, his teacher was a famous and devout Sufi, Abū al-Maʿālī ʿAbd al-Mālik al-Juwaynī, better known as Imām al-Ḥaramayn. Ghazālī remained with him as his pupil and probably also his assistant until the death of the Imam. He was a faithful student and acquired a broad knowledge of many branches of learning. By his diligent application and constant study he probably did lasting injury to his health at this period of his life.

1 Editor's note: The sources used by the translator are now somewhat dated. The following biographical references are readily accessible: Eric Ormsby, *Ghazali: The Revival of Islam* (Oxford, UK: Oneworld, 2008); Margaret Smith, *Al-Ghazali, The Mystic* (London: Luzac & Co., 1944); W. Montgomery Watt, *Muslim Intellectual: A Study of al-Ghazali* (Edinburgh: Edinburgh University Press, 1963); Frank Griffel, *Al-Ghazālī's Philosophical Theology* (New York: Oxford University Press, 2009); and Ebrahim Moosa, *Ghazālī and the Poetics of Imagination* (Chapel Hill: University of North Carolina Press, 2005).

After the death of the Imām al-Ḥaramayn, Ghazālī went to the court of the great vizier, Niẓām al-Mulk,[2] where he won fame and praise for his learning. He was later appointed to teach in the great school at Baghdad, and there he lectured to some three hundred students and gave legal opinions of great importance. He preached to large and appreciative crowds in the mosque, and he prospered in material things.

But although he was outwardly successful, he had no peace of heart. He experienced a deep and lasting change in his life. In all his study and learning he had not found reality, and he was now plunged into the depths of skepticism. He sought the answer to the doubts of his soul in scholastic theology, in the teaching of the Taʿlīmīs,[3] who said that one must follow an infallible living teacher, and in the study of philosophy, but the result was not satisfying. He turned to the study of Sufism, and then realized that what he needed was not so much religious instruction as religious experience. He saw that his own life was so full of sham and covetousness that if he continued thus he could not possibly find rest or reality. His mental state so affected his physical condition that it was impossible for him to continue teaching.

In the year 488/1095, he suddenly forsook position, wealth, and fame, and withdrew from the world. The brilliant teacher who had gloried in worldly success and royal favor now turned his back upon it all and became a wandering dervish ascetic. He had been given divine grace to renounce all for an experiential knowledge of God. He lived in Damascus, visited Jerusalem, and Hebron, and made the pilgrimage to Mecca and Medina. Finally, drawn by the ties of family affection, and recognizing the propriety of such relationships, he returned to Baghdad. This period of retirement and wandering was filled with the practice of devotional exercises and the study and writing of books. Early in this period he wrote his masterpiece, *Iḥyāʾ ʿulūm al-dīn*, and he taught it in Damascus and Baghdad. It is quite possible that he revised this work at a later period in his life.

Ghazālī's return to public life came in 499/1106 when he was appointed to teach in the school at Nīshāpūr, but he only remained there for a short time. He desired a life of retirement and meditation on spiritual things, and so removed to his native city of Ṭūs, where he established a Sufi school

2 The Seljuq vizier, Niẓām al-Mulk, r. 451 or 455–485/1059 or 1063–1092. See *EI*², 8:69.

3 The Taʿlīmīs were Nizārī Ismāʿīlīs.

and *khānaqā*. There he spent his time in study and meditation until his end came quietly in the year 505/1111.

From his own day up to the present time, Ghazālī has held a secure position of leadership in Islam. With him the religious philosophy and experience of Islam reached its zenith, and the system of ethics which he produced has become the final authority for orthodox Islam. His was a warming and revitalizing influence upon Islam in his own day, and it has continued to be such in a potent way to this day. The vitality of his experience, the breadth of his learning, the high plane on which he lived his own transformed life, and the depth of his desire to serve God and his fellow people in complete and self denying devotion made him the man whose influence is considered by many to have been second to none among the leaders of Islam, save that of Muḥammad ﷺ himself.

Al-Sayyid al-Murtaḍā al-Zabīdī, in his commentary on the *Iḥyāʾ* called *Itḥāf al-sāda al-muttaqīn*, has a lengthy treatise on the life and influence of Ghazālī. In it he shows how many Muslim writers have used Ghazālī's books and ideas as a basis for their own thinking and writing. The fact that new books on Ghazālī are still being written by modern Muslim writers and by Western orientalists is conclusive evidence of his high place in the world of Muslim thought. Jibrān Khalīl Jibrān, well-known as a writer both in English and Arabic, wrote of Ghazālī in his book *al-Badāʾiʿ wa-l-ṭarāʾif*, as follows:

> Al-Ghazālī holds a very high place in the minds of Western orientalists and scholars. They place him along with Ibn Sīnā and Ibn Rushd in the first rank of oriental philosophers. The spiritually minded among them consider him to represent the noblest and highest thought which has appeared in Islam. Strange to say, I saw on the walls of a church in Florence, Italy, built in the fifteenth century, a picture of al-Ghazālī among the pictures of other philosophers, saints, and theologians whom the leaders of the Church in the middle ages considered as the pillars and columns in the temple of Absolute Spirit.
>
> Perhaps stranger than this is the fact that the people of the West know more about al-Ghazālī than do the people of the East. They translate his works and investigate his teachings and search out carefully his philosophic contentions and mystic aims. But we, who still speak and write Arabic, seldom mention al-Ghazālī or discuss him. We are still busied with the shells, as though shells

> were all that come out from the sea of life to the shores of days and nights.[4]

Another quotation will be given from a book used in Egyptian secondary and teacher training schools in the study of the history of Arabic literature. It is *al-Wasīṭ fī-l-ādāb al-ʿarabī wa-tārīkhihi* by Shaykh Aḥmad al-Iskandarī and Shaykh Muṣṭafā ʿInānī, as follows:

> There is a real soul bond between al-Ghazālī and St. Augustine. They are two similar appearances of one principle, in spite of the sectarian and social differences existing between their times and environments. This principle is an instinctive inclination within the soul which leads its possessor on step by step from things seen and their external appearances to the things of reason, philosophy, and divinity.
>
> Al-Ghazālī separated himself from the world and from the luxury and high position which he had in it, and lived the lonely solitary life of a mystic, penetrating deeply into the search for those fine threads which join the utmost limits of science to the beginnings of religion; and searching diligently for that hidden vessel in which men's perceptions and experiences are mingled with their feelings and dreams.
>
> Augustine had done this five centuries before him. Whoever reads his book *Confessions* will find that he took the earth and everything derived therefrom as a ladder on which to mount up to the secret thought of the Supreme Being.
>
> However I have found al-Ghazālī to be nearer to the real essence of things and their secrets than St. Augustine was. Perhaps the reason for this lies in the difference between the Arab and Greek scientific theories which preceded his time to which the former fell heir, and the theology which occupied the fathers of the Church in the second and third centuries C.E., which the latter inherited. By inheritance I mean the thing which is passed on with the age from one mind to another, just as certain physical attainments are constant in the external appearance of peoples from age to age.

---

4 Jibrān Khalīl Jibrān, *al-Badāʾiʿ wa-l-ṭarāʾif* (Cairo, 1923), pp. 116–8.

> I found in al-Ghazālī that which makes him a golden link joining the mystics of India who had preceded him with the seekers for the divine who followed him. For in the attainments of Buddhist thought there is something akin to al-Ghazālī; and likewise in what Spinoza and William Blake have written in modern times there is something of his feelings.
>
> Al-Ghazālī is considered as a supporter of the Ashʿarī sect called the people of the Sunna, and as one of the greatest of Shāfiʿī imams. He is reckoned as the best of those who spoke on asceticism, being unlike to the Sufi sects which went beyond the ordinary experience of the human reason. His book, *Iḥyāʾ ʿUlūm al-Dīn*, is one of the finest books on asceticism, ethics, and exposition of the wisdom of the Qurʾān and the Sharīʿa. His writings on these subjects are most eloquent, and his style of writing is aimed at by scholars in this field and by other reformers even up to the present time.[5]

As a writer, Ghazālī was not original in the use of the material that he incorporated in his many books. This was only natural in the light of his experience of studying and searching for truth from so many different sources. He was influenced by all of the systems that he studied, and he appropriated for his own teaching what he deemed to be the truth, wherever he found it. He followed the teaching of the proverb he quoted (page 109), "Eat the vegetable wherever it comes from, and do not ask where the garden is." He took such from his study of the philosophy of al-Fārābī and Ibn Sīnā, especially the latter. He frequently quotes the *Qūt al-qulūb* of Abū Ṭālib al-Makkī and [al-Qushayrī's] *al-Risāla al-Qushayriyya*, and he shows the influence of al-Ḥārith al-Muḥāsibī, Abū Yazīd al-Bisṭāmī, al-Shiblī, and others whose works he studied.[6]

In summing up an article on Ghazālī's debt to al-Muḥāsibī, Margaret Smith writes:

> These examples ... show clearly al-Ghazālī's indebtedness to his great predecessor, both for the main trend of his ascetical, devotional, and mystical teaching and for many of the ideas and

5 Aḥmad al-Iskandarī and Muṣṭafā ʿInānī, *al-Wasīṭ fi-l-ādāb al-ʿarabī wa-tārīkhihi* (Cairo, 1925).

6 Abū Ḥāmid al-Ghazālī, *al-Munqidh min al-ḍalāl*, trans. Claud Field as *The Confessions of Al-Ghazzali* (New York: E. P. Dutton and Co., 1909), p. 41.

> illustrations of which he makes use in his rule for the religious life .... The foundations of that great system of orthodox Islamic mysticism which al-Ghazālī made it his business to bring to completion, had already been well and truly laid.[7]

But Ghazālī did more than merely cite quotations from these sources; he wove them into a harmonious system based upon his own experience of gaining and realizing reality. His whole moral philosophy was a synthesis and a practical expression of the golden mean. He took the rigid framework of the scholastic theologian and clothed it with the warm personal faith of the mystic. To the knowledge of the philosopher, gained through the processes of study, reasoning, and deduction, he added the inner knowledge of the Sufi who sees with the light of certainty, and experiences direct revelations and unveilings of the divine Reality. He was careful, however, to avoid the vagaries of extreme Sufism and especially its tendencies to antinomianism and pantheism. He united the best results of philosophic speculation with Islam, and, while denying the materialism of the philosophers, he nevertheless used their methods to develop his own thought and to refute them where they differed with the teachings of Islam.

Ghazālī put great emphasis upon man's need for spiritual leaders, and his *Iḥyāʾ* gives the ethical teachings of a kindly shepherd who cares for his flock. He was considerate and humane in his dealings with men in general, and, although he was criticized by some, he was slow to refute those who disagreed with him. Even when he did engage the philosophers, his chief concern was to point out the errors of their system of thought and teaching, rather than to denounce them personally.

A Sketch of Ghazālī's Psychology

Introduction

The fact that Ghazālī uses the term "heart" instead of soul in the title of this book is an indication of the primary position this word had in the vocabulary of Muslim religious teachers, and also in that of the philosophers. The term was used in Islam for the seat of intellectual and emotional life even as it had already been used by Judaism and Christianity. Among the Greeks and Romans, the heart took the place of the liver as the seat

7 Margaret Smith, "The Forerunner of al-Ghazzālī," *JRAS* (January 1936), pp. 65–76.

of life, soul, intellect, and emotion.[8] Aristotle gave the heart the place of honor as the seat of the noblest emotions.[9]

Although Ghazālī uses the term 'secrets' of the heart as a synonym for its 'marvels,' it apparently does not connote any special mystical signification, though it has such a meaning in Sufi usage. The heart is the seat of secrets.[10]

Ghazālī limits the discussion of the subject largely to the field of knowledge of proper conduct (*ʿilm al-muʿāmala*). His aim is ethical, and, although he does, sometimes, inevitably deal with questions of metaphysics, it is nevertheless with ethics that he is primarily concerned. He would not go as far as Zeno and reduce all virtues to practical wisdom (*phronēis*),[11] yet that was, for him, the important way of achieving his desired end, the good life.[12] He agreed with Aristotle that understanding included both wisdom (*sophia*) and practical sense (*phronēis*);[13] but what he stressed was the latter, which they both held to be "practical ability, under rational direction, in the choice of things good and avoidance of things which are evil for man."[14] This practical end was kept ever in view by Ghazālī as the logical outcome of man's knowledge and experience.

The Nature of the Soul

In order to understand clearly Ghazālī's concept of the nature of the heart, or soul, it is necessary to discuss four terms that are applied to it. They are: 'heart' (*qalb*); 'spirit' (*rūḥ*); 'soul' (*nafs*); and 'intelligence' (*ʿaql*). Each of these terms has two meanings, but the second meaning of each term is the same as the second meaning of each of the other three terms.

---

8 *Encyclopaedia of Religion and Ethics*, ed. James Hastings, 13 vols. (New York: C. Scribner's Sons, 1908–27), 6:557.

9 George Sidney Brett, *A History of Psychology*, 3 vols. (London: Allen and Unwin, 1912–21), 1:106; *Aristotle*, ed. W. D. Ross (London, 1923), p. 143n1.

10 Muḥammad Aʿlā b. ʿAlī Tahānawī, *Kitāb kashshāf iṣṭilāḥāt al-funūn*, trans. as *Dictionary of the Technical Terms used in the Sciences of the Musulmans*, 2 vols. (Calcutta, 1862), p. 653.

11 Friedrich Ueberweg, *A History of Philosophy*, 2 vols. (New York: Scribners, 1901), 1:200.

12 *Aristotle*, ed. G. R. G. Mure (New York, 1932), p. 129.

13 Brett, *Psychology*, 1:144.

14 Ueberweg, *Philosophy*, 1:176.

The term 'heart' (*qalb*) means the heart of flesh in the body of a man or animal, whether living or dead; but it also means that subtle tenuous substance, spiritual in nature, which is the knowing and perceiving essence of man. There is some connection between the physical heart and this spiritual 'heart,' but practical wisdom and prophetic precedent do not demand nor warrant the explanation of this relationship.

'Spirit' (*rūḥ*) means that refined material substance which is produced by the blood in the left cavity of the heart and which rises up to the brain and passes to all parts of the body through the blood vessels carrying the animal powers of life and sense perception.[15] This resembles Aristotle's theory of the *pneuma* as a "sentient organism of a subtle nature spread through the body and acting as the universal medium of sensation."[16] 'Spirit' also means the above-mentioned subtle spiritual substance which is the second meaning of 'heart.'

The third term is 'soul' (*nafs*). This may mean the life-giving soul whose seat is in the heart.[17] Jurjānī defines *nafs* as "that refined vaporous substance (*jawhar*) which bears the powers of life, sense perception, and voluntary motion," and says that al-Ḥakīm (Ibn Sīnā) called it the animal spirit (*al-rūḥ al-ḥayawaniyya*). Ghazālī and other Sufi writers commonly bring the word *nafs*, which is the ordinary Arabic equivalent for the *psychē* of Greek philosophy, down to the appetitive soul (*epithymia*), in which are united man's blameworthy qualities. This is the *psychē* of Pauline theology and the *nephesh* of Hebrew. It is not clear from this book of the *Iḥyāʾ*, nor from his *Maʿārij al-quds fī madārij maʿrifat al-nafs*, or *al-Risāla al-ladunniyya*, or *Kīmiyāʾ al-saʿāda*, whether or not Ghazālī held that the 'soul' in this sense was material or immaterial in its nature. Some hints of a material soul are found, for example in *Kīmiyāʾ al-saʿāda*,[18] where he speaks of the *nafs* as the vehicle (*markab*) of the heart, a term usually applied to the body; and again in *al-Risāla al-ladunniyya*[19] where he says that Sufis call the animal spirit (*al-rūḥ al-ḥayawānī*) a *nafs*. The clearest hint is perhaps that in *Mīzān al-ʿamal*,[20] where he speaks of the two meanings of the soul

15 Murtaḍa al-Zabīdī, *Itḥāf al-sāda al-muttaqīn*, 10 vols. (Cairo: Būlāq, 1311/1893), 7:203; see note on page 7.

16 Brett, *Psychology*, 1:119.

17 Hastings, *Religion and Ethics*, 1:679b.

18 Ghazālī, *Kīmiyāʾ al-saʿāda* (Cairo: Saʿāda Press, 1343), pp. 8, 10.

19 Ibid., p. 27.

20 Ibid., pp. 18, 20.

as the animal soul (*al-nafs al-ḥayawāniyya*) and the human soul (*al-nafs al-insāniyya*). It is clear that there is in Islam the concept of a material *nafs*.[21] But Ghazālī does not stress the nature of this appetitive soul as regards its materiality or immateriality, but rather as regards its characteristic of uniting the blameworthy qualities of man. These blameworthy qualities are the animal powers in man that are opposed to his rational powers.[22] It is thus, like Plato's irrational soul, made up of anger (*ghaḍab, thymos*) and appetence (*shahwa, epithymia*).

The second meaning of *nafs* is that subtle spiritual substance which is the real essence of man.

The fourth term is 'intelligence' or 'reason' (*ʿaql*). This word is commonly used to translate the Greek *nous*. *ʿAql* is applied to man's knowledge of the true nature of things, and also to his power to perceive and know. This latter meaning is that same subtle spiritual substance of which Aristotle said, "Reason, more than anything else, is man."[23]

It is this second meaning, common to all four terms, of which al-Ghazālī writes in the volume before us. Thus his concept of 'heart,' or 'soul,' may be defined as that subtle tenuous substance, spiritual in nature, which is the perceiving and knowing essence of man, and in reality is man. Its seat is the physical heart. It is immaterial and immortal. It is created directly by God, capable of knowing Him, and is morally responsible to Him.

Ghazālī, following Ibn Sīnā and other Arab philosophers, conceived of the human soul as being between the lower realm of the animal and the higher realm of the divine, and as partaking of the characteristics of each of these realms.[24] In the elaboration of their doctrine of the soul they combined the ideas of Plato and Aristotle, and joined to them additional ideas from Neoplatonic sources. Perhaps the most systematic statement of the resulting doctrine of the soul is that given by Ibn Sīnā, which may be summarized in the following scheme, as adapted from Hastings, *Encyclo-*

---

21 Macdonald, "The Development of the Idea of Spirit in Islam," *Acta Orientalia* 9 (1931), reprinted in *Moslem World* 22 (1932), pp. 25–46. ʿAlī b. Muḥammad al-Jurjānī, *Kitāb al-taʿrīfāt*, ed. Gustav Flügel (Leipzig: Sumptibus F. C. G. Vogelii, 1845), pp. 1396ff.

22 Ghazālī, *Maʿārij al-quds* (Cairo 1346/1927), p. 11.

23 *Nicomachean Ethics*, 1177 b 26–78 a 7, in *Aristotle*, ed. Mure, p. 165.

24 Brett, *Psychology*, 2:484; Plotinus, *The Essence of Plotinus*, based on the translation of Stephen Mackenna (New York: Oxford University Press, 1934), III, ii, 8.

paedia of Religion and Ethics.[25] [The soul is divided into three: vegetative, animal, and human (rational) soul.] Each one of these divisions is further subdivided as follows:

Vegetative Soul	Powers of nutrition		
	Powers of growth		
	Powers of reproduction		
Animal Soul	Motive faculties	Appetitive power	attractive power (concupiscence)
			repulsive power (irascibility and passion)
		Efficient power	in motor nerves and muscles
	Perceptive faculties	External	sight hearing smell taste touch
		Internal	common sense formative faculty cognitive faculty estimative faculty memory
Human or Rational Soul	Active Intelligence (practical reason)		
	Speculative Intelligence (theoretical reason) perceives ideas by		material intellect or potentiality of knowledge
			intellect of possession recognizes axiomatic knowledge
			perfected intellect lays hold on intelligibles

This system was adopted in large part by Ghazālī, and it formed the framework of his philosophy of mind.

25 *Religion and Ethics*, 2:274ff. Cf. Brett, *Psychology*, 2:54ff.; Muʿtazid Weliur-Rahman, "The Psychology of Ibn-i-Sina," *Islamic Culture* 9, no. 2 (April 1935), pp. 341ff.

In analyzing the above scheme as developed by Ghazālī in this book we find ideas corresponding to the Platonic thought of the rational and irrational souls.[26] The rational soul, according to Plato, was created by God and placed in the head, but the irrational part was the creation of the *demiourgoi*. Its nobler part is anger, or the spirited, irascible nature (*thymos*), and has its seat in the heart or thorax; while the base part, which is appetence, or the concupiscible nature (*epithymia*), has its seat in the abdominal cavity.

For Ghazālī, of course, God is the Creator of all that man is and does, and he follows Aristotle in holding that the heart is the seat of the rational soul. But, in spite of these differences, the Platonic division is an important part of the thinking of Ghazālī.[27] Plato's 'rational soul' is Ghazālī's 'soul,' or 'heart,' or 'intellect,' depending on the illustrations he uses. The irrational soul of Plato includes the powers of appetence and anger which, for him and for Ghazālī too, must be held in check by the rational soul or intellect. When the intellect dominates these lower powers, justice is established for both soul and body, but when the lower powers dominate the intellect, it becomes their slave. The excellence or virtue of the rational soul is wisdom, that of anger is courage, and that of appetence is temperance.[28]

Even more clearly do we see the Aristotelian analysis in Ghazālī's psychology with its vegetative, animal, and human 'souls.'[29] Aristotle tried to explain accurately the phenomena of psychic life, approaching it from the side of metaphysics.[30] All known things are included in an ascending scale from pure matter to pure form. The body alone is matter, and the soul alone is form. The sphere of psychology is the relationship of the two (*to empsychon*). Soul and body must be defined in relation to each other. The soul is the true essence of that which we call body, and is man in reality. It is the first actualization (*entelechy*) of the body, and represents a possibility of psychic activity. The second entelechy is the actual realization of this possibility. This is illustrated in the eye that has the power to see

---

26 Brett, *Psychology*, 1:68; Plato, *Timaeus*, trans. R. G. Bury (London: Loeb Classical Library, 1929), 44 E, 69 E, 70 B D E. Cf. Aristotle, *De Anima*, trans. W. S. Hett (London: W. Heinemann, 1935), I, i; III, ix; Plotinus, *Essence*, IV, viii, 5–8.

27 Cf. note on page 7.

28 Brett, *Psychology*, 1:97.

29 Aristotle, *De Anima*, II, i; III, ix; *Aristotle*, ed. Mure, pp. 95ff. Cf. Plotinus, *Essence*, III, iv, 2. See note on page 25.

30 Brett, *Psychology*, 1:100ff.

even when that power is inactive, as in sleep; and the eye that is actually seeing. Ghazālī holds quite a similar position, and gives the same illustration of powers, potential and actual.

Man's power of reaction is threefold: He absorbs nourishment and reproduces, as does the plant. He has sense perceptions, powers of discrimination, and voluntary movement like the animal. He differs from them both in possessing rational power, and is capable of that higher knowledge that includes the knowledge of God. By virtue of this quality of experiential knowledge, man occupies a place between the animals and the angels. "There are in him the desires of the beast united with a reason that is godlike."[31] By neglecting the rational soul he can sink toward the level of the animal, and by cultivating it he can strive toward the level of the angels.

The Soul's Knowledge and Its Acquisition

According to the Neoplatonic idea of man, "Knowledge is always an activity of the soul."[32] Through this activity man gains a firm and lasting grasp of reality. Ghazālī held that man's peculiar glory is the aptitude which he has for that highest of all kinds of knowledge, the knowledge of God. In this knowledge is man's joy and happiness. The seat of this knowledge is the heart, which was created to know Him, just as the eye was created to see objective forms. The physical members are used by the heart to attain the end of knowledge even as the craftsman uses his tool to accomplish his purposes. Man's potential capacity for knowledge is practically unlimited, that is, save by infinity itself.

Although knowledge may, to a certain degree, be the result of man's activity, yet it requires a cause outside of man himself to bestow true wisdom. Plato found this outside cause in the world of Ideas. Aristotle said that intelligence (*nous*) comes into man "from without as something divine and immortal."[33] Intelligence is not a mere function of the natural body. "Knowledge seemed to the Arab to be an eternal and abiding reality, … which for a time reproduced itself in the individual."[34]

31 Ibid., 1:137.

32 Ibid., 1:305.

33 Ueberweg, *Philosophy,* 1:168. Cf. Brett, *Psychology,* 1:153ff.

34 Brett, *Psychology,* 2:51.

Man is potentially capable of knowledge because of the principle that like can know like.[35] The old Greek idea of man as a microcosm[36] is accepted by Ghazālī, who said, "were it not that He has placed an image of the whole world within your very being you would have no knowledge of that which is apart from yourself."[37] He further develops this idea in *Kīmiyāʾ al-saʿāda.*

> Know that man is an epitomy (*mukhtaṣara*) of the world in which there is a trace of every form in the world. For these bones are like the mountains, his flesh as the dust, his hair as the plants, his head as heaven, his senses as the planets.... The power in the stomach is like the cook, that in the liver like the baker, that in the intestines like the fuller, and that which makes milk white and blood red is like the dyer.[38]

In man there are many worlds represented, all of which serve him tirelessly although he does not know of them nor give thanks to Him who bestowed them upon him.

Ghazālī also considers the platonic idea of man being the copy of the archetype.[39] He connects this with the Muslim doctrine of the Preserved Tablet (*al-lawḥ al-maḥfūẓ*).[40] The Archetype of the world was written on the Tablet. The real nature of things is made known to man by disclosure to him of what is there written through the reflection of these truths in the mirror of the heart.

This introduces us to the example of the mirror[41]—a favorite of Ghazālī's. Man's heart, as a mirror, is potentially capable of having reflected in it the real essence of all things, and thus of coming to know them. In this knowledge there are three factors: (1) The intellect, or heart, in which exists the image of the specific natures of things, is like the mirror; (2) The intelligible, or specific nature of the known thing, is like the object reflected in

---

35 Plato, *Timaeus*, 37 B C; see introduction, p. 10.

36 See note on page 59.

37 See page 59, where this is translated.

38 Ghazālī, *Kīmiyāʾ*, p. 19.

39 Plato, *Timaeus*, 37 D E; translation, p. 79. Cf. Plotinus, *Essence*, III, viii, 10; V, i, 4; VI, vii, 15.

40 See "al-lawḥ al-maḥfūẓ," *EI*, 3:19ff.; *EI²*, "lawḥ," 5:698. Also Wensinck, *Gazālī's Cosmology*, pp. 16ff.

41 Cf. Plotinus, *Essence*, I, i, 8.

the mirror; (3) The intelligence, or the representation of the known thing in the heart, is like the representation of the image in the mirror.

The reflection of knowledge in the heart may be prevented by one or more of five causes: (1) The heart of a youth is in a crude unformed condition and is incapable of knowledge, just as a crude unpolished piece of metal is incapable of reflecting objects; (2) Disobedient acts tarnish and corrode the mirror of the heart so that the reflection of reality therein is dimmed or destroyed; (3) Man may not know God because his heart is not turned toward Him: even as the mirror does not reflect the desired object unless it is turned toward it; (4) The heart may be veiled to true knowledge by blindly accepting dogmatic teaching without understanding or thought; (5) The heart may not even know in which direction to turn in order to have reality reflected in it.

Man can polish and burnish the mirror of his heart by means of acts of obedience so that it will reflect the image of true reality. He thus gains knowledge by making it possible for the image of the archetype to be reflected in his heart.

The sum total of man's knowledge is thus rooted in his knowledge of himself. He knows only himself in the proper sense, and knows other things only through himself. This is true also of man's highest attainment of knowledge, the knowledge of God; for the quality of the divine Being is reflected in the human soul. "He who knows himself knows his Lord" is the true statement of tradition. Every heart is thus a microcosm and a mirror, and being thus constituted is capable of knowing itself and the divine.[42]

The heart of man has two kinds of knowledge: intellectual and religious. Intellectual knowledge may be the intuitive knowledge of axioms, or acquired knowledge that is the result of study. Acquired knowledge may deal with the things of this world, such as medicine, geometry, astronomy, and the various professions and trades; or it may be concerned with the things of the world to come, such as the doctrines of religion. Speculative theologians stress this sort of acquired knowledge as being most important.

Religious knowledge is the knowledge of God, His attributes, and His acts. It is accepted on authority by the common people as an unquestionable creed that does not involve direct inspiration. To people of deep religious experience, however, this knowledge is given directly. Saints and

---

42 Cf. development of microcosm and macrocosm in Wilhelm Windelband, *A History of Philosophy*, trans. James Tufts (New York: Macmillan, 1907), pp. 366ff.

mystics receive it through general inspiration (*ilhām*), while it is received by prophets directly from the angel[43] through prophetic inspiration (*waḥy*).

Both intellectual and religious knowledge are needed and neither one is sufficient without the other. This is true in spite of the fact that each tends to exclude the other except in the case of unusual men who are both learned and saintly. Intellectual knowledge may be compared to food, and religious knowledge to medicine. Both are needed for the preservation of health.

Even as there are two kinds of knowledge which enter the heart, so also the heart has two doors by which this knowledge comes into it.[44] There is an outer door to the knowledge of material things and this is sense perception. The inner door is that of divine inspiration and mystical revelation.[45] Here again the principle obtains that like knows like, for the senses belong to this present world for which they were created, while the heart belongs also to the invisible world of spirits (*al-malakūt*).

The external senses of sight, hearing, smell, taste, and touch act through the bodily members: the eyes, ears, nose, tongue, and fingers. Sense perceptions reach the individual by means of these external senses, but they are perceived and understood only by means of the five inner senses which are (1) shared sense or sensus communis (*ḥiss mushtarak*), (2) retentive imagination (*khayāl, takhayyul*), (3) reflection (*tafakkur*), (4) recollection (*tadhakkur*), and (5) memory (*ḥifẓ*). These are internal powers and their seats are internal.

The shared sense is the power that receives the impressions which come through the different external senses and unites them into a harmonious and unified whole. Retentive imagination is the power that takes from the shared sense the physical sensation and transforms it into a psychic possession. This power is located in the front part of the brain. Reflection is the pondering, cogitative faculty of the heart. Recollection is the power to recall the mental images of past sensations that have been forgotten for a time. Memory is the storehouse for the meanings of sensible objects formerly perceived. Its seat is in the back part of the brain.

---

43 Editor's note: this refers to the Angel Gabriel, who delivered revelation to the prophets.

44 Tahānawī, *Iṣṭilāḥāt al-funūn*, p. 371; M. Palacios, *Algazel, Dogmática, Moral, Ascética* (Zaragoza, 1901), pp. 79f.

45 Cf. Plotinus, *Essence*, V, i, 12; III, viii, 9.

This list of the internal senses differs from some of Ghazālī's other classifications. Five other lists are presented in tabular form. [See following tables.] In this book Ghazālī deals with practical and ethical ends, and perhaps did not feel that it was necessary to be scientifically accurate in his statement. It will be noted that the classifications given in the first four of the books as tabulated below are definite attempts to present the subject systematically.

	Maqāṣid al-falāsifa	*Tahāfut al-falāsifa*	*Mīzān al-ʿamal*
1	Common sense *ḥiss mushtarak*	Common sense; imagination *ḥiss mushtarak*; *khayāliyya*	Common sense; imagination *ḥiss mushtarak*; *khayāliyya* anterior ventricle of brain
2	Retentive imagination; conservation *mutaṣawwira; ḥāfiẓa* anterior ventricle	Retentive imagination *ḥāfiẓa*	Retentive imagination *ḥāfiẓa* anterior ventricle
3	Estimation *wahmiyya* posterior ventricle	Estimation *wahmiyya* posterior ventricle	Estimation *wahmiyya* end of middle ventricle
4	Compositive animal and human imagination *mutakhayyila* *mufakkira* middle ventricle	Compositive animal and human imagination *mutakhayyila* *mufakkira* middle ventricle	Compositive animal and human imagination *mutakhayyila* *mufakkira* middle ventricle
5	Memory *dhākira* posterior ventricle	Memory *dhākira* posterior ventricle	Memory *dhākira* posterior ventricle

	Maʿārij al-quds	*Kīmiyāʾ al-saʿāda*	*Iḥyāʾ ʿulūm al-dīn*
1	Common sense; phantasia; tablet *ḥiss mushtarak; binṭāsiyya; lawḥ* front of anterior ventricle	Imagination *khayāl*	Common sense *ḥiss mushtarak*
2	Retentive imagination *khayāl; khayāliyya muṣawwira* back of anterior ventricle	Estimation *wahm*	Retentive imagination *khayāl; takhayyul* anterior ventricle
3	Estimation (*wahmiyya*) whole of brain, esp. back of middle ventricle	Reflection *tafakkur*	Reflection *tafakkur*
4	Compositive imagination, animal and human *takhayyul; mutakhayyila; mufakkira* front of middle ventricle	Recollection *tadhakkur*	Recollection *tadhakkur*
5	Memory (*ḥāfiẓa; dhākira*) posterior ventricle	Memory *ḥifẓ*	Memory *ḥifẓ* posterior ventricle

It would be of added interest if we could know for certain the chronological order of these books. It appears to be quite safe to put the *Maqāṣid* and *Tahāfut* first. *Mīzān al-ʿamal* is placed third because it seems logically nearer to the first two than does *Maʿārij al-quds fī madārij maʿrifat al-nafs* (also known as *Maʿārij al-sālikīn*).[46]

The analyses given in the *Mīzān* and *Maʿārij* are particularly noteworthy for being systematic and detailed in form, and as coming from the

46 Carl Brockelmann, *Geschichte der Arabischer Litteratur, Supplementband*, 3 vols. (1936–7), 1:751.

later period of Ghazālī's life. The list from *Kīmiyāʾ al-saʿāda* is given as an interesting parallel to that in this book of the *Iḥyāʾ*.

Another interesting parallel is found in *al-Risāla al-ladunniyya*,[47] where Ghazālī speaks of the soul's activities as recollection (*tadhakkur*), memorizing (*taḥaffuẓ*), reflection (*tafakkur*), discrimination (*tamyīz*), and deliberation (*rawiyya*). But it is evident that this also is not an attempt at a systematic analysis.

In his *Maʿārij*[48] Ghazālī gives a suggestion regarding the inner senses which enables us to understand more clearly their varying names and functions. He says that they include: (1) that which perceives but does not conserve; (2) that which conserves but does not reason; and (3) that which perceives (understands) and deals with perceptions. These three powers in their relation to the forms of sense impressions and to their ideal meanings place before us the entire range of the internal senses. These relationships are shown in the following table.

<table>
<tr><td rowspan="2">That which perceives (al-mudrik)</td><td>the form received through sense impression (lil-ṣūra) is</td><td colspan="2">common sense (ḥiss mushtarak)</td></tr>
<tr><td>the ideal meaning (lil-maʿnā) is</td><td colspan="2">the estimative faculty (wahm; wahmiyya)</td></tr>
<tr><td rowspan="2">That which conserves (al-ḥāfiẓ)</td><td>the form received through sense impression (lil-ṣūra) is</td><td colspan="2">retentive imagination (al-khayāl; al-ḥāfiẓa)</td></tr>
<tr><td>the ideal meaning (lil-maʿnā) is</td><td colspan="2">memory; recollection (al-ḥāfiẓa; al-dhākira)</td></tr>
<tr><td rowspan="2">That which deals with (al-mutaṣarrif fī)</td><td>the form received through sense impression (al-ṣūra) is</td><td rowspan="2">compositive imagination</td><td>of human intellect (mufakkira)</td></tr>
<tr><td>the ideal meaning (lil-maʿnā) is</td><td>of animal powers (mutakhayyila)</td></tr>
</table>

47 Published with Ghazālī, *Kīmiyāʾ al-saʿāda* (Cairo: Saʿāda Press, 1343), p. 27.

48 Ghazālī, *Maʿārij*, p. 46.

From this arrangement it is also easy to see how these functions are sometines combined and other times separated in the different classifications, and also how the terms may easily vary in their meanings in the different books.

From the foregoing discussion we see that Ghazālī was respectful of Aristotle, Galen, and the later philosophers of the Aristotelian school in his ideas of the body and sense perceptions, both outer and inner. We shall now see that in the realm of intuition, mystic revelation, and ecstasy there is a more pronounced Sufi trend in his thought, and this involves elements from Neoplatonic sources.[49]

Turning then to the inner door of the heart we find Ghazālī's second source of knowledge in divine inspiration and mystical revelation. The experience of this sort of knowledge is given to only a few people, but everyone is obligated to believe in its reality. It is attested by the Qurʾān, by *ḥadīth*, and by many experiences and stories of the saints. Revelation does not differ from acquisition with regard to the knowledge itself, its seat, and its cause, but only in the removal of the veil which does not come about by man's volition. Mystical revelation comes to him whose heart is prepared to receive it, either through the medium of dream-vision during sleep, or, more rarely, in a vision seen during waking hours.[50]

In the case of the prophets, inspiration (*waḥy*) is accompanied by a vision of the angel who imparts knowledge. The inspiration (*ilhām*) of saints differs from it, in that there is no such vision of the angel that brings the knowledge. Ghazālī is not quite consistent in his statements of the part which the angel plays in imparting the knowledge given through revelation. His position seems to be that general inspiration (*ilhām*) is always the result of angelic activity, even though the angel does not appear to the recipient of the revelation. He goes so far as to say that "our hearts attain knowledge only by means of the angels."[51] But in another place he speaks of directly given divine knowledge (*ʿilm ladunnī*) apart from the usual means from without. In *al-Risāla al-ladunniyya* (p. 42) he says that *ʿilm ladunnī* is from the Creator directly, with no mediating agent. This inconsistency is probably explained by his ideas about involuntary suggestions (*khawāṭir*), which will be dealt with later. The mediated knowledge corresponds to the suggestion of the angel (*al-khāṭir al-malakī*), while

49 Cf. Brett, *Psychology,* 1:200ff.; 2:48.

50 Cf. *The Hebrew Tradition* in Brett, *Psychology,* 2:233ff.

51 Translation, page 53.

the immediate and direct knowledge corresponds to the suggestion of the Lord (*al-khāṭir al-rabbānī*).

Through divine inspiration the true nature of reality is revealed to the heart of man. The veils of sense are drawn aside by divine power, and man's heart can perceive, even if it is but for a moment, the truth of the eternal reflected from the Preserved Tablet which is in the world of the unseen. At death the veils of sense are removed entirely and reality is clearly seen by the heart.

Man must prepare his heart to receive this gift of divine unveiling. He can do this by cutting off all earthly ties and making the thought of God not only supreme in every part of his being, but the sole idea which occupies his heart and mind. This is done by withdrawing from the world and engaging in the devotional exercise of *dhikr*, in addition to the prescribed worship. He continues repeating the name of God, with his mind fixed on Him, until the motion of the tongue ceases and the word seems to be flowing over it. He continues until every trace of the word and of its form and letters and appearance is effaced from his heart and nothing remains save its ideal meaning. All dualism is removed. The heart loses all consciousness of anything other than God, and in its contemplation of Him reaches the highest possible state.[52] Man is then prepared to receive the gift of divine unveiling. He had done all that he can do for he has reached the state of ecstasy. God then bestows such gifts as He pleases.

Such are the two ways that man receives knowledge and the two types of knowledge that he may have. Both intellectual and religious knowledge were important to Ghazālī. Both acquired and revealed knowledge played a large part in his scheme of life. He himself was a learned man, and he could never cease to give learning a place of honor and to account it a factor of great importance in human life and experience. But even his learning had not saved him from falling into skepticism, leading to a crisis in his life, while in the experience of mystical revelation he had found certainty and peace. The two factors are strangely intermingled in his writings. At one moment he seems to show his frustration with the common man, who does not have the intellectual power to comprehend knowledge; and at another time we find him praising an almost illiterate saint because of the miraculous gifts (*karāmāt*) and divinely unveiled knowledge that has been revealed to him. Intellectual knowledge is great, but even it must

52 Cf. Brett, *Psychology*, 1:313, 2:43; Plotinus, *Essence*, VI, vii, 34.

bow before that which is manifestly a divine bestowment. This Ghazālī knew from experience.

The Relation of Soul to Body and of Thought to Act

The relation of the soul to the body has already been touched upon in the discussion of the nature of the soul. Plato said that the soul was imprisoned in the body, while Aristotle made it an entelechy or actualization. Both of these ideas are considered in Ghazālī's thought. But the metaphor that Ghazālī chooses to express this relationship appears to come from Plato's *Timaeus*,[53] where the body is spoken of as the vehicle of the soul. Plato's word is *ὄχημα*; Ghazālī's is *markab*.

For Ghazālī, as for Ibn Sīnā, the soul is "a separate independent reality, which is only united to the body accidentally, that is to say, without any relation which affects its essence."[54] Both the vegetal and animal powers "are made possible by the union of the soul with the body; but if we go beyond these we come to other activities which belong to the soul itself."[55] Such soul activity is first of all potential, then nascent, then developed. This is illustrated by a youth who is at first potentially capable of learning to write. Then he comes to know the inkstand, pen, and the letters in their separate forms. And finally he becomes skilled in writing and composition.

The heart is the center for both the psychic and physical actions of man and thus in it are to be found the threads which bind thought to act.[56] The question of moral qualities and responsibilities as related to the soul's activity and the resultant physical action will be dealt with in the following section of this sketch. The first link in the chain connecting the psychic and the physical is the involuntary suggestion (*khāṭir*) which comes to the heart. This is of such importance in Ghazālī's scheme that it must be examined in some detail.

The *khāṭir* (pl. *khawāṭir*), (also *khaṭra*, pl. *khaṭarāt*), is an opinion, idea, or object of thought bestirring itself in the mind.[57] It is the allocution or suggestion that comes to the heart of man; man himself has noth-

53 Plato, *Timaeus* 44 E; 69 C.

54 Brett, *Psychology*, 2:57.

55 Ibid.

56 Ibid., 1:141ff.

57 E. W. Lane, *Arabic-English Lexicon* (London, 1863–93), p. 765.

ing to do with its coming.[58] This term is used largely in Sufi writings, and especially by Ghazālī.

There are various divisions of the *khawāṭir*, the most common being fourfold. (1) The suggestion of the Lord (of the Absolute Reality), (*al-khāṭir al-rabbānī; al-ḥaqqānī*). It is that which is cast directly into the heart of mystics who dwell, as it were, in His Presence. Nothing can oppose it, but the other sorts of *khawāṭir* fade away and disappear before it. To deny it vexes the soul. It is a warning and a sign for guidance. (2) The suggestion of the angel (*al-khāṭir al-malakī*) exhorts to obedience and good acts, and warns against acts of disobedience and things that are disapproved. It blames man for committing acts contrary to divine law and for being slow in doing that which is in agreement therewith. (3) The suggestion of the self (*al-khāṭir al-nafsī*) demands the pleasant favors of this swiftly passing world, and sets forth its invitations to vanity. It is not cut off by the light of the devotional practice of the remembrance of God but continues to demand its desire, unless it comes to enjoy divinely given success (*tawfīq*), in which case its demands are uprooted. (4) The suggestion of the demon (*al-khāṭir al-shayṭānī*). This is the suggestion of the enemy who summons to acts of disobedience and to things that are forbidden and disapproved.

Some say that all *khawāṭir* are from the angels, and may be approved or disapproved by the individual. An exception to this is the suggestion of Absolute Reality with which man never disagrees. By the light of the divine unity (*al-tawḥīd*) man receives the suggestion of God, and by the light of experiential knowledge the suggestion of the angel. By the light of faith an end is put to the suggestion of the self, and by the light of Islam it is restored to obedience.

All types of suggestions come ultimately from God, but some come directly, and others indirectly. Those which come from Him directly, and those which come through the angel, are good. The commentator on *al-Risāla al-Qushayriyya* says that the suggestion of the Lord is equivalent to true insight (*firāsa*) and is a miraculous gift (*karāma*). The suggestions that come from the self may be either good or evil, although the latter is to be expected. The suggestion that comes from the demon is always evil. Some have added to the foregoing division the following: the suggestion of the spirit (*khāṭir al-rūḥ*); the suggestion of the shaykh (*khāṭir al-shaykh*); the suggestion of the intellect (*khāṭir al-ʿaql*); and the suggestion of cer-

58 Cf. Jurjānī, *al-Taʿrīfāt*, p. 101.

tainty (*khāṭir al-yaqīn*). But all of these can be properly placed under the fourfold division already given.

The correct differentiation of these suggestions and their sources can be made only when the mirror of the heart is carefully cleared of all undue fleshly and natural desires by means of asceticism, piety, and remembrance; and then the true nature of the suggestions will be manifest. He who has not reached this stage in the ascetic life should weigh the suggestion in the balances of the divine law to determine its nature. If it is an obligation or a virtue he should do it; but if it is a thing forbidden or disapproved he should put it away from himself. If it is something permitted and rather inclines toward disagreeing with the self, then he should do it; for most of the suggestions of the self are base. Some of the demands of the self are its just rights to things which are necessary, and these must be satisfied. Other demands of the self are for fortune's favors, and these should be denied. He who succeeds in properly recognizing and dealing with these suggestions enters into the way of abundunt life and mystic vision, where the suggestions which seek for fortune's favors pass away and trouble man no more.

Sayyid Murtaḍā al-Zabīdī, the commentator on the *Iḥyāʾ*, says that the novice must put away the suggestions of the self, the angel, and the demon, and give the primary place to the suggestion of the Absolute Reality. Ghazālī makes the suggestion of the angel equivalent to general inspiration (*ilhām*), and that of the demon the same as evil prompting (*wiswās*). Sometimes he speaks as though there were but this twofold division, and he refers to these two as 'calls' (*lammatān*).

The sorts of *khawāṭir* found in *Qūt al-qulūb* by Abū Ṭālib al-Makkī, one of Ghazālī's principal source books, are found in a list given by Zabīdī.[59] They are:

1. General inspiration (*ilhām*).
2. Evil prompting (*wiswās*).
3. Dread (*ījās*).
4. Intention (*niyya*).
5. Hope and desire (*amal; umniya*).
6. Recollection and reflection (*tadhakkur; tafakkur*).
7. Mystic vision (*mushāhadan*).
8. Anxious desire (*hamm*).
9. Seizure of madness (*lamam*).

---

59 Zabīdī, *Itḥāf*, 7:266; Abū Ṭālib al-Makkī, *Qūt al-qulūb* (Cairo: al-Maymaniyya Press, 1310/1893), 1:187ff.

Zabīdī mentions the sixfold division, adding intellect (*ʿaql*) and certainty (*yaqīn*) to the usual four, but denies that the intellect has a *khāṭir*.[60]

The other states of the heart that lead up to physical action are dealt with quite summarily by Ghazālī. For when a man once gives heed to the suggestion in his heart, the other stages follow almost automatically. Thus the suggestion stirs up the inherent inclination of the nature (*mayl al-ṭabʿ*) to do the thing suggested. Inclination of the nature leads to a conviction (*iʿtiqād*), or a reasoned judgment that the thing must be done. This conviction leads to a definite decision (*hamm*) to do it. Thereupon the physical members act in obedience to the decision and command of the heart, and the act is done.

Ghazālī illustrates the various kinds of suggestions (*khawāṭir*) by many *ḥadīth*s and parables. All of the different stages between suggestion and action are made clear by an illustration of which a brief summary is here given. The suggestion comes into the mind of a man that there is a woman behind him in the way, and that, if he were to turn around, he would see her. The inclination of his nature is then to turn and see her. But his inhibitions of modesty and fear must first be removed before he reaches the stage of conviction that he must turn and look. Next he determines and decides finally to look and see her. This state of the heart is followed by the act of turning and looking, unless some new influence is brought to bear upon the man to prevent the act.

The Soul's Experience of Good and Evil

It has already been stated that Ghazālī's purpose in the *Iḥyāʾ* is primarily ethical. His aim is the enlightenment of the soul in order that it may attain its perfection in the full and immediate knowledge of God. There are potent forces that help man toward this end. But there are also evil tendencies that appeal to his lower nature and constantly drag him down and prevent him from reaching the desired goal. The soul is constantly swaying backwards and forwards between these forces for good and evil. Sometimes the good prevails, and again the evil influence predominates.

---

60 Sources of above are: Tahānawī, *Iṣṭilāḥāt al-funūn*, pp. 415–7; Zabīdī, *Itḥāf*, 7:199, 249, 266, 301ff.; ʿAbd al-Karīm b. Hawāzin al-Qushayrī, *al-Risāla al-Qushayriyya* (Egypt: Maṭbʿat Muṣṭafā al-Bābī al-Halabī, 1940), 2:96; Aḥmad b. Muṣṭafā Kumushkhānawī, *Jāmiʿ al-uṣūl fī al-awliyāʾ* (Egypt: Maṭbaʿat al-Jamāliyya, 1328/1910), p. 100; Reynold A. Nicholson, *Studies in Islamic Mysticism* (Cambridge: Cambridge University Press, 1921), p. 212.

If we ask about the source of these good and evil influences that act upon the soul we find that God is the First Cause of all. Here Ghazālī follows established Sunnī theology. "There is no doer (*fāʿil*) save God. Every existing thing, whether creature or provision, gift or prohibition, life or death, wealth, or poverty, or whatever is called by a name, has been created by God alone."[61] He creates men and what they do.

But although God is the ultimate cause of all suggestions and acts, both good and evil, there are also secondary causes. These are angels and demons. Here again we see the Neoplatonic influence at work providing a parallel in the realm of morals to what the Neoplatonic chain does in metaphysics in putting the Absolute Cause far away from the individual. There are a great many angels[62] and a corresponding host of demons. Each type of good or evil act is the result of the soul's acceptance of the suggestion of a particular angel or demon. A number of demons are mentioned by name and their specific fields of activity mentioned. Thabr is the demon who stirs up strife and affliction. Al-Aʿwar incites to adultery, and Miswaṭ to lying. Dāsim stirs up trouble between a man and his family. Zalanbūr leads to dishonesty in the marketplace. Khinzib interrupts a man during the ritual prayer, and al-Walhān interferes with ceremonial purification.

In this development we find suggestions of Eastern influences, especiallly Persian and Hebrew, in the angelology and demonology, as well as in the apparent dualism.[63] In certain passages Ghazālī seems to say that each individual has a demon and an angel that accompany him in his life. This suggests the 'daemon' of Socrates and Plutarch.[64]

The heart has many doors through which the demons enter in order to lead it astray. All of these are related to the qualities of the irrational soul. Man must know these doors, which are: anger and appetence; envy and greed; overeating; love of adornment; striving to gain the favor of men; haste; love of money; stinginess; sectarianism; the study of theology by the common people; thinking evil of Muslims.

There is but one door, however, by which the angels may gain access to the heart. Ghazālī does not explicitly define this door, but it is clear that he is speaking of the rational soul as illuminated by inner piety and outer conformity to the teachings of the Qurʾān and the Sunna.

---

61 Zabīdī, *Itḥaf*, 9:400.

62 Cf. the further development in *Iḥyāʾ*, 4:104ff.

63 Cf. Brett, *Psychology*, 1:221.

64 Ibid., 1:62, 258.

Ghazālī is careful also to show that, although good and evil are both inevitably present in man's experience, every individual is responsible for the development of his character. Man must discipline his soul. The book of the *Iḥyāʾ* that immediately follows this one deals with the subject of this discipline. But in the present book we find the subject constantly stressed. The rational soul must be made and kept the master, while anger and appetence must be kept in the position of servants. The demands of the appetitive and spirited natures must be balanced against each other so that desire and will may all be harmoniously developed into a complete character.[65] But when man habitually yields to the demands of his lower nature, his intellect becomes the slave of his passions and is entirely occupied with schemes to attain the ends of his lower desires. The master has become enslaved, and the soul is overcome by confusion, immorality, and sin.

The discipline of the soul is accomplished through ascetic and devotional practices. This present world and the desire for the things of the world must be denied, and the entrances of Satan may thus be closed. There must be complete dependence upon God and submission to Him. As long as man truly desires any of the things of this world, be it but a stone to use for a pillow, just so long will Satan find in his desire a way to approach his heart and lead it astray.

Ghazālī uses another figure to express the same idea. Satan's food is man's appetence or desire. It therefore becomes man's duty to empty his heart of all desire for worldly things, and thus remove that upon which Satan feeds.

The *dhikr*, or the devotional practice of the remembrance of God and the repeated mention of His name, is the best way to fix the heart's desire upon Him, and so to ward off the attacks of Satan. *Ḥadīth* says that the *dhikr* causes Satan to slink away and hide himself. It is therefore the best means of defense against the evil promptings that Satan suggests to the human heart. It is conceivable that some of Satan's evil promptings may thus be cut off entirely, but for the most part there is no complete victory over Satan in this life. Man may triumph over him for a moment or for an hour by means of pious practices, but he returns to man again and again. Only the prophets, who are preserved from sin (*maʿṣūmūn*), are able to baffle Satan indefinitely. It is therefore essential that man shall maintain a

65 Cf. Brett's dicussion of Aristotle, *Psychology,* 1:142ff.

constant lifelong struggle against Satan, for only thus can he develop his character as he ought to do.

In dealing with man's moral responsibility for his own good and evil acts, Ghazālī lays down one clear rule. Man is held accountable for his own voluntary choices. He will be judged in accordance with the purpose (*qaṣd*) on which he has fixed his heart, his determination (*ʿazm*), his intention (*niyya*), and his decision (*hamm*). When two men engage in a sword fight both slayer and slain will be condemned to the fire, because each one intended to kill the other.

On the other hand, man is not held accountable for the involuntary suggestion (*khāṭir*) that occurs to his mind, nor for the inclination of his nature (*mayl al-ṭabʿ*), since there is no element of volition on his part in either of them. In regard to man's conviction (*iʿtiqād*) that he must do a certain thing, Ghazālī says that this may have been reached involuntarily through circumstances beyond his control, and in such a case the man is not accountable. But when the conviction has been reached as the result of voluntary deliberation, then he is held morally responsible for it.

Ghazālī deals with the subject of the soul's destiny. Because of the fact that he was able to accept so many of the positions of the Aristotelian philosophers and to find a harmony between their teachings and those of Islam, we may naturally expect him to say, with Ibn Sīnā, that the rational soul, prepared by the practice of the virtues, attains perfection after death.[66] In fact, Ghazālī does make almost that same statement. But he does it quite incidentally when he says that at death the veils of sense are removed, and the soul sees clearly and knows fully the true nature of reality.

But in the closing portion of this book Ghazālī does not stress the philosophical position; indeed he turns toward the position of Islam. The general and particular decrees (*qaḍāʾ wa qadr*) of God determine inevitably and inexorably the fate of the soul. Some hearts are built up by means of piety and purified through discipline. Others are burdened by passion and utterly corrupted by foul actions, so that they have no place for good. The hearts of most men sway between the good and the evil, the angel and the demon, until the dominant factor obtains the victory. But this factor has been caused to predominate by the predestination of God. Because of the divine decree, obedience has been made easy for some, and disobedience for others, God guides aright and leads astray.

---

66 Hastings, *Religion and Ethics*, 2:276a.

THE MARVELS OF THE HEART

بِسْمِ اللَّهِ الرَّحْمَٰنِ الرَّحِيمِ

Author's Foreword

In the Name of God the Merciful, the Compassionate.[1]

Praise belongs to God,[2] whose majesty perplexes the hearts and thoughts of those who seek in vain to comprehend it;[3] whose shining light at its beginning is such as to bewilder eye and sight; who is acquainted with all hidden secrets; who knows all that conscience conceals; who has no need of counselor or helper in ruling His kingdom; the Overturner of hearts and the Forgiver of sins; the Concealer of faults; the Deliverer from anxieties. And may blessings and peace rest in abundance upon the master of the messengers, who unites religion and defeats heretics, and upon his descendants, the righteous, and the pure.

The honor and excellence of man, in which he surpasses all other sorts of creatures, is his aptitude for knowing God, praise be to Him. This knowledge is man's beauty and perfection and glory in the present world, and his provision and store for the world to come. He is prepared for this knowledge only through his heart, and not by means of any of his members. For it is the heart that knows God, and works for God, and strives toward God, and draws near to Him, and reveals that which is in the presence of God. The members of the body, on the other hand, are merely

1 A pious phrase known as the *basmala*. It confers blessings, and is used at the beginning of formal writings as well as in many other connections touching all phases of Muslim life.

2 The *ḥamdala* is an ascription of praise to God; it is used as one of the fixed introductory phrases to every formal writing.

3 Zabīdī says that the mystics' knowledge of God is in the fact that they come experientially to know that they can never know Him in the sense of having a complete experiential knowledge of His being and attributes. This knowledge is His alone.

followers, servants, and instruments that the heart uses and employs as the king uses his slave, as the shepherd makes use of his flock, or as the craftsman uses his tool.

For it is the heart that is accepted by God when it is free from all save Him, but veiled from God when it becomes wholly occupied with anything other than Him. It is the heart upon which claims are made, with which conversations are carried on, and with which remonstrance is made, and which is punished. It rejoices in nearness to God and prospers if kept true, and is undone and miserable if debased and corrupted.[4] It is that which in reality is obedient to God, the Exalted, and the acts of devotion that are manifest in the members of the body are but its light. It is that also which is disobedient and rebellious against God, the Exalted, and the acts of turpitude that course through the members are but its effects. By its darkness and its light there appear the good and evil qualities of its external appearance, since "every vessel drips that which it contains."[5] The heart is that which, if a man knows it, he knows himself, and if he knows himself, he knows his Lord. It is that which, if a man knows it not, he knows not himself, and if he knows not himself, he knows not his Lord.[6] He who knows not his own heart is still more ignorant of everything else, since the majority of mankind know not their own hearts and their own selves, for intervention has been made between them and their own selves. For *God intervenes between a man and his heart* (8:24). His intervention consists in preventing man from observing it [i.e., his heart], and watching over it, and becoming acquainted with its qualities, and perceiving how

4 Cf. Qurʾān 91:9–10.

5 An Arabic proverb, poetic in form according to MSS texts, quoted in G. W. Freytag, *Arabum Proverbia*, 3 vols. (Bonn, 1839), 2:371, no. 179. Aḥmad b. Muḥammad al-Maydanī, *Majmaʿ al-amthāl* (Egypt: al-Maṭbaʿa al-Bahiyya al-Miṣriyya, 1342/1923), 2:73.

6 This is a proverb often quoted by Muslim writers of all shades of belief. It corresponds to the 'know thyself' of Socrates and other early Greek philosophers. To this was added the idea that man's soul is an inbreathing of divine life, Qurʾān 32:8. Bayḍāwī, in his comment on this verse, quotes this proverb. Philosophical Muslims of different groups, including the Ikhwān al-Ṣafāʾ and Ibn Sīnā use this proverb. Ibn al-ʿArabī and Ghazālī, among other mystics, use the phrase repeatedly, sometimes speaking of it as a *ḥadīth* from the Prophet. See *Kīmiyāʾ*, p. 4. Zabīdī says that this is reported to be a saying of Yaḥyā b. Muʿādh al-Rāzī (d. 258/872), a famous preacher. See Ibn Khallikān, *Kitāb wafayāt al-ʿayān*, trans. MacGuckin de Slane as *Ibn Khallikan's Biographical Dictionary*, 4 vols. (Paris, 1842–71), 4:51ff.

it is turned between two of the fingers of the Merciful;[7] and how at one time it lusts for the lowest of the low and is brought down to the plane of the demons; and at another time, it mounts up to the highest of the high, and advances to the world of the angels who are drawn near to God (*al-malāʾika al-muqarrabūn*).[8] He who knows not his heart, to watch over it and be mindful of it, and to observe what shines on it and in it of the treasures of the world of spirits (*al-malakūt*),[9] he is one of those of whom God, the Exalted, has said, *those who forget God; and He made them to forget their own souls. Such are the rebellious transgressors!* (59:19). Thus the knowledge of the heart and of the real nature of its qualities is the root of religion and the foundation of the mystic traveler's way.

Since we have completed the first part of this book,[10] which deals with those acts of worship and customs that are carried out by the external bodily members, which is external knowledge, and since we have promised[11] to explain in the second part those mortal vices and saving virtues that come upon the heart, which is inner knowledge, we must preface this part with two books. One book will deal with the explanation of the heart's qualities and characteristics, and the second with the manner of disciplining the heart and improving its characteristics.[12] After that we will launch forth into a detailed discussion of the things that destroy and save. So we shall now mention that which can be most readily understood of the exposition of the wonders of the heart by means of examples. Most minds are too dull to comprehend a plain statement of its wonders and of its secrets that pertain to the realm of the world of spirits.

---

7 A much quoted *ḥadīth*, ʿAbdallāh b. Muslim Ibn Qutayba, *Taʾwīl mukhtalaf al-ḥadīth* (Cairo: Maṭbaʿa Kurdistān al-ʿIlmiyya, 1326/1908), p. 263. Muslim also relates it from ʿAbdallāh b. ʿAmr.

8 "Al-malāʾika al-muqarrabūn"; see *Encyclopaedia of Islam*, ed. M. Th. Houtsma, et al. (Leiden, 1913–37), 3:189ff. esp. 3:190a, Also Wensinck, *The Muslim Creed* (Cambridge: Cambridge University Press, 1932), p. 198.

9 For a treatment of *mulk* and *malakūt* see Macdonald, "The Life of al-Ghazālī," pp. 116ff.; Wensinck, *On the Relation between Ghazālī's Cosmology and his Mysticism* (Amsterdam, 1933).

10 I.e., the first half of the *Iḥyāʾ*.

11 See *Iḥyaʾ* text in Zabīdī, *Itḥāf*, 1:63.

12 Editor's note: The second book of the third quarter has been translated by T. J. Winter, *On Disciplining the Soul and Breaking the Two Desires* (Cambridge: Islamic Texts Society, 1995.)

Chapter 1

An Exposition of the Meaning of 'Soul,' 'Spirit,' 'Heart,' and 'Intelligence,' and of the Purport of these Names

Know that there are four names that are used in these chapters. But few of the leading savants have a comprehensive knowledge of these names and their different meanings, and of the definitions of the things named. Most of the mistakes regarding them originate in ignorance of the meaning of these names, and of the way in which they are applied to different objects. We will explain as much of the meaning of these names as pertains to our purpose.

One of these is the term 'heart' (*qalb*), and it is used with two meanings. One of them is the cone-shaped organ of flesh that is located at the left side of the chest. It is flesh of a particular sort within which there is a cavity, and in this cavity there is black blood that is the source (*manbaʿ*) and seat (*maʿdan*) of the spirit (*rūḥ*).[1] We do not now propose to explain its shape nor its mode of operation since religious ends have no connection therewith, but only the aim of physicians.[2] Animals and even the dead have this heart of flesh. Whenever we use the term 'heart' in this book, we do not mean this sort of heart, for it is but an impotent bit of

---

1 "Nafs," *EI*. *EI*², 7:880. Cf. "The blood round the heart is the thought of men." H. Diels, *Die Fragmente der Vorsokratiker*, quoted in Brett, *Psychology*, 1:359. Editor's note: seat (*maʿdan*) may also be translated as origin, or source.

2 For the early ideas of Arabian physiology, see Edward G. Browne, *Arabian Medicine* (Cambridge, 1921), pp. 121ff. Cf. Brett, *Psychology*, 1:283ff.

flesh, belonging to the visible material world (*ʿālam al-mulk wa-l-shahāda*), and is perceived by the sense of sight, by animals as well as by mankind.

The second meaning of the 'heart' is a subtle tenuous substance[3] of an ethereal spiritual sort (*laṭīfa rabbāniyya rūḥāniyya*), which is connected with the physical heart. This subtle tenuous substance is the real essence of man. The heart is the part of man that perceives and knows and experiences; it is addressed, punished, rebuked, and held responsible, and it has some connection with the physical heart. The majority of men have been become perplexed when they tried to perceive the nature of this connection. Its connection therewith resembles the connection of accidents with substances, of qualities with the things they qualify, of the user of a tool with the tool, or of that which occupies a place with the place. We will guard against trying to explain this for two reasons: first, because it deals with mystical sciences (*ʿulūm al-mukāshafa*),[4] and our aim in this book includes only the knowledge of proper conduct (*ʿilm al muʿāmala*); and second, because to ascertain it calls for a disclosing of the secret of the spirit (*rūḥ*), concerning which the Messenger[5] of God ﷺ did not speak, and therefore no one else should speak.[6] Our aim then is this: whenever we use the term 'heart' (*qalb*) in this book we mean by it this subtle tenuous substance. And what we propose is to mention its characteristics (*awṣāf*) and states (*aḥwāl*),[7] not its real nature (*ḥaqīqa*)[8] in itself, for the science of practical religion does not require the mention of its real nature.

The second term is the 'spirit' (*rūḥ*), and it is also used with two meanings relevant to our purpose. One of these [meanings] is a subtle body whose source is the cavity of the physical heart, and which spreads by means of the pulsative arteries to all the other parts of the body.[9] Its circulation in

---

3 This concept has been expressed by the word 'subtlety,' following the usage of the older philosophy. See Macdonald, *The Religious Life and Attitude in Islam* (Chicago: University of Chicago Press, 1912), pp. 221, 229ff. The nearest parallel in modern psychology to the refined nature of this 'subtle tenuous substance' is probably found in the ectoplasm or teleplasm of psychical research.

4 For the different kinds of science and knowledge see "ʿilm," *EI*² and the references there given.

5 "Rasūl," *EI*, 3:1127ff. *EI*², 13:454.

6 A *ḥadīth* given by Bukhārī and Muslim from Ibn Masʿūd.

7 "Aḥwāl," *EI*, 1:227. *EI*², 12:343.

8 "Ḥaqīqa," *EI*, 1:223ff.

9 Zabīdī says that this 'spirit' is a very refined substance, the animal life principle.

the body and the overflowing from it of the light of life, sense perception, sight, hearing, and smell to the members of the body resemble the flood of light from a lamp that is moved around throughout a house. Whenever the lamp is brought to any part of the house it is lit by it. Life is like the light that falls upon the walls; the spirit is like the lamp; the circulation of the spirit and its movement within correspond to the movement of the lamp throughout the house by the moving of the one who moves it. Whenever physicians use the term 'spirit' they have in mind this meaning, which is a subtle vapor produced by the heat of the heart. It is not our purpose to explain this usage of the term since its connections are within the scope of physicians who treat the body. The purpose of physicians of religion who treat the heart that it may be led near to the Lord of the worlds has no connection at all with the explanation of this 'spirit.'

The second meaning is that subtle tenuous substance in man which knows and perceives, which we have already explained in one of the meanings of the 'heart.' It is the meaning intended by God, the Exalted, in His statement, *Say: "the spirit is my Lord's affair"* (17:85). It is a marvelous and lordly (*rabbānī*) affair,[10] the real and ultimate nature of which most intellects (*ʿuqūl*) and [people's] understandings (*afhām*) are unable to grasp.

The third term, 'soul' (*nafs*),[11] partakes of many meanings, two of which pertain to our purpose. By one is denoted that meaning which includes both the faculty of anger (*ghaḍab*) and of appetence (*shahwa*)[12] in man,

---

The arteries are made doubly strong so as to be able to carry the subtle body (*jism laṭīf*) which is the spirit. Zabīdī quotes Suhrawardī's *ʿAwārif al-maʿārif* on the spirit. Animals have it. It gives the power of sense perception. It is strengthened by nourishment. Zabīdī says further that the learned say that this spirit is a tenuous vaporous body produced from the blood that comes to its left chamber. Its value lies in the way it bears the physical powers so that they are circulated in the body.

10 Zabīdī says that thinkers and writers have differed much about the true nature of the spirit (*rūḥ*).

11 The *nafs* is the appetitive soul or self, the 'flesh' of Pauline usage; see *EI* 3:827–30, and *EI*[2] 7:880. Macdonald, *Religious Life and Attitude*, pp. 228–30.

12 The twofold division of the irrational soul according to Plato was (1) *thymos*, anger or the irascible faculty, including courage, energy, and ambition. This is the higher of the two and its seat is the heart. (2) *Epithymia*, the appetence or the concupiscible faculty, including the appetites. It is the lower part and its seat is in the abdominal cavity. This idea with slight variation is a basic factor in the psychology of Ghazālī.

which we will explain later. This meaning predominates among Sufis,[13] for they mean by the 'soul' that principle in man that includes his blameworthy qualities (*ṣifāt madhmūma*). So they say, "The soul must be striven against and broken." This is alluded to by [the Prophet] ﷺ in his statement, "Your soul, which is between your two sides, is your worst enemy."[14]

The second meaning is that subtle tenuous substance that we have mentioned, which is, in reality, man. It is the soul of man and his essence. But it is described by different descriptives according to its differing states. When it is at rest under His command, and agitation has left it on account of its opposition to the fleshly appetites, it is called 'the soul at rest' (*al-nafs al-muṭmaʾinna*). Of such a soul did God, the Exalted, say, *Oh, you soul at peace, return to your Lord, pleased, and pleasing Him* (89:27–8). The soul, according to the first definition, cannot be conceived of as returning to God, the Exalted, for it is far removed from God and belongs to the party of Satan.[15] But when the soul is not completely at rest, but is striving to drive off and oppose the appetitive soul, it is called 'the upbraiding soul' (*al-nafs al-lawwāma*); for it upbraids its possessor whenever he falls short in the worship of his Master. God, the Exalted, said, *Nay, and I swear by the upbraiding soul* (75:2). But if the soul leaves its opposition and becomes submissive and obedient to the demands of the fleshly appetites and the invitations of Satan, it is called 'the soul that commands to evil' (*al-nafs al-ammāra bil-sūʾ*) God, the Exalted, said, relating the words of Joseph ﷺ or the wife of the prince *And I do not acquit myself, for verily the soul commands to evil* (12:53). Yet it may sometimes be said, "By the 'soul that commands to evil,' is meant the soul according to the first definition," for that 'soul' is most blameworthy. But the soul according to the second definition is praiseworthy, for it is man's very self, or his essence and real nature, which knows God, the Exalted, and all other knowable things.[16]

---

13 "Sufi," a Muslim mystic; see "taṣawwuf," *EI*, 4:681ff. *EI*², 10:313.

14 A *ḥadīth* quoted by Bayhaqī from Ibn ʿAbbās.

15 Editor's note: throughout the translation, *shayṭān* is translated alternately as 'demon,' 'devil,' or 'Satan,' and can refer to the Devil or any of his progeny. When referred to by Imam al-Ghazālī as Iblīs, it is left as such and denotes the Devil.

16 Zabīdī gives an additional list of types of souls: (1) *al-nafs al-dassāsa*, or the concealing soul (Qurʾān 91:10); (2) *al-nafs al-mushtarā*, or the bought soul (Qurʾān 9:112); (3) *al-nafs al-sawwāla al-dassāsa al-qattāla*, or the soul that makes evil seem inconsequential, which conceals and slays; (4) *al-nafs al-zākiyya*, or the purifying soul (Qurʾān 91:9); (5) *al-nafs al-dhākira*, or the remembering soul (Qurʾān 7:204);

The fourth term, which is intellect (*ʿaql*),[17] also partakes of various meanings that we have mentioned in the *Book of Knowledge*.[18] Of these, two pertain to our purpose. 'Intellect' may be used with the force of knowledge (*ʿilm*) of the real nature of things, and is thus an expression for the quality of knowledge whose seat is the heart. Second, 'intellect' may be used to denote that which perceives knowledge, or the heart in the sense of the subtle tenuous substance. And we know that every knower has within himself an entity (*wujūd*) which is a self-existing principle (*aṣl qāʾim bi-nafsihi*), and knowledge is a quality (*ṣifa*) residing in it, and the quality is other than the thing qualified. So 'intellect' may be used as meaning the quality of the knower, and it may be used to mean the seat of perception, the mind which perceives. The latter meaning is that referred to in the saying of the Prophet ﷺ, "The first thing God created was the intellect."[19] For knowledge is an accident that cannot be conceived as the first created thing; indeed its seat had to have been created before it or along with it, and because one cannot converse with it [i.e., knowledge, *ʿilm*]. A *ḥadīth* also relates that He, the Exalted, said to the intellect, "Draw near," and it drew near. Then He said, "Retreat," and it retreated.

So it is now made clear to you that there exist the following meanings of these names: the corporeal heart, the corporeal spirit, the appetitive soul, and intelligence. These are four meanings that are denoted by four

---

(6) *al-nafs al-mamlūka*, or the controlled (possessed) soul (Qurʾān 5:28); and (7) *al-nafs al-ʿilmiyya*, or the knowledgeable (ideal) soul.

17 See "ʿaql," *EI*, 1:242ff. for discussion and bibliography. *EI*², 1:341.

18 *The Book of Knowledge* is the first book of the *Iḥyāʾ*. The discussion referred to is in Zabīdī, *Itḥāf*, 1:458ff. Editor's note: see the published translation of this book, *The Book of Knowledge*, trans. Nabih Amin Faris (Lahore: Sh. Muhammad Ashraf, 1966). Also see the PhD thesis of William McCall, "The Book of Knowledge," Being a Translation, with Introduction and Notes of al-Ghazzali's Book of the '*Ihya, Kitab al-Ilm*' (Hartford Seminary, 1940), (available at www.ghazali.org).

19 A weak *ḥadīth* with many variations, discussed at length in Zabīdī, *Itḥāf*, 1:453ff. Zabīdī here gives one fuller form of it as follows: When God created the intellect He said to it, "Draw near," and it drew near. Then He said, "Retreat," and it retreated. Then He said, "I have created nothing that I love more than you; by you I take and by you I give." The idea to which Ghazālī refers in this passage is comparable to the Neoplatonic concept of the intellect being the first emanation from the Absolute. See Browne, *Arabian Medicine*, pp. 121ff. Cf. also the Active Intellect of Fārābī and Ibn Sīnā, Ueberweg, *Philosophy*, 1:412ff.; Brett, *Psychology*, 2:53.

terms.[20] There is also a fifth meaning, which is that subtle tenuous substance in man that knows and perceives, and all four of these names are successively applied to it. There are then five meanings and four terms, and each term is used with two meanings.

Most of the learned (*ʿulamāʾ*) are confused in distinguishing between these terms, and in regard to their successive use. So you find them talking about involuntary suggestions (*khawāṭir*),[21] and saying, "This is the suggestion of the intellect, this is the suggestion of the spirit, this is the suggestion of the heart, and this is the suggestion of the soul," and the observer does not understand the distinction in the meanings of these names. So for the sake of uncovering this matter we have put here at the beginning an explanation of these names. Wherever the expression 'heart' occurs in the Qurʾān and in the Sunna, its intended meaning is that in man which discerns and comes to know the real nature of things. This may be alluded to by metonymy as the heart which is in the breast, because between that subtle tenuous substance and the physical heart there is a special connection.[22] For although this subtle tenuous substance is connected with and used by the rest of the body as well, yet this connection is by means of the heart, so therefore its primary connection is with the heart. It is as though the heart were its seat, its kingdom, its world, and its mount. Therefore Sahl al-Tustarī[23] has likened the heart to the throne and the breast to the seat. He said, "The heart is the throne (*ʿarsh*) and the breast is the seat (*kursī*)." But it must not be supposed that he meant that it is the throne of God and His seat, for that is impossible. But he meant that the heart is its [i.e., the subtle tenuous substance's] kingdom and the primary channel for its planning and activity. These then [i.e., the physical heart and the breast] stand in the same relationship to the heart [the subtle tenuous substance] as do the throne and seat to God, the Exalted.[24]

---

20 Editor's note: Zabīdī comments that they are soul, spirit, heart, and intellect.

21 *Khawāṭir*, see Introduction, pp. xxixff.

22 Ghazālī gives the heart the place of honor; it is the seat of the noblest functions, the brain being given an inferior position. For this concept as it was held in the Aristotelian psychology see Brett, *Psychology*, 1:106.

23 Sahl al-Tustarī, Abū Muḥammad Sahl b. ʿAbdallāh b. Yūnus (203–63/818–96 or 897), was a Sunnī theologian, a mystic, and a strict ascetic. He held that in interpreting the Qurʾān it was necessary to seek four meanings: literal, allegorical, moral, and analogical. See *EI*², 8:840.

24 See "kursī," *EI*², 5:509.

This metaphor is appropriate only in certain respects. The explanation of this is not vital to our purpose and so let us pass it by.

Chapter 2

An Exposition of the Armies of the Heart

GOD, THE EXALTED, HAS said, *And none knows the armies of your Lord except Him* (74:31). For in hearts and spirits and in other worlds God, praise be to Him, has "armies levied,"[1] whose nature and the details of whose number none knows save He. We will now refer to some of the armies of the heart such as pertain to our purpose.

The heart has two armies: an army seen with the eyes, and an army seen only by insight. The heart is as king, and the armies are as servants and helpers, and this is the meaning of 'army' (*jund*). Now its army, which is visible to the eye, includes the hand, the foot, the eye, the ear, the tongue, and the rest of the members, both outer and inner. These all serve the heart and are in subjection thereto, and it is the disposition of them, and repels for them. They were created with an inherent disposition to obey it, and cannot disobey it or rebel against it. For if it orders the eye to be opened, it is opened; if it orders the foot to move, it moves; if it orders the tongue to speak and is fully determined in the matter, it speaks; and so also for the rest of the members. The subjection of the members and the senses to the heart resembles, from one point of view, the subjection of the angels to God, the Exalted; for they were created with an inherent disposition to obedience, and they cannot disobey Him. *They do not disobey God in what He commands them, but do what they are commanded* (66:6). There

---

1 An allusion to the well-known *ḥadīth* narrated by Muslim, "Spirits are armies levied (set in array)." See Wensinck, *Concordance et Indices de la Tradition Musulmane* (Leiden: E. J. Brill, 1933–7), 1:365.

is, however, this one difference: the angels عليهم السلام know their own obedience and conformity, whereas the eyelids obey the heart in opening and closing because they are in subjection to it, and they have no knowledge of themselves nor of their obedience to the heart.

The heart needs these armies because of its need for a vehicle, and for provision for that journey for which it was created, the journey to God, praise be to Him, and for passing through its stages (*manāzil*) until He is met face to face. For this cause hearts were created, as God, the Exalted, has said, *I have not created the jinn and humans save that they may worship me* (51:56). The vehicle of the heart is the body alone; its provision is knowledge alone; and the means of attaining the provision for the journey and supplying one's self therewith lie only in righteous acts.

It is impossible for the creature to reach God, praise be to Him, except by dwelling in the body and passing through this present world (*al-dunyā*),[2] for the nearest stage must be passed through in order that the most distant stage may be attained. This present world is the seedbed (*mazraʿa*) of the world to come (*al-ākhira*),[3] and it is one of the stages of right guidance (*hudā*). It is called 'nearer' (*dunyā*) only because it is the nearer of the two abodes. The heart must therefore get its supply of provision from this world. The body is its vehicle by which it comes into contact with this world. Thus the body needs to be cared for and preserved, and it is preserved only by procuring for it such food and other things as are suitable for it, and by warding off from it the causes of destruction which are repugnant to it and destroy it.

The heart thus needs two armies in order to procure food: an internal army which is the appetite, and an external [army] which is the hand and the members that procure food. So the needed appetites are created in the heart, and the members of the body are created which are the instruments of the appetites.

Likewise the heart needs two armies to drive off the things that lead to destruction: an internal army of anger (*ghaḍab*), by which it drives off things that lead to destruction and takes revenge upon its enemies, and an external [army], which is the hand and the foot by which it carries out the dictates of anger. This is completed by means of things outside the body, such as weapons, and the like.

---

2 See "dunyā," *EI*[2], 2:626.

3 See "ākhira," *EI*, 1:231. *EI*[2], 1:325.

Then, too, the appetite for food and the means of securing it are of no profit to him who needs food as long as he has no knowledge of food. So in order to gain this knowledge, the heart needs two armies: an internal army, which is the perception of sight, taste, smelling, hearing, and touch; and an external [army], which is the eye, ear, nose, etc. A detailed account of the need for these and the wisdom in them would be very long, and many volumes would not contain it. We have referred to a small portion of it in the *Book of [Patience and] Thankfulness*,[4] and this will suffice.

All the armies of the heart are limited to three classes. One class incites and instigates either to obtain that which is profitable and suitable, as, for example, appetence (*shahwa*); or to the ward off that which is harmful and destructive, as, for example, anger (*ghaḍab*). This impulse may be called the will (*irāda*). The second class is that which moves the members to the attainment of these desired ends, and it is called power (*qudra*). These are armies which are diffused throughout the rest of the members, especially the muscles and tendons. The third class is that which perceives and gathers information as spies. These include the power of sight, hearing, smell, taste, etc., which are divided among certain appointed members. This is called knowledge (*ʿilm*) and perception (*idrāk*).

Corresponding to each of these internal armies there are external armies, which are the physical members. These are made up of fat, flesh, nerve, blood, and bone, which are prepared as the instruments of these armies. Thus the power to seize lies only in the fingers, the power to see only in the eye and so on for the other powers. We are not now speaking of the external armies, I mean the physical members, for they belong to the visible material world, but rather of those unseen armies by which the heart is helped. This third class, which alone of this group perceives, is divided into that which is lodged in the outer abodes, or the five senses, I mean hearing, sight, smell, taste, and touch; and that which has been lodged in inner abodes, or the ventricles of the brain, which are also five. Thus after seeing an object a man closes his eye and perceives its image (*ṣūra*) within himself. This is the retentive imagination (*khayāl*). This image then remains with him by reason of something which preserves it, which is the army of memory (*al-jund al-ḥāfiẓ*). He then thinks about what he has remembered and combines part with part, after which he recalls what

4 The second book of the fourth quarter of the *Iḥyāʾ*. Editor's note: forthcoming translation by Henry Littlejohn, *On Patience and Thankfulness* (Cambridge: Islamic Texts Society, 2010).

he had forgotten and it comes back to him again. Then he gathers together in his retentive imagination all the meanings of his sense impressions by means of the common [i.e., shared] sense (*ḥiss mushtarak*).[5] For there are within man common sense, imagination (*takhayyul*), reflection (*tafakkur*), recollection (*tadhakkur*), and memory (*ḥifẓ*).[6] Were it not that God created the powers of memory, thought, recollection, and imagination, the brain would be devoid of them even as is the hand and the leg. Thus these powers are internal armies and their seats are internal.

Such then are the armies of the heart. It would take a long time to explain this by citing examples so that the understanding of the weak could comprehend it, while our purpose in such a book as this is that the strong and masterful from among the learned can profit thereby. Yet we will strive to make the weak understand by citing examples so that this is brought within the range of their understanding.

5 *Sensus communis*. See Brett, *Psychology*, 1:120ff.; 2:55; Howard C. Warren, *Dictionary of Psychology* (Cambridge, MA, 1934), p. 51.

6 For a discussion of these internal senses see Harry Wolfson, "The Internal Senses in Latin, Arabic, and Hebrew Philosophic Texts," *Harvard Theological Review* 28, no. 2 (April 1935), pp. 69–133. See also Brett, *Psychology*, 2:55ff.

Chapter 3

An Exposition of the Similitudes of the Heart and its Internal Armies

KNOW THAT THE TWO armies of anger and appetence are sometimes perfectly obedient to the heart, which helps it along the path it journeys, and their companionship on the journey that lies before it is desirable. But these two also disobey the heart at times, in trespass and revolt, until they gain the mastery over it and bring it into subjection. This results in destroying it and cutting it off from its journey, by which it might reach eternal happiness.

The heart has another army, which is knowledge, wisdom (*ḥikma*), and reflection, the explanation of which will follow. It should gain the assistance of this army, for it is the party of God,[1] the Exalted, against the other two armies, for they may join themselves to the party of Satan. If it neglects this help and gives the army of anger and appetence dominion over itself, it will surely perish and suffer a manifest loss. This is the state of the majority of people, for their intellects have been forced by their appetence to labor at devising stratagems to satisfy the appetence, whereas appetence should be forced by their intellects to labor at that which the mind needs. We will make this clearer to your understanding[2] by means of three examples.

1 Cf. Qurʾān 5:56, 58:22. See *EI*, 2:322ff; "ḥizb," *EI²*, 3:513.

2 Zabīdī, *Itḥāf* and Princeton MS read 'heart.'

Example One.[3] We may say that the soul (I mean by the soul the aforementioned subtle tenuous substance) is like a ruler in his city and his kingdom, for the body is the kingdom of the soul, its world, its abode, and its city. The powers and members of the body occupy the place of craftsmen and laborers. The intelligent reflective power is like the sincere adviser and intelligent minister. Appetence is like an evil slave who brings food and provisions to the city. Anger and ardor (*ḥamiyya*) are like the chief of police. The slave who brings the provisions is a liar, a deceiver, an impostor, and a malicious person who plays the part of a sincere adviser, while beneath his advice there is dreadful evil and deadly poison. It is his wont and his custom to contend against every plan that the wise minister makes, so that not even for an hour does he cease his contention and opposition to his [the minister's] opinions. When the ruler in his kingdom seeks the advice of his minister and shuns the counsel of this vile slave, inferring indeed from his counsel that the right course is that which is contradictory to his opinion; and [when] the chief of police disciplines him and brings him under the authority of the minister and causes him to be under his orders, empowering him on his part over this vile slave and his followers and helpers, so that the slave is under authority and not the possessor of it, and so that he [the slave] is subject to orders and directions and not the one who gives orders and directs; then the rule of his [the king's] state is upright and then justice is ordered because of him.

Thus when the soul seeks the aid of the intellect and is disciplined by the ardor of anger, which it empowers over appetence, seeking the aid of one of the two against the other; sometimes by lessening the degree and excess of anger by making an ally of appetence and gradually modifying it; sometimes by subduing and overcoming the appetence by giving anger and ardor power over it and by disapproving of its demands; then its powers are made harmonious and its character comely. Whoever turns aside from this path is like the one of whom God, the Exalted, has said, *Have you seen such a one as takes as his god his own vain desire? God has, knowing (him as such), left him astray* (45:23). He, the Exalted, also said, *and followed his lust and his likeness was as the likeness of a dog; if you chase him, he pants, or if you leave him, he [still] pants* (7:176). Again He ﷻ said about the one who restrains his soul from lust, *[But] as for he who feared standing before his Lord, and restrained his soul from lower desires, then indeed Paradise will be [his] refuge* (79:40–1). The way in which these armies strive, and

3 Cf. Weliur-Rahman, "The Psychology of Ibn-i-Sina," p. 355.

the way in which some of them are given power over others will be told, if God, the Exalted, so wills, in the *Book of Disciplining the Soul.*

Example Two. Know that the body is like a city and the mind (*ʿaql*), I mean the perceptive power in man, is like a king who rules over it. Its perceptive powers of the senses, both externel and internal, are like its armies and helpers. Its members are like the people of the city. 'The soul that commands to evil,'[4] which is appetence and anger, is like the enemy who opposes him in his kingdom and strives to destroy his people. His body thus becomes, as it were, a frontier outpost, and his soul the place in which guards are stationed. So if he is one who strives against the enemy and routs him and conquers him as he ought, then will his deeds be praised on the day when he returns to the Presence [i.e., of God]. As God, the Exalted, says, *and those who strive in God's way with their wealth and their persons, God has preferred those who strive with their wealth and their persons a rank above those who sit still* (4:95). But if he loses the frontier and neglects his people, his deeds will be blamed and vengeance will be taken against him [from those he neglected] when he meets God the Exalted. A *ḥadīth* says, "It will be said to him on the day of resurrection, 'O evil shepherd, you ate meat and drank milk and did not bring back the lost nor restore the broken; today will I [the one neglected] be revenged against you.'"[5] It is also to this struggle that reference is made in the saying of the Prophet, "We have returned from the lesser struggle (*jihād*) to the greater."[6]

Example Three. The intellect is like a horseman who has gone hunting. His appetence is his horse and his anger is his dog. When the horseman is skilled and his horse well broken and his dog trained and taught, then he is able to succeed. But when he is himself clumsy, his horse ungovernable, and his dog vicious, then his horse is neither guided under him, nor does his dog go forth in obedience to his signs. So he himself deserves to perish

---

4 Cf. Qurʾān 12:53.

5 A weak *ḥadīth*, not found in the well-known collections. ʿAbd al-Raḥīm b. al-Ḥusayn al-ʿIrāqī (725–806/1325–1404), the famous Egyptian *ḥadīth* scholar who traced the sources of the *ḥadīths* that Ghazālī quotes in the *Iḥyāʾ*, says that he did not find a source for this *ḥadīth*. Editor's note: Zabīdī says it was narrated by Abū Nuʿaym in the biography of Mālik b. Dīnār.

6 ʿIrāqī says that this was a weak *ḥadīth*, found in the collection of Bayhaqī. See Ghazālī, *Ayyuhā al-walad*, trans. George H. Scherer, *O Youth!* (Beirut: American Press, 1933), p. 62n2.

rather than to gain that which he seeks. The clumsiness of the horseman is like the ignorance of a man, his paucity of wisdom, and his dim insight. The restiveness of the horse is like the victory of appetence, and especially the appetite for food and for sexual indulgence. The viciousness of the dog is like the victory of anger and its domination. We ask God in His grace to grant us success.[7]

7 Success (*tawfīq*) is the divine favor by which success is attained. Theologians differed in explaining it. The Ashʿarī position is that it was the creation of the power needed for obedience. See Tahānawī, *Iṣṭilāḥāt al-funūn*, p. 1501; Asín, *Algazel*, pp. 447ff.

Chapter 4

An Exposition of the Special Properties of the Heart of Man

KNOW THAT GOD HAS bestowed on all animals other than man all of these things that we have mentioned. For animals have appetence and anger, and the senses, both outer and inner. Thus the sheep sees the wolf with her eye and knows in her heart its enmity, and so flees from it. That is an inner perception.

We will now mention that which peculiarly characterizes the heart of man, and because of which he has been given great honor and is qualified to draw near to God, the Exalted. This special characteristic has its basis in knowledge and will. By 'knowledge' is meant that knowledge which deals with the things of this world[1] and the world to come, and with intellectual realities (*ḥaqāʾiq ʿaqliyya*). These things are beyond the objects of sense perception, and animals do not share with man in them. Nay, rather, knowledge of axioms and universals (*al-ʿulūm al-kulliyya al-ḍarūriyya*) is a peculiar property of the intellect. Thus a man judges that a single individual[2] cannot be imagined to be in two places at one time. This is his judgment for every individual, although it is well known that he has only observed some individuals by his sense perception. So his judgment passed on all individuals goes beyond that which sense has perceived. If you understand this in regard to this obvious axiomatic knowledge, it is even more obvious in the rest of the theoretical sciences (*naẓariyyāt*).

---

1 Zabīdī and Princeton MS read 'of religion.'

2 Zabīdī text reads 'horse' instead of 'individual' throughout this illustration.

Now regarding the will, when a man perceives by his intellect the consequences of an act and the best way to do [something], there is aroused within his essential self (*dhāt*) a desire for the advantageous way, a desire to exert himself in the means to attain it, and also the will to this end. This differs from the will of appetence and the will power that animals have, indeed it is quite the opposite of appetence. For appetence shuns bleeding and cupping,[3] while the intelligent [man] wants them, seeks them, and freely spends money for them. The appetite inclines to savory foods in time of sickness, while the intelligent [man] finds within himself that which causes him to abstain from them. This abstinence does not come from appetence. Had God created the intellect that gives information regarding the consequences of things, and not created this cause that moves the members to carry out the mandates of the intellect, then the judgment of the intellect would, in reality, be lost. Thus the heart of man has the special properties of knowledge and will which separate it from the other animals, nay, rather, which separate it from the youth in his original constitution,[4] for this comes to him only with maturity.

Now appetence, anger, and the external and internal senses exist potentially in youth, but in attaining them the youth must pass through two stages. One stage is that his heart must comprehend the knowledge of axioms and first principles, such as the knowledge of the impossibility of impossible things, and the possibility of things manifestly possible. But in this stage he has not as yet attained to the speculative sciences, save that they have become possible and within easy reach of attainment. His status in relation to knowledge is like that of the writer whose knowledge of writing consists merely in knowing inkstand, pen, and the letters as they are written separately but not in their combined forms, for such a person is well on the way to writing but has not as yet achieved it.

The second stage is that he shall gain that knowledge which is acquired by experiment and thought, so that it is stored up in him and he can return to it whenever he wills. His status is like that of a man skilled in writing, who, on account of his ability therein, is called a writer, even when he is not actually engaged in writing. This is the highest stage of humanity, but in this stage there are innumerable degrees of contrast among men in the abundance or paucity of knowledge, in the dignity of knowledge or its sordidness, and in the way of attaining it. [This knowledge] comes

3 See Browne, *Arabian Medicine*, pp. 12, 43.

4 "Fiṭra," *EI*, 2:115ff. *EI*^{2}, 2:931.

to some hearts through divine revelation (*ilhām ilāhī*)[5] by way of immediate disclosure (*mubādaʾa*) and unveiling (*mukāshafa*), and for some it is a thing to be learned and acquired. Sometimes it is gained quickly and sometimes slowly. In this stage are seen the varying degrees of the learned (*ʿulamāʾ*), the wise (*ḥukamāʾ*),[6] prophets (*anbiyāʾ*),[7] and saints (*awliyāʾ*).[8]

The degrees of advancement in knowledge are unlimited inasmuch as the knowledge of God, praise be to Him, is infinite. The highest rank is that of the prophet to whom is revealed all realities, or most of them, not by a process of acquisition nor after difficulty, but by a divine unveiling in the shortest possible time. In this happiness man draws near to God, the Exalted, in idea (*maʿnā*), reality, and quality, not in respect to place and distance. The levels up to these various degrees are the stages (*manāzil*) reached by those journeying (*sāʾirīn*) toward God, the Exalted, and there is no limitation to these stages. Each traveler knows only his own stage, to which he has attained on his journey. He knows it and he knows also those stages that are behind him. He does not know the real nature of that which is just ahead of him, but he may believe in it as he believes in the unseen. Even as we believe in prophecy and the prophet and accept his existence as true, while no one but a prophet knows the real nature of prophecy; and even as the embryo knows not the state of the infant, nor the infant the state of the discerning child and what has been opened up to him of axiomatic knowledge; nor the discerning child the state of the intelligent man and what he has acquired of speculative knowledge; so also the intelligent man knows not what attainments of the grace and mercy of God have been revealed to His saints and prophets. *The mercy which God grants to humanity none can withhold* (35:2). This mercy is generously bestowed by reason of the goodness and generosity of God ﷻ who does not begrudge it to anyone, but it only appears in those hearts that are exposed to the gifts of God. The Prophet ﷺ said, "Verily your Lord, in the days of your generation, has gifts; will you then not expose yourselves to them?"[9] This exposing of one's self to them is done by cleansing and purifying the heart from evil and from the turbidity that comes from a blameworthy

5 *Ilhām* is the general inspiration given to saints; see *EI*, 2:467ff. *EI*², 3:1119.

6 "Ḥukamāʾ," *EI*, 2:224. *EI*², "ḥikma," 3:377.

7 "Anbiyāʾ," *EI*, 3:802ff. *EI*², "nubuwwa," 8:93.

8 "Awliyāʾ," *EI*, 4:1109ff. *EI*², "walī," pl. "awliyāʾ," 11:109.

9 A *ḥadīth* described by ʿIrāqī as disagreed upon (*mukhtalaf al-isnād*), quoted also in *Iḥyāʾ*, 1:186.

character, as will be set forth later. This liberality is that which is referred to in the statement of the Prophet ﷺ, "God descends every night to the lowest heaven and says, 'Is there anyone who asks, that I may grant his request?'"[10] Again the Prophet ﷺ said, quoting the statement of his Lord, ﷻ "Great indeed is the longing of the righteous to meet me, and I long even more to meet them."[11] There is also the saying of [God], the Exalted,[12] "Whoever draws near to me by a span, I approach him by a cubit."[13]

All of this is an indication that the light of knowledge is not veiled from men's hearts by any stinginess or prohibition on the part of the Giver, who is far removed from such acts, but rather it is veiled by wickedness, turbidity, and anxiety within the heart. For hearts are like vessels; as long as they are filled with water, air cannot enter them. So the knowledge of the majesty of God, the Exalted, cannot enter into hearts that are occupied with anything apart from Him. It is to this that reference is made in the saying of the Prophet ﷺ, "The sons of Adam would look unto the kingdom of Heaven were it not that the demons hover over their hearts."[14] From all of this it is clear that the special characteristic peculiar to man is knowledge and wisdom,[15] and that the noblest kind of knowledge is the knowledge of God, His attributes, and His deeds. By this comes man's perfection, and in his perfection is his happiness and worthiness to live near the divine majesty and perfection. The body then is a vehicle for the soul, and the soul is the seat of knowledge. Knowledge is the end destined for man and his special characteristic for which he was created.

---

10 An authentic *ḥadīth* given by Malik, Bukhārī, Muslim, Abū Dāwūd, Tirmidhī and Ibn Māja. Wensinck, *Concordance*, 2:152b.; Muḥammad al-Madanī, *al-Itḥāfāt al-saniyya fi-l-aḥādīth al-qudsiyya* (Hyderabad 1323), nos. 422, 796, 844–50; Ibn Qutayba, *Mukhtalaf al-ḥadīth*, p. 243. It is quoted also in Zabīdī, *Itḥāf*, 3:3.

11 ʿIrāqī says that he did not find a source for this *ḥadīth*.

12 Zabīdī says this a *ḥadīth qudsī*.

13 An authentic *ḥadīth* given by Bukhārī from Abū Hurayra, and accepted by all. Wensinck, *Handbook of Early Muḥammadan Tradition* (Leiden: E. J. Brill, 1927), p. 18b.; Ibn Qutayba, *Mukhtalaf al-ḥadīth*, p. 284.

14 A *ḥadīth* quoted by Aḥmad b. Ḥanbal from Abū Hurayra. Previously quoted in *Iḥyā*ʾ, 1:264.

15 This was one of the teachings of the Aristotelian system; see Windelband, *Philosophy*, p. 154.

The horse shares with the donkey the power to carry burdens and is distinguished from it by its own special characteristics of charging and fleeing, and beauty of form, and therefore the horse was created for the sake of these special characteristics, the removal of which from it would bring it to the low rank of the donkey. Likewise man shares in some things with the donkey and the horse, and differs from them in others, which are his own special characteristics. These distinguishing characteristics are among the qualities of the angels who are drawn near to [God,] the Lord of the worlds.

Man has a rank between the beasts and the angels. Man, in that he takes nourishment and reproduces, is a plant; and in that he has sense perceptions and moves by his own free will, he is an animal; and with regard to his figure and his stature, he is like the relief figure on the wall; but his distinguishing characteristic is his experiential knowledge (*maʿrifa*) of the real nature of things.[16] Whoever makes use of all of his members and powers in such a way as to seek their aid in attaining to knowledge and work, is like the angels and is worthy to be joined to them, and deserves to be called an angel and a lordly being (*rabbānī*). Thus God, the Exalted, has declared, by the mouths of the women who beheld Joseph ﷺ, *This is no mortal; this can be no other than a noble angel* (12:31). But whoever spends his energy in following after bodily pleasures and eats as do the animals is brought down to the low depths of the beasts. So he becomes ignorant as an ox, gluttonous as a hog, greedy as a dog, or a cat, malevolent as a camel, vain as a leopard, or sly as a fox. Or he may unite all of these and become a rebellious demon (*shayṭān marīd*).

There is not a single one of the bodily members nor a single sense perception but that it helps along the path that leads to God, the Exalted, as will be shown, in part, in the *Book of [Patience and] Thankfulness*. Whoever uses them therein wins the victory, but whoever turns aside therefrom loses and is disappointed. The totality of man's happiness therein lies in making the meeting with God, the Exalted, his aim, the abode of the world

---

16 For the Aristotelian development of the vegetative soul, the animal soul, and the rational soul, which is the basis of this section, see Windelband, *Philosophy*, pp. 149–54; Brett, *Psychology*, 1:128ff., 2:54ff. For the Muslim development of this thought before Ghazālī, see Weliur-Rahman, "The Psychology of Ibn-i-Sina," pp. 335–58.

to come his dwelling place, this present world his temporary stopping place,[17] the body his vehicle, and its members his servants.

So the perceptive part of man dwells in the heart, as a king in the midst of his kingdom. The imaginative faculty, whose seat is in the front of the brain,[18] acts as the master of his couriers, for the reports of sense perceptions (*maḥsūsāt*) are gathered therein. The faculty of retentive memory (*ḥāfiẓa*), whose seat is the back of the brain, acts as his storage keeper. The tongue is his interpreter and the active members of his body [are] his scribes. The five senses act as his spies, and he makes each one of them responsible in a certain domain. Thus he sets the eye over the world of colors, hearing over the world of sounds, smell over the world of odors, and so on for the others. These are the bearers of tidings that they collect from their different worlds and transmit to the imaginative faculty, which is like the master of the couriers. The latter in turn delivers them to the storage keeper, which is memory. The storage keeper sets them forth before the king, who selects therefrom that which he has need of in managing his kingdom, in completing the journey ahead of him, in subjugating his enemy by whom he is afflicted, and in warding off from himself those who cut off his path. If [the king] does this he is successful, happy, and thankful for the blessings of God, the Exalted. But if he neglects all of these things, or uses them for the welfare of his enemies, which are appetence, anger, and other transient pleasures, and in the building of his path instead of his abode—for this present world is his path through which he must pass, while his own country and his permanent abode is the world to come—then he is forsaken, wretched, ungrateful for the blessings of God, the Exalted, being one who makes ill use of the armies of God, the Exalted, and forsakes the party of God. So he deserves hatred and exile on the day of overturn[ing] and resurrection. May God protect us from such.

Kaʿb al-Aḥbār[19] referred to this example, which we have given, when he said, "I went to ʿĀʾisha[20] 🙵 and said to her, 'Man's eyes are a guide, his ears a funnel, his tongue an interpreter, his hands wings, his feet couriers,

---

17 Zabīdī reads 'path.'

18 This localization of the seat of the imaginative power was an older idea of Greek philosophers and was given new life by Ibn Sīnā; Brett, *Psychology*, 2:56.

19 Kaʿb al-Aḥbār, Abū Isḥāq b. Matīʿ b. Haisūʿ, was a Yemeni Jew, converted to Islam in the caliphate of Abū Bakr or ʿUmar. He was the oldest authority for Jewish–Muslim traditions; see *EI*, 2:582ff. *EI²*, 4:316.

20 ʿĀʾisha b. Abī Bakr, the favorite wife of the Prophet; see *EI*, 1:216. *EI²*, 1:307.

and the heart is his king. If the king enjoys good health, so also do his armies.'" She said, "Thus have I heard the Messenger of God ﷺ speak."[21]

ʿAlī[22] ؓ also, in illustrating the heart of man, said, "Verily, God, the Exalted, in His earth has vessels, and they are the hearts of men. Those most beloved by Him, the Exalted, are the gentlest, the clearest, and the most robust."[23] Then he explained, saying, "The most robust in religion, the clearest in certainty, and the gentlest to the brethren." This is a reference to the statement of [God] the Exalted, *hard against the unbelievers and merciful among themselves* (48:29), and the statement of [God] the Exalted, *His light is like a niche within which is a lamp* (24:35). Ubayy b. Kaʿb[24] ؓ said, "This means 'as the light of a believer and his heart.'" Again there is the statement of [God] the Exalted, *Or like the darkness in a vast deep ocean* (24:40), which is an illustration of the heart of the hypocrite. Zayd b. Aslam[25] said of the statement of [God] the Exalted, *in a preserved tablet* (85:22), "It is the heart of the believer." Sahl said, "The heart and the breast are like the throne and the seat." These then are the examples of the heart.

---

21 ʿIrāqī says that this *ḥadīth* was not authentic.

22 ʿAlī b. Abī Ṭālib, the cousin of the Prophet and his son-in-law, was the fourth caliph; see *EI*, 1:283ff. *EI*², 1:381.

23 A weak *ḥadīth* quoted from Makkī, *Qūt al-qulūb*.

24 Ubayy b. Kaʿb, a Helper (d. 22 or 30/643 or 650). He wrote down some of the prophetic revelation for Muḥammad. See Ibn Ḥajar al-ʿAsqalānī, *A Biographical Dictionary of Persons who knew Mohammed* (Calcutta, 1856), 1:30ff. Ibn Qutayba, *Ibn Coteiba's Handbuch der Geschichte*, ed. Ferdinand Wüstenfeld (Götingen: bei Vandenhoeck und Ruprecht, 1850), p. 133.

25 Zayd b. Aslam al-ʿAdawī (d. 36/656) was a freedman of the caliph ʿUmar and a reliable *ḥadīth* scholar. Ibn Ḥajar, 2:39; Ibn al-Nadīm, *Kitāb al-fihrist*, ed. Gustav Flügel (Leipzig: F. C. W. Vogel, 1871–2), pp. 23, 225.

Chapter 5

An Exposition Summarizing the Qualities and Similitudes of the Heart

Know that there are four mingled factors that dwell together in man's nature and make-up, and therefore four kinds of qualities are united against him. These are the qualities (*ṣifāt*) of the beasts of prey (*sabuʿiyya*), brutish qualities (*bahīmiyya*), demonic qualities (*shayṭāniyya*), and lordly qualities (*rabbāniyya*).

Insofar as anger rules over him he is overcome by the deeds of a beast of prey, such as enmity, detestation, and attacking people by beating and cursing them. Insofar as appetence rules him he is overcome by brutish acts of gluttony, greed, carnal desire, and so on. Insofar as there is within his soul something lordly, as God, the Exalted, has said, *The Spirit is my Lord's affair* (17:85), he claims lordship for himself and loves mastery, superiority, exclusiveness, and despotism in all things; and to be the sole ruler, and to slip away from the noose of servitude and humility. He longs to study all [branches] of knowledge, nay, rather he claims for himself knowledge and gnosis and the comprehension of the real nature of things. He rejoices when knowledge is attributed to him, and is grieved when accused of ignorance. The comprehension of all realities, and seeking to rule by force over all creatures are among the lordly qualities, and man is greedy for them. Insofar as he differs from the beasts in having the faculty of discernment, although sharing anger (*ghaḍab*) and appetence (*shahwa*) with them, he attains to demonic qualities. Thus he becomes wicked and uses his discernment in the discovery of ways of evil. He seeks to attain his ends by guile, deceit, and cunning, and sets forth evil as though it were good. These are the characteristics of demons (*shayāṭīn*).

Every man has within him a mixture of these four qualities, i.e., lordly, demonic, beastly, and brutish; and all of these are gathered together in the heart. So there are gathered inside of a man's skin, as it were, a pig, a dog, a demon, and a sage. The pig is appetence, for the pig is not blamed for his color, his shape or appearance, but for his covetousness, his voracity, and his greed. The dog is anger, for the carniverous beast and the savage dog are not dog and beast from the standpoint of their appearance or color or shape, but because the spirit and meaning of this bestial quality is savagery and enmity and slaughter. Now within man there is the savagery and anger of the beast, and the greed and lechery (*shabaq*) of the pig. Thus the pig through gluttony invites man to excess and abomination, and the wild beast by means of anger calls him to oppression and harmful acts. The demon continues to stir up the appetite of the pig and the wrath of the wild beast, and to incite the one by means of the other; and he makes their inborn dispositions appear good to them.

The sage, who represents the intellect, is in duty bound to ward off the plotting and guile of the demon by revealing his deception by means of his [i.e., the sage's] penetrating insight and evident clear illumination; and to destroy the gluttony of this pig by setting the dog over him, for by means of anger he breaks down the assault of appetence. He wards off the savagery of the dog by setting the pig over him and bringing the dog in subjection under his rule. If he does this successfully his affairs are set right, equity is manifest in the kingdom of the body, and all proceeds on the straight path.

But if he is unable to overcome them they overcome him and bring him into servitude, and so he continues to seek crafty tricks and careful plans to satisfy his pig and please his dog. Thus he is constantly in servitude to a dog or a pig. This is the condition of the majority of mankind whenever their primary concern is for the belly, loins, and vying with the enemy. The strange thing is that he disapproves of idolators worshipping stones, whereas if the veil were removed and his true state were disclosed and his true condition set before him as it is set before mystics (*al-mukāshafūn*), either in sleep or when awake, he would see himself standing before a pig, now prostrating himself before him and again kneeling, awaiting his signal and his command. So whenever the pig is roused up to seek the satisfying of any of his appetites, the man is sent forth at once to serve him and to bring that for which he lusts. Or else the man would see himself standing before a savage dog worshipping him, obeying him and giving ear to his demands and requests, and carefully planning schemes to render obedience to him. Thus he endeavors to please his demon, for it is he who stirs up the pig and arouses the dog and sends them forth to bring [the man] into subjection. In this way he worships the demon in his worship of these two.

So let every servant watch over his times of activity and of inactivity, his silence and his speech, his rising up and his sitting down, and let him look to them with careful insight, and he will find, if he is honest with himself, nothing but an effort all day long to serve these base impulses. This is the utmost oppression, for it makes the possessor possessed, the lord lorded over, the master a slave, and the conqueror conquered, in that [man] forces the mind that is worthy of lordship, conquest, and rule to serve these low impulses. And undoubtedly from obedience to these three qualities are spread to the heart that are heaped up thereupon so that they become a dirty stain and a rust that is destructive and deadly to the heart.[1]

From obedience to the pig of appetence there result the following characteristics: shamelessness, wickedness, wastefulness, avarice, hypocrisy, defamation, wantonness, nonsense, greed, covetousness, flattery, envy, rancor, rejoicing at another's evil, and so on. As for obedience to the dog of anger there are spread thereby into the heart the qualities of rashness, squandering, haughtiness, boasting, hot temper, pride, conceit, sneering, disregard, despising of creatures, the will to evil, the lust of oppression, and others. In regard to obedience to the demon through obedience to appetence and anger, there results from it the qualities of guile, deceit, craftiness, cunning, deception, audacity,[2] dissembling, violence, fraud, mischief, obscenity, and such like.

But if the matter is reversed and man overcomes all these, bringing them under the rule of the lordly element within him, then his heart becomes the abode of such lordly qualities as knowledge, wisdom, certainty, the comprehension of the real nature of things, the knowledge of matters as they really are, the subjugation of all by the power of knowledge and insight, and worthiness to advance beyond all creatures because of the perfection and majesty of his knowledge. Then too he dispenses with the worship of appetence and anger, and, by holding in check the

1 Cf. Qurʾān 9:88, 94; 83:14.

2 The rest of this list is omitted in Zabīdī.

pig of appetence and returning him to his proper limits, he acquires such honorable qualities as chastity, contentment, quietness, abstemiousness, godliness, piety, happiness, goodly aspect, modesty, sagacity, helpfulness, and such like. By holding in check the power of anger and conquering it, and returning it to its proper limits, man attains to the qualities of courage, generosity, gallantry, self-control, patience, gentleness, endurance, pardoning, steadfastness, nobility, valor,[3] dignity, and others.

The heart is as a mirror that is surrounded by these factors which exert their influence upon it. These influences reach the heart in uninterrupted succession. The praiseworthy influences that we have mentioned add to the clearness, shining, illumination, and brightness of the mirror so that the clear statement of the Real[4] (*jalliyyat al-Ḥaqq*) shines therein, and there is revealed in it the real nature of the thing sought in religion. To such a heart as this is the reference of the Prophet ﷺ in his saying, "Whenever God wills good for a man He causes his heart to exhort him";[5] and in his saying ﷺ, "The man whose heart is his exhorter has a protector from God over him."[6] This is the heart in which there abides the remembrance (*dhikr*) [of God]. God, the Exalted said, *Verily in remembrance of God do hearts find rest!* (13:28).

The blameworthy influences are like a darkening smoke that rises up over the mirror of the heart and is heaped up upon it time after time until it becomes dark and murky and entirely veiled from God the Exalted. This is corrosion and rust. God, the Exalted, said, *Nay, but that which they have earned is rust upon their hearts* (83:14). He ﷻ also said, *if We will, We can affilict them in their sins, and imprint their hearts, so that they hear not* (7:100). Here He connected their lack of hearing with their being corroded by sins, even as He connected hearing with godly fear. He, the Exalted, said, *but fear God and listen* (5:108), and *fear God, and God teaches you* (2:282). Whenever sins are heaped up the heart is corroded, and thereupon it is blinded to the perception of reality and the correctness of [one's practice of] religion. It scorns the world to come and magnifies this present world, feeling concern for it alone. So if anything concerning the world to come and the dangers therein knocks at its hearing, it goes into one ear and out the other. It does not find an abode in the heart nor stir it to repentance

3 Zabīdī omits the last two of the list.

4 *Al-Ḥaqq*, God as the Absolute Reality.

5 ʿIrāqī says that the chain of narrators for this *ḥadīth* is good (*jayyid*).

6 ʿIrāqī says that he did not find a source for this *ḥadīth*.

and to make amends. These are they who despair of the world to come even as the infidels despair of those who are in their graves.[7] This is the meaning of the blackening of the heart by sins according to the statement of the Qurʾān and the Sunna.[8]

Maymūn b. Mihrān[9] said, "Whenever a man commits a sin he makes a black spot upon his heart, and whenever he turns away from it and repents, the spot is polished away, and if he returns to sin it increases until it covers the heart." This is rust. The Prophet ﷺ said, "The heart of the believer is stripped clean and a lamp shines therein, but the heart of the unbeliever is black and upside down."[10] Obedience to God, praise be to Him, by striving against the appetites polishes the heart, but disobedience to Him blackens it. So whoever engages in acts of disobedience blackens his heart; and whoever does a good deed after he has done an evil one, and thereby removes its effect, does not have his heart darkened, but its light is decreased. It is like a mirror which [one] breathes upon and then wipes off, and then breathes upon again and wipes off, which is not without a certain cloudiness.[11]

The Prophet ﷺ said, "There are four kinds of hearts:[12] a heart that is stripped clean, in which a lamp shines and this is the believer's heart; a heart that is black and upside down, which is the heart of the unbeliever; a hardened heart bound in its sheath of evil, which is the heart of the hypocrite; and a broad heart in which there is both belief and hypocrisy. Its belief is like green herbage that pure water causes to abound, and its hypocrisy is like an ulcer which purulent matter and pus cause to spread.

---

7 Cf. Qurʾān 60:13.

8 "Sunna," usage or way of life; see *EI*, 4:555ff. *EI*², 9:878. Zabīdī says in Qurʾān, 83:14; in the Sunna [editor's note: *ḥadīth* literature].

9 Maymūn b. Mihrān, Abū ʿAmr b. Mihrān al-Jazarī (d. 116 or 117/734 or 735), a Follower. He was a cloth merchant and tax collector under ʿUmar b. ʿAbd al-ʿAzīz. Ibn Qutayba, *Mukhtalaf al-ḥadīth*, p. 228; Ibn Taghrībirdī, *Abū al-Maḥāsin Ibn Ṭagri Bardii Annales* [Nujūm al-zāhira fī mulūk Miṣr wa-l-Qāhira], ed. T. W. J. Juynboll and B. F. Matthes, 2 vols. (Leiden: E. J. Brill, 1851–5), 1:291, 308.

10 A part of the following *ḥadīth*; see the next note.

11 Editor's note: see Hamza Yusuf, trans., *Purification of the Heart* (Starlatch, 2004).

12 A *ḥadīth* given by Aḥmad from Abū Saʿīd al-Khudrī, Wensinck, *Handbook*, p. 95a. Previously quoted in the *Iḥyāʾ*. Cf. Massignon, *Essai sur les Origines du Lexique Technique de la Mystique Musulmane* (Paris: P. Geuthner, 1922), p. 138.

This heart is judged to belong to whichever of the two gains the mastery." Another reading is, "is carried away by whichever."

God, the Exalted, said, *Indeed, those who fear God, when a thought touches them from Satan, they remember [God] and at once they have insight* (7:201). Thus He stated that the clearness of the heart and its perspicacity are attained by the practice of remembrance (*dhikr*),[13] and none achieve this except those who fear Him. For the fear of God is the door to remembrance of Him; remembrance is the door to mystical unveiling (*kashf*);[14] and mystical unveiling is the door to the greatest success (*fawz*) which is the success of meeting (*liqāʾ*) God the Exalted.

13 *Dhikr*, often written *zikr*, includes the remembrance of the heart and the act of making mention with the tongue; see *EI*, 1:958. *EI*², 2:223.

14 "Kashf," mystic unveiling; see *EI*, 2:787ff. *EI*², 4:696.

Chapter 6

An Exposition of the Similitudes of the Heart as Related Specifically to Knowledge

KNOW THAT THE SEAT (*maḥall*) of knowledge (*ʿilm*) is the heart, by which I mean the subtle tenuous substance (*laṭīfa*) that rules all the parts of the body and is obeyed and served by all its members. In its relationship to the real nature of intelligibles (*maʿlūmāt*), it is like a mirror in its relationship to the forms (*ṣuwar*) of changing appearances (*mutalawwināt*). For even as that which changes has a form, and the image (*mithāl*) of that form is reflected in the mirror and represented therein, so also every intelligible has its specific nature, and this specific nature has a form that is reflected and made manifest in the mirror of the heart. Even as the mirror is one thing, the forms of individuals another, and the representation of their image in the mirror another, being thus three things in all, so here, too, there are three things: the heart, the specific natures of things, and the representation and presence of these in the heart. The 'intellect' (*al-ʿālim*) is an expression for the heart in which there exists the image of the specific natures of things. The 'intelligible' (*al-maʿlūm*) is an expression for the specific natures of things. 'Intelligence' (*al-ʿilm*) is an expression for the representation of the image in the mirror.

Even as the act of grasping, for example, requires that which grasps, such as the hand, and that which is grasped, such as the sword, and an act bringing together the sword and the hand by placing the sword in the hand, which is called the act of grasping, so also the coming of the image of the intelligible into the heart is called intelligence. The reality was in existence and so also the heart, but there was no intelligence present, for intelligence is an expression for the coming of the reality into the heart. Similarly the sword was in existence and also the hand, but there was nothing named 'the act of grasping and taking' present because the sword had not actually come into the hand. It is true that 'grasping' is an expression for the presence of the sword itself in the hand, while the intelligible itself does not actually come into the heart. For fire itself does not actually come into the heart of one who knows fire, but that which is actually present is its definition and its real nature that corresponds to its form. So the comparison of [the heart] with the mirror is more apt, for man himself is not really present in the mirror, but there is present merely an image that corresponds to him, and thus the presence of an image in the heart corresponding to the real nature of the intelligible is called intelligence.[1]

The mirror may not reflect the forms for five reasons: first, a defect in its formation, as, for example, a piece of crude iron before it is turned and shaped and polished; second, because of its dirt and rust and dullness, even though it is perfect in formation; third, because it is turned away from the direction of the object toward something else, as, for example, if the object were behind the mirror; fourth, because of a veil placed between the mirror and the object; and fifth, because of ignorance of the direction of the object desired, so that it is impossible to place it in front of the position and direction of the object.

Thus too is the heart a mirror, ready to have reflected in it the true nature of reality in all things. Hearts are destitute of the knowledge that they lack only because of the following five reasons.

The first reason is an imperfection in its own nature, such as the heart of a youth that does not reflect intelligibles because of its imperfection.

The second reason is because of dullness that is a result of acts of disobedience, and the filth from many lusts that are heaped upon the face of the heart, for these prevent the purity and cleanness of heart. Reality ceases to be manifest therein in proportion to its darkness and the filth heaped upon it. To this the Prophet ﷺ referred in his statement, "When [a man] commits a sin something of his intelligence forsakes him and does not return to him again."[2] That is to say, there comes over his heart a dullness whose influence abides forever, even when his purpose is to follow it with a good deed that will erase it. But if he had done the good

1 Cf. the separated form or intellectus agens of Ibn Sīnā's doctrine of the intellect. Brett, *Psychology*, 2:57ff.

2 ʿIrāqī says that he did not find a source for this *ḥadīth*.

deed without the preceding evil deed, then the illumination of the heart would unquestionably have increased. However when the evil deed preceded [it], the value of the good deed was lost, although the heart was restored by it to its state previous to the evil deed, but its light was not increased thereby. This is an evident loss and an inescapable defect. The mirror that has been stained and then wiped off with a polishing cloth is not like that which has been wiped with the polisher to increase its clearness without any previous stain. So undertaking obedience to God and opposing the demands of the appetites is that which brightens the heart and purifies it. Therefore God, the Exalted, said, *And those who strive for Us—We will surely guide to Our ways* (29:69). The Prophet ﷺ said, "God causes him who does the best he knows to become the heir to knowledge that he knows not."[3]

The third reason is that the heart may be turned away from the direction of reality which is sought. For the heart of the good and obedient man, although it is bright, does not have the clear statement of the Real revealed in it, for he does not seek the Real and does not have his mirror opposite to the direction of the thing sought. Perhaps all of his attention is taken up by the details of bodily submission or arranging the means of his livelihood, and his thought is not free to contemplate the Lordly Presence and the hidden divine realities. So there is revealed to him only that which he thinks about, whether it is the minute defects of his [religious] works or the hidden faults of the soul, if it is these which occupy his mind, or the interests of gaining a livelihood if he thinks of them. Now if limiting one's attention to works and the details of acts of obedience prevents the revelation of the clearness of the Real, what is your estimation (*ẓann*)[4] of one who expends his energies in the lusts and pleasures of this present world and the things connected therewith? And how should true revelation not be denied to such a person?

The fourth reason is the veil. The obedient man who has overcome his appetites and devotes himself exclusively to a certain specific reality may not have this revealed to him because it is veiled from him by some belief that he has held from his youth, and which he has blindly followed (*taqlīd*) and accepted in good faith. This belief walls him off from the true nature of the Real and prevents there being revealed to his heart

---

3 A weak *ḥadīth* quoted from Makkī, *Qūt al-qulūb*; it precedes in *Iḥyā*ʾ, 1:63.

4 See Wolfson, "Internal Senses," p. 93n.; also Weliur-Rahman, "The Psychology of Ibn-i-Sina," p. 354.

anything contrary to the strict interpretation of the doctrines that he has blindly accepted. This too is a great veil that overshadows most Muslim theologians (*mutakallimūn*)[5] and those who are zealous followers of the schools (*madhāhib*),[6] and indeed most righteous men who think upon the kingdom of the heavens and the earth, for they are veiled by their blindly followed creeds that are hardened in their souls and firmly fixed in their hearts, and have become a veil between them and the perception of realities.

The fifth reason is ignorance of the direction from which the knowledge of the thing sought must be obtained. For the seeker after knowledge cannot obtain knowledge of that which is unknown except by recalling the knowledge that is related to what he desires, so that when he recalls it and arranges it within himself in a special order, to which the learned give the name of 'process of deduction' (*ṭarīq al-iʿtibār*), he will then have found the direction of the thing sought, and its true nature will be clearly revealed to his heart. For the things that are not instinctive, which one desires to know, cannot be caught save in the net of acquired knowledge; indeed no item of knowledge is acquired except from two preceding items of knowledge that are related and combined in a special way, and from their combination a third item of knowledge is gained.[7] This is like the result of the union of a stallion and a mare. Here even as he who wishes to produce a mare cannot do so from donkey, cow, nor man, but from a special source, from male and female horses, and this if there takes place a special union; so also every item of knowledge has two special sources and a way for their combination, and from this combination there is gained the derived item of knowledge that is sought. Ignorance of these sources and of the inner aspect of combining them is what prevents understanding. An example of this already mentioned is the ignorance of the direction in which the object is.

Another example is that of a man who desires to see the back of his neck in a mirror. If he holds up the mirror in front of his face he does not have it placed opposite to the position of the back of the neck, and the back of his neck does not appear in it. If he holds it behind the back of his neck and facing it, he has turned the mirror away from his eyes and so cannot see either the mirror or the reflection of the back of his neck in it. So he

---

5 "Mutakallimūn," theologians; see *EI*, 2:672ff. *EI*², "ʿilm al-kalām," 3:1141.

6 Generally the four Sunnī schools of law: Mālikī, Shāfiʿī, Ḥanafī, and Ḥanbalī. See *EI*, 2:104ff; cf. also 4:252. *EI*², "madhhab," 12:551.

7 The reference is to the syllogism.

needs another mirror to place behind the back of his neck, with the first mirror facing it in such a way that he can see it, and he must observe the proper relationship between the placing of the two mirrors so that the image of the back of his neck is reflected in the mirror opposite to it, and the image of this mirror is reflected in the other mirror that faces the eye. Then the eye perceives the image of the back of his neck. So in the hunt for knowledge there are strange ways in which there are devious turnings and oblique shiftings, stranger than those we have mentioned concerning the mirror; and rare indeed upon the face of the earth is he who is guided to the way of clearly seeing through those devious ways.

These are the reasons that prevent the heart from coming to know the real nature of things. Otherwise every heart is innately able to come to know realities, for it is a lordly and noble thing, differing from other substances in the world by this special property and noble quality. To it is the reference in the statement of [God] ﷻ, *Indeed, We offered the Trust to the heavens and the earth and the mountains, but they declined to bear it, but man [undertook to] bear it* (33:72). This refers to his possession of a special characteristic that distinguishes him from the heavens, the earth, and the mountains, by which he is enabled to bear the trust of God the Exalted. This trust is gnosis and divine unity (*tawḥīd*).[8]

The heart of every human being is, [in its original constitution], able and capable of bearing this trust, but the causes that we have mentioned prevent it from carrying this burden and arriving at the realization of the trust. In this connection the Prophet ﷺ said, "Every child is born with a natural conformity to religious truth (i.e., of Islam, *fiṭra*), and it is only his parents who make him a Jew or a Christian or a Magian."[9] The Messenger of God ﷺ also said, "Were it not that the demons hover over the hearts of the children of Adam they would turn their eyes toward the heavenly

8 *Tawḥīd*. Jurjānī, *al-Taʿrīfāt*, p. 73, says that *tawḥīd* consists in: experientially knowing God's lordship; declaring His unity; and denying that there is any other like Him. The term is thus practically synonymous with Muslim 'theology' in the narrower sense of that term. See *EI*, 1:306, 2:704. *EI*², 10:389. See also Abū Ḥāmid al-Ghazālī, *Iḥyāʾ ʿulūm al-dīn: Kitāb al-tawḥīd waʾl-tawakkul*, trans. David Burrell, *Faith in Divine Unity and Trust in Divine Providence* (Louisville, KY: Fons Vitae, 2001).

9 Lane, *Lexicon*, p. 2416, says, "Every infant is born in a state of conformity to the natural constitution with which he is created in his mother's womb, either prosperous or unprosperous (in relation to the soul)." See also 'fiṭra,' *EI*, 2:115ff. *EI*², 2:931. This is a *ḥadīth* from Abū Hurayra related by all. Wensinck, *Handbook*, p. 43a.

kingdom."[10] This is a reference to some of these hindrances, which are the veil between the heart and the kingdom.

To this also is the reference in the *ḥadīth* that has come down from Ibn ʿUmar[11]. He said, "The Messenger was asked, 'O Messenger of God, where is God in the earth or in heaven?' He replied, 'In the hearts of His believing creatures.'"[12] There is also a narration [*ḥadīth qudsī*] that God, the Exalted, said, "My earth cannot contain me, neither my heaven, but the tender and calm heart of my servant can contain Me."[13]

Another narration says that the Messenger of God was asked, "Who are the best of men?"

He replied, "Every believer whose heart is cleansed."

They asked, "What is the cleansed heart?"

He answered, "It is the godfearing, pure heart, in which there is no fraud, nor iniquity, nor treachery, nor rancor, nor envy."[14]

On that account ʿUmar[15] said, "My heart saw my Lord when, because of godly fear, He raised the veil." For whomsoever the veil is lifted between himself and God,[16] the form of the material world (*al-mulk*) and of the world of spirits (*al-malakūt*) is clearly manifest in his heart, and he sees a Garden the width of a part of which is that of the heavens and the earth. Its total expanse is greater than the heavens and the earth, for 'the heavens and the earth' is only an expression for the visible material world, which, although broad in extent and far-reaching in compass, is still but a part of the whole. But the world of spirits is boundless, consisting of those secrets hidden from the sight of the eyes and perceived only by insight. It is true that only a part of it appears to the heart, but in itself and in its relation to the knowledge of God it is infinite. The material world and the world of spirits taken together under one classification are called the

---

10 A very uncertain *ḥadīth*, possibly confused with that mentioned on page 27, says ʿIrāqī.

11 Ibn ʿUmar, ʿAbdallāh b. ʿUmar b. al-Khaṭṭāb (d. 73/692), a Companion and the son of the second caliph; see *EI*, 1:28ff. *EI*², "ʿAbd Allāh b. ʿUmar b. al-Khaṭṭāb," 1:53.

12 A *ḥadīth* given in Makkī, *Qūt al-qulūb* and Qushayrī, *al-Risāla al-Qushayriyya;* ʿIrāqī says that he did not locate a source with this exact wording.

13 ʿIrāqī says that he did not find a source for this *ḥadīth*.

14 ʿIrāqī says that the chain of narrators for this *ḥadīth* is authentic (*ṣaḥiḥ*), given by Ibn Māja from ʿAbdallāh b. ʿUmar. Wensinck, *Concordance*, 2:78b.

15 ʿUmar b. al-Khaṭṭāb (d. 23/644) was the second caliph; see *EI*, 3:982ff. *EI*², 10:818.

16 Zabīdī text reads, 'between himself and his heart.'

Lordly Presence (*al-ḥaḍra al-rubūbiyya*),[17] for the Lordly Presence encompasses all existing things. For there exists nothing except God, the Exalted, His works, and His Kingdom; and His servants are a part of His works.[18] What appears of this to the heart is, according to some, Paradise[19] itself, and according to the people of reality (*ahl al-ḥaqq*),[20] it is the means of deserving Paradise. The extent of his possession in Paradise is in proportion to[21] the extent of his knowledge and the measure to which God and His attributes and works have been revealed to him.

The intent of all of these acts of obedience and actions of the members is the purification, improvement, and enlightenment of the heart. *Prosperous is he who purifies it* (91:9). The purpose of improvement is to achieve the illumination of faith in it; I mean the shining of the light of knowledge [of God]. That is the point in the statement of the Exalted, *Whomsoever God wants to guide, He expands his breast to [accept] Islam* (6:125); and in His statement, *So is one whose breast God has expanded to [accept] Islam, and he is upon light from his Lord* [like one whose heart rejects it] (39:22). This illumination and this faith have indeed three degrees. The first degree is the faith of the rank and file, which is purely blind imitation (*taqlīd*).[22] The second is the faith of the theologians (*mutakallimīn*), which is mingled with a sort of logical reasoning but its degree is nearly the same as that of the faith of the rank and file. The third degree is the faith of the mystics (*ʿārifūn*), which is seeing [clearly] with the light of certainty.[23]

---

17 "Ḥaḍra," *EI*, 2:207. *EI*², 3:51.

18 Zabīdī gives another reading: "and His Kingdom is made up of His servants and His works" (*Itḥāf*, 7:235) This passage is an assertion of the unity of God, the Self-existent One, which also guards against the possibility of there being anything in the universe that owes its existence to other than Him.

19 "Djanna," *EI*, 1:1014ff. *EI*², 2:447.

20 *Ahl al-ḥaqq*, a general term for Muslim mystics, 'the followers of reality,' according to the usage here by Ghazālī. See Nicholson, *The Mystics of Islam* (London: G. Bell and Sons, 1914), p. 1.

21 Zabīdī reads, 'because of.'

22 "Taqlīd," faith based on acceptance of custom and authority; see *EI*, 4:630ff. *EI*², 10:137.

23 Zabīdī gives a further analysis of these degrees of faith, taken from other writings of Ghazālī. The first two are from Ghazālī, *Iljām al-ʿawāmm ʿan ʿilm al-kalām* (Cairo, 1309/1891) and the third from *Mishkāt al-anwār* (Cairo 1322/1904). Also see W. H. T. Gairdner, "Al-Ghazālī's Mishkāt al-Anwār and the Ghazālī Problem," *Der Islam* 5, no. 2 (1914), pp. 121–53. The first degree of faith, or that of the rank and

We will make clear to you these degrees, with an example, your acceptance that Zayd, for instance, is in the house. This has three degrees. The first is that someone has told you, someone whom you have experienced to be truthful, and never known to lie and never doubted his word. Your heart, by the mere hearing, calmly receives his report and is satisfied with it. This is belief by mere blind acceptance, and of such nature is the faith of the rank and file. For when they reached the age of discrimination they heard from their fathers and mothers of the existence of God, the Exalted, of His knowledge, will, and power, and the rest of His attributes; also of the sending of the messengers and their veracity, and their message.[24] They received even as they heard and became established therein and satisfied therewith; and it never occurred to their minds to disagree with what their fathers and mothers and teachers told them because of the high esteem in which they held them. This faith is the efficient cause of salvation in the world to come, and those who embrace it are in the first [i.e., lowest] ranks of the people of the right hand,[25] but not among those who are drawn near [to God]. For this [faith] has in it no mystical unveiling, nor insight, nor

---

file, is blind imitation. It comes through: (1) hearing the doctrine from someone who is an authority worthy of trust, as a child trusts a parent or teacher; (2) hearing, in convincing circumstances, something known about previously; (3) hearing a doctrine that appeals to the nature of the individual, which is the weakest of all types of faith. The faith of the theologians is the second degree, and it is mingled with some logical reasoning. It may be (1) belief resting on complete proof that has been worked out step by step, which is the highest rank of this sort; or (2) belief resting on the well-known stock arguments of leading teachers; or (3) belief resting on written proofs, such as those used in debates and correspondence. The third degree of faith, which is that of mystics, is seeing with the light of certainty. (1) It is belief that all other than God has no essential existence, but has only contingent and figurative existence. Man, therefore, is the absolute possession of the One Unique Ruler who has no partner. (2) This is followed by advancement from the level of the figurative to an ascent to the summit of reality, until a clear vision is experienced that the face of God is the One Existence, and all else is eternally perishing. Cf. Qurʾān 28:68. (3) After attaining the heaven of reality there is no existence seen save God and the believer is devoid of all feeling of self or of other than God, and is lost in contemplation of Him. This state, in which a 'passing away' (*fanāʾ*) takes place, is an experience of the divine Unity (*tawḥīd*). Editor's note: see also Abū Jaʿfar al-Ṭaḥāwī, *The Creed of Imam al-Ṭaḥāwī*, trans. Hamza Yusuf (Zaytuna Institute, 2007).

24 Zabīdī text reads, "the Messenger, his veracity, and his message" (7:238).

25 Cf. Qurʾān 56:26.

enlargement of the breast by the light of certainty, since it is possible for there to be an error in what is heard from individuals, nay, indeed, from groups, in that which pertains to creed. The hearts of Jews and Christians are also satisfied with what they hear from their fathers and mothers, only their belief is a mistaken one because an error has been passed on to them. Muslims believe the truth, not because they have studied it, but because the word of truth has been passed on to them.

The second degree of belief is that you hear the words and voice of Zayd from within the house, but from behind a wall, and you deduce from this the fact of his being in the house. Then your belief, your acceptance as true, and your certainty that he is in the house are stronger than your belief through hearsay alone. For if you are told, "He is in the house," and then hear his voice, you become more certain of it, for the voice indicates shape and form to him who hears it, on condition of seeing the form. So his heart judges this to be the voice of that person. This is belief mingled with proof. It is also possible for error to follow because one voice might resemble another. Also pretense is possible by means of imitating the voice. This might not occur to the mind of the hearer, for he had no thought of any such accusation, or that anyone had a purpose in such deception and imitation.

The third degree of belief is to enter the house and look at him with your own eyes and see him. This is real experiential knowledge and sure observation. It is like the knowledge of those who are drawn near [to God] and of the veracious (*ṣiddīqūn*), for their belief is based on eyewitness [account]. This belief includes that of the rank and file and that of the theologians; and they have this very evident additional advantage that the possibility of error is taken away. It is true that believers of this class differ in rank according to their attainments in knowledge, and the degrees of unveiling. An example of the difference in degrees of knowledge is that one man sees Zayd in the house when he is near at hand in the courtyard and while the sun is shining, and so he sees him perfectly; while another sees him in a room, or at a distance, or in the evening, so that his form is sufficiently plain that he can be sure that it is he, but the minute details and hidden features of his form are not made clear to him. The variance in degree in seeing divine things is of this sort. Regarding the difference in the attainments of knowledge, it is as though one sees Zayd, ʿAmr, Bakr, and others in the house, while another sees Zayd only. The knowledge of the former is unquestionably greater than that of the latter because of the abundance of things known.

This is the state of the heart in relation to knowledge, and God, the Exalted, knows best that which is right.

Chapter 7

An Exposition of the Condition of the Heart as Related to the Categories of Knowledge: Intellectual, Religious, Worldly, and Otherworldly

KNOW THAT THE HEART is innately prepared to apprehend the real nature of ideas as has been stated previously. But the kinds of knowledge that exist in it may be divided into those which pertain to the intellect, and those which pertain to divine law. Intellectual knowledge (*ʿulūm ʿaqliyya*) is subdivided into axiomatic (*ḍarūriyya*) and acquired (*muktasaba*) [knowledge]. Acquired [knowledge] is further divided into that which deals with this [present] world, and with the world to come. By intellectual knowledge we mean that by which the innate intellect makes its judgments and which does not come into existence through blind imitation and instruction. It is divided into axiomatic and acquired [knowledge]. No one knows whence or how the axiomatic is attained. Such is a man's knowledge [for example], that one person cannot be in two places, and that one thing cannot be both created and eternal, existent and nonexistent at the same time. For man finds this knowledge to be a natural endowment of his soul from his youth, and does not know when or whence he attained it. I mean that he does not know any proximate cause for it. Otherwise it would not be hidden from him that it is God who has created him and guided him aright. Acquired knowledge is that which is gained by learning and deduction. Both of these are sometimes called intellectual. ʿAlī ﷺ said, "I beheld the intellect as though it were twofold: innately endowed, and developed through instruction. That which is developed through instruction is of no avail, apart from the innate endowment, even as the sun is of no avail apart from a seeing eye."[1]

The first of these is referred to in the saying of [the Prophet] ﷺ to ʿAlī, "God certainly has not created anything more honorable to Him than the intellect."[2] The second is referred to in his ﷺ statement to ʿAlī ؓ "Then men draw near to God by different kinds of good deeds; you draw near by your intellect."[3] For it is not possible to draw near by innate constitutional endowment, nor by axiomatic knowledge, but by that which is acquired. In ʿAlī's ؓ case, he was able to draw near by using his intellect to acquire the knowledge for which close proximity to the Lord of the worlds is bestowed. The heart is like the eye, and the innate intelligence in it is like the potentiality of sight in the eye. The potentiality of sight is a subtlety which is lost in blindness, but which is present in sight, even though a man may have closed his eyes or the darkness of night may have enfolded him. The knowledge attained thereby in the heart is like the potentiality of perception of sight in the eye, and its vision of the essences of things. The fact that knowledge is held back from the eye of the intellect during youth until the age of discretion and maturity is like the holding back of the vision from the sight until the time when the sun shines with its flood of light upon the objects of the sight.

The pen with which God has written knowledge upon the pages of the heart is like the disk of the sun. Knowledge is not achieved within the heart of the youth before the age of discretion only because the tablet of his heart is not yet prepared to receive the engraving of knowledge. The pen (*al-qalam*)[4] is a term for one of the creations of God, the Exalted, which He has made a cause by which knowledge is inscribed upon the

---

1 This quotation is in poetic form and might be reproduced approximately as follows:

Man's mind a twofold intellect appears:
    The one instinctive; the other what he hears
That which is heard avails naught, save when joined
    To that which is instinctive in the mind.
Just as the sun which shines in the sky
    is of no worth without a seeing eye.

2 A *ḥadīth* quoted by Tirmidhī al-Ḥakīm (*Nawādir al-uṣūl*), which ʿIrāqī says has a weakness (*ḍaʿf*) in the chain of narrators. For Zabīdī's discussion of this and the following *ḥadīth* see *Itḥāf*, 1:461ff.

3 ʿIrāqī says that there is a weakness (*ḍaʿf*) in the chain of narrators of this *ḥadīth*.

4 "Qalam (kalam)," pen; see *EI*, 2:675ff. *EI*², 4:471.

hearts of men. God, the Exalted, said, *Who taught by the pen, taught man that which he knew not* (96:4–5). The pen of God, the Exalted, does not resemble the pen of His creatures, even as His description does not resemble the characterization of His creation. Thus His pen is not made from a reed nor from a piece of wood, even as He Himself is not made up of substance (*jawhar*)[5] nor of accident (*ʿaraḍ*).[6]

So the comparison between the inner insight and the outer vision is valid from these points of view, save that there is no comparison between them in honor. For the inner insight is the very soul itself, which is the subtlety that perceives. This is like the rider, and the body like his mount; and blindness in the rider is more dangerous to the rider than blindness in his mount. Indeed there is no relation between the one affliction and the other, nor any comparison of the inner insight with the outer vision. God, the Exalted, has called it by its name, for He said, *The heart lied not [about] what it saw* (53:11), thus calling the perception of the mind a vision (*ruʾya*). Like this is the statement of the Exalted, *Thus did we show Abraham the realm of the heavens and the earth* (6:75). In this He did not mean the outer vision of the eye, for that was not granted exclusively to Abraham عليه السلام that it should be set forth as having been a special favor. Therefore the non-perception is called blindness. The Exalted said, *For it is not eyes which are blind, but blinded are the hearts which are within the breasts* (22:46). And again, the Exalted said, *And whoever in this life is blind, will be blind in the hereafter, and more astray in way* (17:72). This is the exposition of intellectual knowledge.

Now, as regards the religious sciences, they are taken by way of acceptance on authority (*taqlīd*) from the prophets (*anbiyāʾ*), on whom be the peace and blessings of God. This is acquired by learning the Book of God, the Exalted, and the Sunna of the Messenger of God, ﷺ and understanding their meaning after having heard them. In this is the heart made perfect in quality and safe from illness and disease. For the intellectual sciences, although needed by the heart, are not sufficient for its safety, just as the intellect is not sufficient to make continuous the causes of physical health, but needs also to gain the experiential knowledge of the properties of

---

5 "Jawhar," substance in the philosophic sense; see *EI*, 1:1027ff.; *EI*^{2}, 2:493. Harry A. Wolfson, *The Philosophy of Spinoza*, 2 vols. (Cambridge, MA: Harvard University Press, 1934), 1:64n2.

6 "ʿAraḍ," an accident that exists in a substance; see *EI*, 1:417. *EI*^{2}, 1:603.

medicines and herbs by learning them from the doctors (*aṭibbāʾ*)[7] and not by reading in books, since the intellect alone cannot find this knowledge. But after it is heard it cannot be understood except by means of the intellect. Thus the intellect cannot dispense with instruction [lit. hearing], nor can instruction dispense with the intellect.

So he who is a proponent of mere blind imitation and of setting aside the intellect entirely is ignorant; and he who is satisfied with the intellect alone, without the light of the Qurʾān and the Sunna, is deluded. Take care that you be not in either of these two groups, but be one who unites the two sources. For the intellectual sciences are like foods, and the sciences of religious law are as medicines. The sick person is harmed by food whenever he neglects the medicine. Thus the diseases of the heart can be treated only by the medicines derived from the religious law (*sharīʿa*),[8] which are the offices of the rites of worship and the works set by the prophets, on whom be the blessings of God, for the reformation of hearts. So he who does not treat his sick heart by the use of ritual worship, but is content to use the intellectual sciences alone, is harmed thereby, even as the sick man is harmed by food.

The supposition of those who think that the intellectual sciences are opposed to the sciences of religious law and that it is impossible to bring them together in harmony, is a supposition that arises from blindness in the eye of insight. We take refuge in God from it. But often such a man finds some of the sciences of religious law contradictory to others and is unable to harmonize them, so he supposes that there is a contradiction in religion and is perplexed thereby, and he withdraws from religion as a hair is withdrawn from dough. This is only because his own impotence has caused him to imagine an inconsistency in [our] religion. How far that is from the truth! He is indeed like a blind man who entered a house and there stumbled over some of the vessels of the house and said, "What are these vessels doing in the path; why are they not put in their place?" They answered him, "Those vessels are in their place, but you did not find the way because of your blindness. How strange it is of you not to blame your stumbling on your blindness, but rather to blame it upon the negligence of someone else." This is the relationship between religious and intellectual sciences.

---

7 "Aṭibbāʾ," doctors of medicine; see "ṭibb," *EI*, 4:740ff. *EI*², 10:451.

8 "Sharīʿa," *EI*, 4:320ff. *EI*², 9:321.

The intellectual sciences are divided into those of the present world and those of the world to come. Those of this present world are such sciences as medicine, mathematics, engineering, astronomy, and the other professions and trades. Those of the world to come are such as the knowledge of the states of the heart, of defects in religious works, and of the knowledge of God, the Exalted, and His attributes and His acts, as we have explained in the *Book of Knowledge*. These two sciences exist in tension, by which I mean that whoever applies himself to one of them and goes deeply into it has his insight into the other lessened for the most part.

ʿAlī ﷺ has given three similes of this present world and the world to come. He said, "They are like the two scales of the balance; and like the East and the West; and like a man's two wives, for when he makes the one content he makes the other angry." So you see those who are wise in the affairs of the present world, in medicine, mathematics, engineering, and philosophy, are ignorant in the affairs of the world to come. Similarly those who are wise in the minutiae of the sciences of the world to come are ignorant, for the most part, of the sciences of this present world; for the power of the intellect cannot accomplish the two things together, as a general rule. Thus one of them obstructs the perfection of the second. The Prophet ﷺ said, "Most of the inhabitants of Paradise are simpletons (*bulh*)."[9] That is, they are simpletons in the things of this present world. Ḥasan[10] said in one of his exhortations, "We perceived a group, which if you saw them, you would say that they are mad; and if they saw you, they would say that you are demons."

So whenever you hear about a strange thing in the field of religion, which people wise in the sciences deny, do not let their denial delude you so that you do not accept it; for it is impossible for one who walks the eastern path to possess [goods] that exist [only] in the West. So also is the case with this present world and that which is to come. The Exalted said, *Those who rest not their hope on their meeting with Us, but are pleased and satisfied with the life of the present [and feel secure therein and those who are heedless of Our signs]* (10:7). Again, the Exalted said, *They know but the outer (things) in the life of this world, but of the End of things they are heedless* (30:7). And again, He ﷻ said, *So turn away from whoever turns his back on Our message and desires not except the worldly life. This*

---

9 Zabīdī says this is a weak and generally denied (*munkar*) *ḥadīth*.

10 Ḥasan b. Abū al-Ḥasan al-Baṣrī (21–110/642–728), a prominent and learned scholar and pious ascetic; see *EI*, 2:273. *EI*², 3:247.

is their sum of knowledge (53:29–30). So to combine a complete attentive observance of the affairs of this present world and of religion is rarely easy, save to those whom God has firmly established for the direction of His servants in their livelihood and their return [to God]. Such are the prophets who are helped by the holy spirit,[11] who receive divine power sufficient for all things, nor does it fall short at all. But when the hearts of creatures are given over completely to that which pertains to this present world, they turn aside from the world to come and fall short of coming to perfection therein.

11 This is apparently an extension of the teaching in the Qurʾān about the supernatural aid given to ʿĪsā (2:81, 254; 5:109), so as to include all the prophets. The meaning of the term 'holy spirit' here is probably explained by the words that follow, 'divine power sufficient for all things.' On the above passages, Bayḍāwī gives this as one meaning of the 'holy spirit', another of course, being Jibrīl. See also "Nafs," *EI*. *EI*², 7:880.

Chapter 8

An Exposition of the Difference between General Inspiration (*ilhām*) and Learning (*taʿallum*); and the Difference between the Sufi Way of Seeking the Unveiling of Reality and the Way of the Speculative Theologians (*nuẓẓār*)

KNOW THAT THE SCIENCES that are not axiomatic, but which come into the heart at certain times, differ in their manner of attainment. Sometimes they come upon the heart as though something were flung into it from a source it knows not.[1] At other times they are gained through deduction (*istidlāl*) and study. That which is not attained by way of acquisition nor through artful proof is called general inspiration (*ilhām*), and that which is attained through inference is called reflection (*iʿtibār*) and mental perception (*istibṣār*). Furthermore that which exists in the heart apart from some expedient or cunning or effort on the part of man is subdivided into two classes. In the first the servant is not aware how he achieved it, nor whence; in the second he is acquainted with the

---

1 For a close and interesting parallel see the statement of Philo quoted in Brett, *Psychology*, 1:249, here given in part: " … and sometimes when I come to my work empty, I have suddenly become full, ideas being in an invisible manner showered upon me and implanted in me from on high; so that through the influence of Divine Inspiration I have become greatly excited, and have known neither the place in which I was nor those who were present, nor myself, nor what I was saying, nor what I was writing."

secondary cause (*sabab*)[2] from which he has derived that knowledge, which is the vision of the angel who casts it into his heart. The former is called general inspiration, and inbreathing into the heart (*nafth fi-l-rawᶜ*). The latter is called prophetic inspiration (*waḥy*),[3] and it is an exclusive characteristic of the prophets (*anbiyāʾ*), whereas the former is given only to the saints (*awliyāʾ*) and the pure (*aṣfiyāʾ*). The preceding type, which is gained through deduction, is that given to the learned (*ᶜulamāʾ*).[4]

The true doctrine is that the heart has the capacity to have revealed in it the true nature of reality in all things. But this is prevented by the intervention of the five aforementioned causes. These are as a veil that hangs down between the mirror of the heart and the Preserved Tablet (*al-lawḥ al-maḥfūẓ*),[5] which is engraved with all that God has decreed until the day of resurrection. The reflection of the real nature of knowledge from the mirror of the Tablet upon the mirror of the heart is like the reflection of an image from one mirror to another mirror opposite it. The veil between the two mirrors is sometimes removed by the hand, and at other times by a gust of wind that moves it. Thus the winds of divine favor sometimes blow and the veils are drawn aside from the eyes of hearts so that there is reflected in them something of that which is written upon the Preserved Tablet. Sometimes this takes place during sleep, and thereby there is revealed (*yuᶜlim*) that which will come into being in the future. The veil is completely lifted by death, when the covering is withdrawn. At other times [inspiration] is made during waking hours and the veil is lifted by a secret favor from God, the Exalted, and some of the marvels of knowl-

---

2 "Sabab," secondary cause; see *EI*, *Supp*. pp. 191ff. *EI*², 8:666.

3 "Waḥy," prophetic inspiration; see *EI*, 4:1091ff. *EI*², 11:53. Zabīdī (7:245) gives six varieties of *waḥy*, as follows: (1) that which comes as the ringing of a bell; (2) that in which an angel appears and addresses man; (3) visions in sleep; (4) that which is cast into the heart; (5) Jibrīl comes (to the Prophet) in his true form, having six hundred wings, each one of which fills the horizon; (6) God speaks to him directly as He did the night of the heavenly journey. This is the highest sort.

4 "ᶜUlamāʾ," the learned; see *EI*, 4:994. *EI*², 10:801. Zabīdī says (7:245), in commenting on this, that there are three kinds of *ᶜilm* mentioned by Ibn al-ᶜArabī, as follows: (1) intellectual knowledge, whether axiomatic or rationally proven; (2) knowledge of states, which is learned only through experience; and (3) knowledge of secrets, which is above the intellect, and is received only through the inbreathing of the holy spirit.

5 See "al-lawḥ al-maḥfūẓ," *EI*, 3:19ff.; *EI*², "lawḥ," 5:698. also Wensinck, *Gazālī's Cosmology*, pp. 16ff.

edge glisten in the heart from behind the curtain of the unknown. This may be like a dazzling flash of lightning, or it may be continuous up to a certain point, but its continuance is most rare. Inspiration (*ilhām*) then does not differ from acquisition as regards the knowledge itself, its seat, and its cause, but it differs only in the removal of the veil, for this is not accomplished by man's volition. General inspiration does not differ from prophetic inspiration in any of these respects, but only in the matter of the vision of the angel who imparts the knowledge; for our hearts attain knowledge only by means of the angels.[6] To this the Exalted refers in the statement, *And it is not for any human being that God should speak to him except by revelation or from behind a partition or that He sends a messenger to reveal, by His permission, what He wills* (42:51).

If you have come to know this, know also that the inclination of the Sufis is toward the knowledge gained through inspiration, more than that gained through instruction. Therefore they do not jealously covet the study of knowledge, nor the acquisition of that which authors have written, nor discussion about the statement of [doctrines] and proofs that have been mentioned. But they say, "The way of knowledge is to put foremost spiritual striving, to abolish blameworthy traits, to cut all ties, and to advance toward God, the Exalted, with utmost concern." Whenever this takes place, God becomes the ruler over the heart of His creature and the surety for his illumination with the light of knowledge. When God becomes the ruler of the heart, He floods it with mercy and sheds His light upon it, and the breast is opened and there is revealed to it the secret of the world of spirits (*malakūt*),[7] and by a gift of mercy there is cleared away from the surface of the heart the veil of whiteness[8] that blinds its eye, and there shines in it the real nature of divine things.

---

6 Zabīdī (7:246) says that knowledge is gained in the following ways: (1) through intuitive intelligence and sense contact; (2) through sight, based on intellectual or sensible premises; (3) through the report of others, hearing, or reading; (4) through inspiration (*waḥy*), (4a) through the tongue of an angel who can be seen, (4b) by hearing the voice of an angel without seeing him, or (4c) through a casting into the heart, either during waking hours or when asleep.

7 Zabīdī says that this elevation above the world of sense is the first ascent (*al-miʿrāj al-awwal*) of the traveler on the mystic's path.

8 *Ghurra*—whiteness. The reference is probably to the white leucoma which so often causes loss of sight in eastern lands.

The servant[9] has only to make himself ready by a thorough purification, by summoning intention along with a sincere desire, by complete yearning, and by watching with constant expectation for the mercy that God, the Exalted, may grant to him. For prophets and saints have had divine things revealed to them, and the light has flooded their breasts, not by learning and study and the writing of books, but by asceticism (*zuhd*)[10] in this present world, by cutting the self off from all of its ties, by emptying the heart of all of its busying affairs, and by advancing with the utmost concern toward God, the Exalted; for whoever belongs to God, God belongs to him.

The [Sufis] assert that the way to this is, first of all, by cutting off ties with this present world and by emptying the heart of them, by taking away concern for family, possessions, children, homeland, knowledge, rule, and rank. Nay rather he must bring his heart into that state in which the existence of all these is the same as their nonexistence.[11] Then he must withdraw alone, apart, into a place of private devotion (*zāwiya*),[12] and limit himself to the prescribed religious duties (*farāʾiḍ*)[13] and the supererogatory prayers (*rawātib*).[14] He must sit with an empty heart and concentrated purpose. He must not divide his thought by reciting the Qurʾān, nor the contemplation of its exposition, nor by books of *ḥadīth*, nor anything else. But he must strive [such] that nothing save God, the Exalted, shall come into his mind. Then after he has seated himself in a place apart (*khalwa*) he shall keep saying continuously with his tongue, "Allāh, Allāh," and his heart shall be fixed on it too, until he comes finally to a state in which the motion of the tongue will cease and it will seem as though the word is flowing over his tongue. He must continue patiently in this until every trace of the word is effaced from the tongue and he finds his heart persevering in this devotional exercise (*dhikr*). Still he shall persevere until the form and letters of the expression and the very appearance of the word is

9 Editor's note: Skellie has 'novice (*murīd*)' here, from Zabīdī, *Itḥāf* (7:246). He then refers the reader to "murīd," novice or neophyte; see *EI*, 3:735. *EI*², 7:608.

10 "Zuhd," asceticism; see *EI*, 4:1239. *EI*², 11:559.

11 Zabīdī says that this is the first stage, or the true beginning, of the mystic's path.

12 "Zāwiya," see *EI*, 4:1220ff. *EI*², 11:466.

13 "Farāʾiḍ" (pl.), "farḍ," see *EI*, 2:61; *EI*², 2:783. Zabīdī, *Itḥāf*, 1:144.

14 "Rawātib" (pl.), supererogatory acts of worship which may precede and follow the prescribed prayers; see *EI*, 3:1129. *EI*², "rātib," 8:459. See also Ghazālī, trans. Calverley, *Worship in Islam*, pp. 21, 186ff.

effaced from the heart and there remains present in it naught save the ideal meaning which is, as it were, adhering to and inseparable from the heart.

To attain to this point is a matter of his choice; so too is the prolonging of this condition by warding off the suggestions of Satan. Not by his choice, however, can he procure the gift of the mercy of God, the Exalted. By what he has done thus far he has exposed himself to the breezes of God's mercy, and it only remains for him to wait for such mercy as God may grant to him, even as He has, in this way, given His mercy to the prophets and saints. Upon doing this, if his desire is sincere, his intention pure, and his perseverance good, and if his lusts do not draw him aside nor the suggestions of the self (*ḥadīth al-nafs*)[15] engross him with the ties of this present world, there will shine forth the gleams of reality into his heart. In its beginning this will be like a blinding flash of lightning. It is not continuous but it returns, although it may delay. If it returns it may continue, and it may be but a flash. If it continues it may be for a longer or shorter time. These different types may appear, the one succeeding the other, or they may be limited to one sort only. The stages (*manāzil*) of the saints of God, the Exalted, in this are unlimited, even as the superiority of their nature and moral characteristics is not to be reckoned. So this way goes back to an absolute purifying and clarifying and brightening of the heart on your part, and then only to make ready and wait in expectation.

The speculative theologians (*nuẓẓār*) and those whose opinions deserve consideration have not denied the fact that this way does exist, that it is a possibility, and that it does, in rare instances, lead to the desired end. Indeed this way has been that of most prophets and saints. But they consider it a difficult way, and think it slow in bearing fruit, and feel that the fulfilment of all of its conditions is very improbable. They claim that to blot out all ties to this extent is practically impossible. If it does happen for a moment, its continuation is even more difficult, since the slightest evil prompting or involuntary suggestion disturbs the heart.

---

15 The *ḥadīth al-nafs* is equivalent to *al-khāṭir al-nafsī* (see page xxx). See Abū al-Qāsim al-Qushayrī, *al-Qushayri's Epistle on Sufism*, trans. Alexander Knysh (Reading, UK: Garnet Publishing, 2007), pp. 106–7. See also ʿAbdallāh b. ʿUmar al-Bayḍāwī, *Anwār al-tanzīl wa asrār al-taʾwīl*, 2 vols. (Leipzig, 1846–8), on Qurʾān 50:15. It is the lightest type of sin, and according to some, is not even to be reckoned as sin on the day of judgment. See *EI*, 2:927a. See also chapter 13 of the present work.

The Prophet ﷺ said, "The heart of the believer is more unsteady than a cooking pot as it boils."[16] He, may the best blessings and peace be upon him, also said, "The heart of the believer is between two of the fingers of the Merciful." During such strenuous effort the physical constitution may be disordered, the intellect confused, and the body may suffer. If progress in the discipline and improvement of the soul is not made by means of the realities of the sciences, then the heart is ensnared with corrupt imaginings in which the soul trusts for a long time before they come to an end; and one may live out his appointed time without succeeding. Many a Sufi has traveled this way and continued to hold a single visionary [state] for twenty years, whereas if he had mastered knowledge beforehand, the point of confusion in his vision (*khayāl*) would have been opened up to him at once. So to busy one's self in the path of learning is a surer and easier means of attaining the aim. They claim that it is as though a man left off the study of jurisprudence (*fiqh*),[17] asserting, "The Prophet ﷺ did not study it and he became one who understood the divine law by means of prophetic and general inspiration without any repetition or application, and perhaps discipline of the soul and steadfastness will bring me finally to that goal." Whoever thinks this wrongs himself and wastes his life. Nay, rather, he is like one who gives up the way of gain through farming, hoping to chance upon some treasure. The latter is indeed possible, but extremely unlikely. So too [in the matter of gaining knowledge]. They say, "It is first of all necessary to attain to that which the learned have achieved and to understand what they said. Then after that there is no harm in expectantly waiting for that which has not been disclosed to the other learned men, and it may be that this will be disclosed afterwards through strenuous effort."

16 An authentic *ḥadīth* quoted by Aḥmad from Miqdād b. al-Aswad.

17 "Fiqh," *EI*, 2:101ff. *EI*², 2:886.

Chapter 9

An Exposition of the Difference in Rank between the Two Positions by a Tangible Example

KNOW THAT THE WONDERS of the heart are outside the realm of things perceived through the senses (*mudrakāt al-ḥawāss*),[1] for the heart is also beyond sense perception. The understandings are too weak to grasp, except by means of a tangible example, that which is not perceived through the senses. So we shall explain this to people of weak understanding by means of two examples.

For the first illustration let us suppose that a reservoir is dug in the earth, into which the water can be conducted from the surface above through streams which empty into it. The bed of the reservoir may also be dug up and the dirt removed from it until the fountain of pure water is reached, and then the water bursts forth from the bottom of the reservoir. This water is purer and more constant, and perhaps more copious and abundant. The heart then is like the reservoir and knowledge like the water. The five external senses are like the streams. Knowledge may possibly be conducted to the heart by means of the streams of the senses and the consideration of things observed until it is thus filled with knowledge. It is also possible to stop up these streams [from flowing into] it by solitude and seclusion and averting the eyes from seeing, and then to resolve in the depths of the heart to purify it and remove from it the layers of veils until the fountain of knowledge bursts forth from within it.

1 *Ḥawāss*, external senses. See Weliur-Rahman, "The Psychology of Ibn-i-Sina," pp. 344–51.

But if you say, "How can knowledge burst forth from the heart itself while it is destitute of it," know that this is one of the wonders of the heart's secrets. It is not permissible to deal with it in the knowledge of proper conduct (*ʿilm al-muʿāmala*). This much, however, can be mentioned, that the real natures of things are written down in the Preserved Tablet (*al-lawḥ al-maḥfūẓ*), and indeed in the hearts of the angels who are brought near [to God].

For just as an architect draws plans for buildings on blank paper and then brings them into actuality in accordance with that archetype (*nuskha*), thus the Creator of the heavens and the earth wrote an archetype of the world from beginning to end upon the Preserved Tablet, and then brought it into actuality in accordance with that archetype.

From the world which has been brought into actuality in the image [of the archetype] there is transmitted to the external senses and the retentive imagination (*khayāl*)[2] still another image. For whoever looks at the sky and the earth and then closes his eyes, sees in his imagination the image of the sky and the earth, so that it is as though he were looking at them; and were the sky and the earth annihilated and he himself remained, he would find within himself the image[3] of the sky and the earth as though he were beholding them and looking at them.

Then from his imagination an effect is transmitted to the heart, so that there is represented in it the real natures of things that have entered into sensation and imagination. The representation in the heart corresponds to the world that is represented in the imagination, which in turn corresponds to the world as it exists in itself, external to the imagination and heart of man. This existing world corresponds to the archetype existing in the Preserved Tablet.

Thus the world has four degrees of existence.[4] There is existence in the Preserved Tablet; this is prior to its corporeal (*jismānī*) existence. Its

---

2 *Khayāl*, the power to preserve the forms of sensibles perceived by the common sense after the objects themselves have been removed. It is a storehouse for the common sense, placed in the back part of the front ventricle of the brain, Jurjānī, *al-Taʿrīfāt*, p. 107. See also Wolfson, "Internal Senses," p. 100n.; Weliur-Rahman, "The Psychology of Ibn-i-Sina," p. 353.

3 Editor's note: here, Imam al-Ghazālī uses the word *ṣūra*, usually translated as form.

4 Cf. Ibn Sīnā's three modes of existence. Things are *ante res*, in the mind of God; *in rebus*, natural existence together with its accidents; and *post res*, as conceived by the human intellect. Ueberweg, *Philosophy*, 1:413. Ghazālī has merely subdivided

real (*ḥaqīqī*) existence follows this, and it is followed in turn by its imaginative (*khayālī*) existence,[5] by which I mean the existence of its image in the imagination. Its imaginative existence is followed by its intellectual existence, by which I mean the existence of its image within the heart. Some of these [orders of] being are immaterial (*rūḥāniyya*) and some [are] corporeal. Of the immaterial, some are more immaterial in their [order of] being than others. This is a kindness (*lutf*) coming from the divine wisdom; for God has made the pupil of your eye in such a way that, in spite of its smallness, there is pictured within it the image of the world, the heavens and the earth, with all their widespread extent. Then it goes on from existence in the realm of sensation to existence in the imagination, and from it to existence in the heart. For you can never apprehend anything save that which has reached you; and were it not that He has placed an image (*mithāl*)[6] of the whole world within your very being you would have no knowledge of that which is apart from yourself. Glory belongs unto Him who has ordered these wonders in the heart and eye, and then blinded the heart and eye to the perception of them so that the hearts of the majority of creatures have become ignorant of themselves and their wonders.

Let us now go back to intended purpose and say, "It is conceivable that the real nature of the world might be represented in the heart, its mental image coming now from the senses and again from the Preserved Tablet; even as it is conceivable that the image of the sun should be represented in the eye, coming now from looking directly at it, and again from looking at the water on which the sun shines which reproduces its image." So whenever the veils are lifted between the heart and the Preserved Tablet, the heart sees the things which are therein, and knowledge bursts forth into it therefrom, so that it does not have to acquire its knowledge through the avenues of the senses. This is like the bursting forth of water from the depths of the earth. Whenever the heart becomes occupied with things

---

this third division, *post res*, into imaginative and intellectual existence. In this chain of modes of existence we see some of the influence of Neoplatonism on Arabic philosophy.

5 Editor's note: On the imagination, see William Chittick, *The Sufi Path of Knowledge* (Albany: State University of New York Press, 1989).

6 Cf. the Aristotelian idea of the human soul as a microcosm, uniting in itself all the faculties of the other orders of animate existence and distinguished by *nous*. Ueberweg, *Philosophy*, 1:168.

in the imagination derived from sensibles (*maḥsūsāt*), this veils it from examining the Preserved Tablet, just as when water is collected from streams [into a reservoir]; it is thereby prevented from bursting forth from the earth; or just as he who looks into the water that reproduces the image of the sun is not looking at the sun itself.

Thus the heart has two doors.[7] One door opens toward the world of spirits (*ʿālam al-malakūt*), which is the Preserved Tablet and the world of the angels (*ʿālam al-malāʾika*). The other door opens toward the five external senses that are tethered to the visible material world. This visible world also resembles the world of spirits to a certain extent. Now the fact that the door of the heart is opened to the acquisition of knowledge through the senses is a thing you understand. But regarding its door that opens to the world of spirits and [is able to] see the Preserved Tablet, you have certain knowledge through meditating upon the wonders of dream-visions (*ruʾyā*) and the heart's observation in sleep of what will be in the future or what was in the past, without any acquisition on the part of the senses.

That door, however, is opened only to one who devotes himself exclusively to the remembrance of God, the Exalted. The Prophet ﷺ said, "Men of a single [thought] have taken the lead."[8] He was asked, O Messenger of God, "Who are they?" He answered, "Those who are devoted to the remembrance of God, the Exalted, for this remembrance (*dhikr*) of theirs has put away from them their load of sin and they come to the resurrection unburdened."[9] Then he described them by relating the statement of God, the Exalted, "Then I shall draw near with my face toward them. Do you think that anyone knows what thing I desire to bestow upon him toward whom I turn my face?" Then He, the Exalted, said, "The first thing I give

---

7 Man's potential intelligence is made actual from two directions: divine inspiration, and reasoning and argumentation. This was taught by Ibn Sīnā (Weliur-Rahman, "The Psychology of Ibn-i-Sina," pp. 356ff.); Ueberweg, *Philosophy*, 1:412ff.; Brett, *Psychology*, 2:51, 57), and further developed by Ghazālī, who added Sufi elements as we find here. The soul of man, or his heart, is between sense perception and divine illumination and is influenced by them both, in the sense that both are sources of knowledge. This is similar to what Ghazālī has already told us of man's being between the angel and the demon, in the sense of being influenced by them both in the sphere of conduct.

8 This first part is an authentic *ḥadīth* given by Muslim from Abū Hurayra.

9 This latter part, which begins 'for this remembrance' and so on, is a weak addition. Wensinck, *Handbook*, p. 97a.

them is that I cast light into their hearts and they give tidings of me even as I give tidings of them."[10] The entrance for these tidings is the inner door.

So this is the difference between the knowledge of the prophets and saints and that of the learned and the philosophers (*ḥukumāʾ*): the knowledge of the former comes from within the heart through the door that is opened toward the world of spirits, whereas the knowledge of the philosophers[11] comes through the doors of the senses that open to the material world. The wonders of the world of the heart and its wavering between the visible and invisible worlds cannot be fully dealt with in a [study of the] knowledge of proper conduct. But this is an example that will teach you the difference of the entrance of the two [kinds of] knowledge.

The second example will explain to you the difference between the two types of action, by which I mean the action of the learned and that of the saints. The learned work to acquire knowledge itself and gather it into the heart, but the saints among the Sufis labor only [with the goal of] polishing, cleansing, clarifying, and brightening the heart.

The story is told that once the Chinese[12] and the Byzantines (Rūm) vied with one another before a certain king as to the beauty of their workmanship in decorating and painting. So the king decided to give over to them a portico so that the Chinese might decorate one side of it and the Byzantines the other side; and to let a curtain hang down between them so as to prevent either group from looking at the other. And he did so. The Byzantines gathered together countless strange colors, but the Chinese entered without any color at all and began to polish their side and to brighten it. When the Byzantines had finished, the Chinese claimed that they had finished also. The king was astonished at their statement and the way in which they had finished the decorating without any color at all. So they were asked, "How have you finished the work without any color?" They replied, "You are not responsible for us; lift the veil." So they lifted it, and behold on their side there shone forth the wonders of the Byzantine skill with added illumination and dazzling brilliance, since that side had

---

10 A "ḥadīth qudsī," see *EI*, 2:190b, 4:336a; *EI*², 3:28. I do not find its source.

11 Editor's note: the Cairo text has *ḥikma* (wisdom), Zabīdī (7:254) has *ḥukamāʾ*, as used above.

12 Zabīdī gives a proverb which says that wisdom descended (in special power) upon three bodily members: the brain of the Greek, the hand of the Chinese, and the tongue of the Arab. See following page for painting representing the contest.

A painting of the contest that takes place between the Chinese and the Byzantines. (From a manuscript of Niẓāmī, *Khamsa,* Shiraz, 1449–50, New York, Metropolitan Museum of Art, 13.228.3, fol. 332r.).

become like unto a polished mirror by reason of much brightening. Thus the beauty of their side was increased by its added clearness.

The care of the saints in cleansing, polishing, purifying, and clarifying the heart until the true nature of the Real shines forth clearly therein with utmost illumination is like the work of the Chinese. The care of the learned and the philosophers in acquiring and adorning knowledge, and the representation of this adornment in the heart, is like the work of the Byzantines.

But whatever the [truth] of this matter, the heart of the believer does not die, nor is its knowledge[13] erased at death nor its clearness clouded. To this Ḥasan, may God have mercy on him, referred in his saying, "Dust will not consume the seat of faith." This knowledge is a means of access that brings him near to God, the Exalted. But what [the heart] has attained of knowledge itself; or what it has attained of purity and the capacity to receive what knowledge writes upon the heart, does not enable it to dispense with more knowledge. There is no happiness for anyone, apart from learning and mystical knowledge and some degrees of happiness are more noble than others, just as there is no wealth without money. For he who has a dirham is 'wealthy' and he who has storehouses crammed full is 'wealthy.' The contrast between the different degrees of [those who are] happy is in accordance with their contrast in mystical knowledge and faith, just as the contrast between the different degrees of men of wealth is in accordance with the scarcity or abundance of their money.

The varieties of mystical knowledge (*maʿārif*) are lights, and believers do not run to meet God, the Exalted, save by their lights. God, the Exalted, said, *their light shining before them and on their right* (57:12). It is related in a narration, "Some of them are given a light the size of a mountain and some smaller. The last of them will be a man who is given a light on his big toe, which sometimes shines and again goes out. Whenever it shines he puts his foot forward and walks, and when it goes out he stands still. Their crossing the Traverse (al-Ṣirāṭ)[14] is in accordance with their light.

---

13 Zabīdī says that the knowledge referred to here is the believer's experiential knowledge of God.

14 Editor's note: a bridge that crosses over Hell. See "Ṣirāṭ," *EI*², 9:670. See also Annabel Keeler: "The 'Traverse' (*ṣīrāṭ*) is traditionally described as a bridge stretched over the gulf of Hell, sharper than a sword and thinner than a hair, which all the believers are made to cross at the Resurrection. It is described in Ghazālī's *Iḥyāʾ ʿulūm al-dīn*, Book 40: *Kitāb Dhikr al-mawt wa-mā baʿdahu*, trans. Timothy J. Win-

Some of them cross in the twinkling of an eye, some as a flash of lightning, some as the passing of a cloud, some as a falling star, and some as a charging horse. He who was given a light on his big toe crawls along on his face and hands and feet. One hand slips off but he holds on with the other, and one foot slips off but the other holds. The fire reaches his sides, but he keeps on in this way until he is saved."[15] Thus the distinction in the faith of men is shown. Were the faith of Abū Bakr[16] to be weighed [on one side of the scales], and on the other side that of all men except prophets and messengers, the first would tip [the scale]. This resembles the statement of him who said, "Were the light of the sun to be placed in the scales over against that of all lamps it would preponderate." For the light of the faith of individuals among the common people is like the light of a lamp, and with some it is as the light of a candle. But the faith of the righteous (*ṣiddiqīn*) gives light comparable to that of the moon and stars, and the faith of the prophets is as the light of the sun. For even as the form of the entire horizon with all its broad expanse is revealed in the light of the sun, while only a narrow corner of the house is revealed in the light of a lamp, thus also is there a distinction in the expansion of the breast by mystical knowledge, and in the unveiling of the breadth of the world of spirits to the hearts of the mystics.

So a narration tells us, "On the day of resurrection the command will be given, 'Remove from the Fire whoever has a *mithqāl*[17] of faith, or half a *mithqāl*, or a quarter of a *mithqāl*, or a grain, or an atom.'"[18] All of this goes to show the distinction in the degrees of faith, and that these quantities of faith do not prevent [one from] entering the Fire. It is also understood from this that whoever has more than a *mithqāl* of faith will not enter the Fire. For if he entered, orders would be given to remove him first. Again whoever has an atom's weight of faith in his heart does not deserve to abide forever in the Fire even though he entered it.

---

ter, as *The Remembrance of Death and the Afterlife* (Cambridge, 1989), pp. 205–10." In *Tafsīr al-Tustarī*, trans. Annabel Keeler and Ali Keeler (Louisville, KY: Fons Vitae and Royal Aal al-Bayt Institute for Islamic Thought, 2010), note to Sūra 23.

15 A *ḥadīth* from Ibn Masʿūd related by Bukhārī and Muslim. Cf. Madanī, *Aḥādīth al-qudsiyya*, nos. 49, 256.

16 Abū Bakr al-Ṣiddīq, the first caliph; see *EI*, 1:60ff., 4:402ff. *EI*², 9:534.

17 *Mithqāl*, here apparently a standard weight, although the passage has some textual variants. Equivalent to one and one-half dirhams or twenty carats, says Lane.

18 An agreed upon *ḥadīth* from Abū Saʿīd. See Wensinck, *Concordance*, 2:22b.

So also is his ﷺ statement, "There is nothing that is better than a thousand like it except a man, that is, a believer,"[19] referring to the superiority of the heart of a gnostic (*ʿārif*) of God, the Exalted, for it is better than a thousand hearts of the common folk. The Exalted said, *You will be superior if you are [true] believers* (3:139): thus giving preference to believers over Muslims. The one referred to is the believing gnostic and not the blind imitator.

He ﷻ said, *God Allah will raise those who have believed among you and those who were given knowledge, by degrees* (58:11). By *those who have believed* here He means those who attest [to belief] without knowledge, and has thus discriminated between them and *those who are given knowledge*. This indicates that the name 'believer' is applied to the blind imitator even though his attestation does not result from insight nor mystical revelation. Ibn ʿAbbās ؓ,[20] in commenting on the statement of the Exalted, *those who are given knowledge*, said, "The learned man is exalted above the believer by seven hundred degrees, between each two of which there is a distance equal to that between heaven and earth." [The Prophet] ﷺ said, "Most of the people of Paradise are simpletons, but the seventh heaven[21] is for men of understanding." He ﷺ also said, "The learned man is as far superior to the ordinary worshipper as I am superior to the least man of my Companions."[22] Another reading has it, "as the moon is superior to the rest of the stars."

So by these evidences it is clear that the distinction in rank among the people of Paradise is in accordance with the distinction in their hearts and their mystical knowledge. Therefore the day of resurrection is 'a day of mutual disillusionment'[23] since he who is deprived of the mercy of God

---

19 A good *ḥadīth* from Ibn ʿUmar.

20 Ibn ʿAbbās, ʿAbdallāh (d. between 68 and 70/687 and 689), a cousin of the Prophet and a celebrated *ḥadīth* narrator and commentator on the Qurʾān; see *EI*, 1:19ff. *EI*², 1:40.

21 The first part of this *ḥadīth* has preceded on page 49. ʿIrāqī says that he finds no authority for the addition. The word *ʿilliyyūn*, seventh heaven, may be related to the Hebrew *ʿelyōn*. Cf. Qurʾān 83:18–9; Genesis 14:18.

22 A *ḥadīth* quoted by Tirmidhī from Abū Umāma; see also *Iḥyāʾ*, 1:6 and 2:215. Wensinck, *Concordance*, 2:151a.

23 Cf. Qurʾān 64:9. Editor's note: *taghābun*, or mutual disillusionment, refers to people's attempt to deceive each other, see Elsaid M. Badawi and Muhammad Abdel Haleem, *Arabic-English Dictionary of Qurʾanic Usage* (Leiden: Brill, 2008), p. 659.

is badly deceived and suffers a great loss. For he who is thus deprived sees high ranks above his own station, and he looks to them in the same way that a rich man who owns ten dirhams looks to the rich man who owns the earth from East to West. Each of them is rich, but how great is the difference between the two! So how greatly has he been cheated who has lost the favor [of God]! *The hereafter is greater in degrees and greater in distinction* (17:21).

It might be literally translated as 'day of bickering' or 'day of mutual neglect.'

Chapter 10

An Exposition of the Testimony of Divine Law to the Validity of the Method of the Mystics in Gaining Experiential Knowledge, not through Instruction nor in the Ordinary Way

KNOW THAT WHOSOEVER HAS had even a small thing revealed to him through general inspiration (*ilhām*), and a coming into his heart from whence he knows not, has learned by experience the truth of this way. He who has never apprehended this must nevertheless believe in it, for the rank of mystical knowledge therein is very rarely attained. It is attested by the proof texts of revelation, experiences, and narrations.

Beginning with the proof texts there is the statement of the Exalted, *But those who strive for Us—We will surely guide to Our ways* (29:69). All wisdom that appears in the heart through steadfastness in worship apart from instruction comes by way of mystical unveiling and general inspiration. The Prophet ﷺ said, "God causes him who does what he knows to inherit the knowledge of that which he knows not,[1] and aids him in what he does so that he comes to deserve Paradise. But he who does not do what he knows goes astray in that which he knows, and is not aided in what he does so that he comes to deserve the Fire." God, the Exalted,

1 The *ḥadīth* proper probably ends here, the rest being a quotation from Makkī, *Qūt al-qulūb*, says Zabīdī. This is also evidenced by ʿIrāqī's statement that the first part is a *ḥadīth* of Anas given by Abū Nuʿaym, but that he finds no source in *ḥadīth* for the rest of the quotation. The first part is also quoted in the *Iḥyāʾ*, 1:63, and by Bayḍāwī in his comment on the preceding Qurʾānic quotation, 29:69.

said, *And whoever fears God, He will make for him a way out.* [This is interpreted, 'He will grant] a prosperous issue from all difficulties and doubts ...*and will provide for him from where he reckoned not* (65:2). And He will cause him to know without instruction and to be sagacious without experiment. God, the Exalted, said, *O you who believe! if you fear God He will grant you a criterion* (8:29). This is said to be a light that distinguishes between reality and falsehood (*bāṭil*), and by which one finds a way out of uncertainties. Therefore [the Prophet] ﷺ used to pray much for light. He said, upon whom be blessings and peace, "God give me light and increase light unto me; grant me light in my heart, light in my grave, light in my hearing, and light in my seeing." He even said, " ... in my hair, my skin, my flesh, and my bones."[2] The Prophet ﷺ was asked about the statement of God, the Exalted, *So is one whose breast God has expanded to [accept] Islam and he is upon a light from his Lord* (39:22), what this *expanding* was. He replied, "It is enlarging, for, when the light is cast into the heart, the chest is enlarged and expanded for it."[3] He ﷺ also said to Ibn ʿAbbās, "O God give him discernment in religion and teach him interpretation."[4] ʿAlī ؓ said, "I have nothing which the Prophet ﷺ divulged to me save that God, the Exalted, gives a servant understanding in His book."[5] This was not by instruction. In commenting on the statement of the Exalted, *He gives wisdom to whom He wills* (2:269), it is said that 'wisdom' is understanding in the Book of God, the Exalted. The Exalted said, *And we gave understanding of the case of Solomon* (21:79), referring especially to what was revealed to him under the name *understanding*. Abū al-Dardāʾ[6] used to say, "The believer sees with the light of God from behind a thin veil." And by God that is the truth. God casts it into their hearts and makes it move upon their tongues. Some of the Predecessors (*al-salaf*)[7] have said, "The estimation (*ẓann*) of the believer is divination." The Prophet ﷺ said,

2 An agreed upon *ḥadīth* from Ibn ʿAbbās.

3 A *ḥadīth* from Ibn Masʿūd; also *Iḥyāʾ*, 1:68.

4 A *ḥadīth* related by Aḥmad and others from Ibn ʿAbbās; also *Iḥyāʾ*, 1:33.

5 An accepted *ḥadīth*, varying considerably in form. In *Iḥyāʾ*, 1:254, it is given as follows: "The Prophet did not disclose to me anything that he concealed from the people save that God gives a servant understanding in His Book."

6 Abū al-Dardāʾ al-Khazrajī al-Anṣārī, a great Qurʾān scholar and judge in Damascus, where he died in 31/651; see *EI*, 1:62. *EI*², 1:113.

7 *Salaf*, that is, Companions, Successors, Followers. Tahānawī, *Iṣṭilāḥāt al-funūn*, p. 676ff.; Thomas Hughes, *Dictionary of Islam* (London: W. H. Allen, 1885), p. 560a.

"Beware of the natural insight (*firāsa*)[8] of the believer, for he sees with the light of God, the Exalted."[9] It is to this that reference is made in the statements of the Exalted, *Indeed in that there are signs for those who discern* (15:75); and statement of the Exalted, *We have shown clearly the signs to a people who are certain [in faith]* (2:118). Ḥasan narrated from the Messenger of God ﷺ, that he said, "Knowledge is twofold—there is an inner knowledge within the heart and it is the profitable knowledge."[10] One of the scholars was asked what this inner knowledge was, and replied, "It is one of the secrets of God, the Exalted, which He casts into the hearts of His beloved (*aḥibbā*ʾ), and with which He has acquainted no angel nor human being."

[The Prophet] ﷺ said, "Verily there are in my nation recipients of [heavenly] discourse (*muḥaddithūn*), ones that are taught, and individuals that are spoken to, and ʿUmar is one of them."[11] Ibn ʿAbbās ﷺ recited, *We have not sent any messenger before you*[12] (21:25), nor any prophet, nor any narrators, that is, any who were trustworthy.[13] The 'recipient of discourse' is he who has been inspired (*mulham*), and he who has been inspired is one in whose heart an unveiling has been made from within, and not from the direction of external senses. The Qurʾān plainly states that godly fear (*taqwā*) is the key to right guidance (*hidāya*) and mystical revelation. This is knowledge without instruction. God, the Exalted, said, *And [in] what God has created in the heavens and the earth are signs for a people who fear God* (10:6), [signs] given especially to them. He, the

8 "Firāsa," divinely given intuition; see *EI*, 2:108b. *EI*², 2:916.

9 A *ḥadīth* quoted by Tirmidhī from Abū Saʿīd; also *Iḥyā*ʾ, 2:259.

10 An accepted *ḥadīth* of Ḥasan al-Baṣrī, quoted by Tirmidhī. In *Iḥyā*ʾ, 1:52 it is given, "Knowledge is twofold: a knowledge on the tongue, which is God's argument (*ḥujja*) against His creatures; and a knowledge in the heart, which is the profitable knowledge."

11 Bukhārī quotes a similar *ḥadīth* from Abū Hurayra, and Muslim from ʿĀʾisha.

12 The meaning apparently given to this quotation here is quite different from that of the Qurʾānic context.

13 *Ṣiddīqūn*, those who accept and assert the truth of God and His Messenger. See Qurʾān 4:71 and 57:16 with Bayḍāwī's comment on the latter verses. For the early usage of the term, see Massignon, *Essai*, p. 193. Cf. the use of *al-ṣiddīq*, the veracious, with the name of Abū Bakr. See *EI*, 4:432b. *EI*², 9:534. Cf. Margaret Smith, *Studies in Early Mysticism* (New York: Macmillan, 1931).

Exalted, said, *Here is a plain statement to men, a guidance and instruction to those who fear God* (3:138).

Abū Yazīd[14] and others used to say, "The scholar is not he who learns something by heart out of a book, for if he forgets what he has memorized he becomes ignorant, but the scholar is he who takes his knowledge directly from his Lord whensoever he wishes without any memorizing or study." Such is divine knowledge (*ʿilm rabbānī*),[15] and to it is reference made in the statement of the Exalted, *We taught him knowledge from our presence* (18:65). Although all knowledge is from His presence (*min ladunhu*), yet some of it comes through the means used in teaching mankind, and this is not called directly-given divine knowledge (*ʿilm ladunnī*).[16] This latter, however, is the knowledge that is opened in the secret of the heart without any usual means from without.

These are the traditional evidences, and were all of the existing evidence of this sort to be gathered together—verses, narrations, and recorded sayings[17]—it would be boundless.

The witness of experience to this is also boundless. This appears from the Companions,[18] the Followers,[19] and those who came after them.

Abū Bakr al-Ṣiddīq ﷺ said to ʿĀʾisha ﷺ just before his death, "They are your two sisters." His wife at the time was pregnant and later bore a daughter, and he knew before her birth that she was a girl. ʿUmar ﷺ said during his sermon[20] one Friday, "O Sāriya,[21] the mountain, the mountain"; since it had been disclosed to him that the enemy was upon them, so he,

---

14 Abū Yazīd al-Bisṭāmī also known as Bāyazīd (d. 261 or 264/874 or 877), a Persian ecstatic Sufi, probably the first to discuss the doctrine of *fanāʾ*, self-annihilation. See *EI*, 1:686 and *Supp*. p. 42; *EI²*, 1:162. Massignon, *Essai*, p. 247ff.

15 Editor's note: Zabīdī (7:260) has *ʿālim rabbānī*, which might best be translated as a 'lordly' scholar.

16 *ʿIlm ladunnī*, the meaning here seems to be knowledge learned directly from God by a spoken word or a vision without the mediation of prophet or angel. The term is also used of a direct certain knowledge of God's essence and attributes, Tahānawī, *Iṣṭilāḥāt al-funūn*, p. 1066; Massignon, *Essai*, p. 111.

17 Ghazālī uses the term *akhbār* for *ḥadīth*s that go back to Muḥammad, and *āthār* for narrations that go back to the Companions. See "khabar," *EI*, 2:859. *EI²*, 4:895.

18 "Ṣaḥāba," the Companions of the Prophet; See "aṣḥāb," *EI*, 1:477ff. *EI²*, 8:827.

19 "Tābiʿūn," the Followers who came after the Companions; see *EI*, 4:583. *EI²*, 10:28.

20 "Khuṭba," the regular Friday sermon in the mosque; see *EI*, 2:980ff. *EI²*, 5:74.

21 *Sāriya*, an expedition that travels at night, here personified in direct address.

since he knew, warned them. The fact that his voice reached them was one of the many miraculous gifts (*karāmāt*).[22]

Anas b. Mālik[23] said, "I entered into the presence of ʿUthmān,[24] and on my way there I had come across a woman and looked at her out of the corner of my eye and reflected on her charms. As I entered, ʿUthmān said, 'One of you comes into my presence with the marks of adultery showing in his eyes. Know you not that adultery of the eyes is the look? So repent or I shall punish you.' I said, 'Is there revelation (*waḥy*) after the Prophet?' He replied, 'No, but mental perception, inference, and true natural insight.'"

Abū Saʿīd al-Kharrāz[25] said, "I entered into the sacred mosque and saw a poor man wearing two tattered cloaks and said to myself, 'This man and his ilk are a burden upon mankind.' But he called me to him and said, *God knows what is in your hearts, so beware of Him* (2:235). Then I asked forgiveness of God secretly, at which he again called me and said, *He it is who accepts repentance from His servants* (9:104). Then he disappeared from me and I did not see him again."

Zakarīyā b. Dāwūd[26] said that Abū al-ʿAbbās b. Masrūq[27] went in to see Abū al-Faḍl al-Ḥāshimī[28] when he was sick; he had children but was without known means of livelihood. Abū al-ʿAbbās said, "when I got up I said to myself, 'Where does this man get anything to eat from?' But he shouted at me, 'O Abū al-ʿAbbās, put away this sordid anxiety, for God, the Exalted, has hidden kindnesses.'"

---

22 "Karāmāt," see *EI*, 2:744. *EI*^{2}, 4:615.

23 Anas b. Mālik, Abū Ḥamza (d. 91 or 93/710 or 712), one of the most prolific *ḥadīth* narrators; see *EI*, 1:345. *EI*^{2}, 6:262.

24 ʿUthmān Abū ʿAmr ʿUthmān b. ʿAffān (d. 35/655), the third caliph; see *EI*, 3:1008ff. *EI*^{2}, 10:946.

25 Abū Saʿīd Aḥmad b. ʿĪsā (Muḥammad) al-Kharrāz al-Baghdādī (d. 277/890), a famous mystic and companion of Dhū al-Nūn and others. Qushayrī, *al-Qushayri's Epistle*, trans. Knysh, pp. 53ff.

26 Zakarīyā b. Dāwūd. I cannot identify him.

27 Abū al-ʿAbbās Aḥmad b. Muḥammad b. Masrūq al-Ṭusī (d. 298 or 299/910 or 911), a mystic and pupil of Muḥāsibī. Qushayrī, *al-Risāla*, trans. Knysh, p. 54; Massignon, *Essai*, pp. 209, 223.

28 Abū al-Faḍl al-Hāshimī; I am not sure of the identification, but he may be the mystic who studied Indian mysticism. See Massignon, *Essai*, pp. 68, 70, 78.

Aḥmad al-Naqīb[29] said, "I went into the presence of Shiblī[30] who said, '[You are] tested, Aḥmad.' I said, 'What do you mean?' He said, 'As I was sitting there the thought came over me, 'you are miserly.' I said, 'I am not miserly,' but my thought continued to reproach me saying, 'but you are miserly.' So I said, 'whatever the day brings to me, I shall give to the first poor man who meets me.' Hardly had I finished the thought when there came to me a companion of Muʾnis al-Khādim[31] who brought fifty dinars and said, 'Use this for your own expenses.' When he had said this I rose up and took it and went out, and behold, a poor blind man [was] sitting in front of a barber who was shaving his head. So I approached him and gave him the dinars. He said, 'Give them to the barber.' I said, 'But their sum is such and such.' He replied, 'Did we not tell you that you are miserly?' When he said this I gave them to the barber, who said, 'When this poor man sat down before me I agreed that I should take no fee from him.' So I cast them into the Tigris and said, 'No one magnifies you but God humbles him.'"

Ḥamza b. ʿAbdallāh al-ʿAlawī[32] said, "I went into the presence of Abū al-Khayr al-Tīnānī,[33] thinking in my heart that I would greet him but not eat food in his house. After I left his house he soon caught up with me, and he was carrying a platter of food. He said, 'Eat, O youth, for you have now passed out from the limits set by your former resolution.'" This man Abū al-Khayr al-Tīnānī was famous for his miraculous gifts. Ibrāhīm al-Raqqī[34] said, "I went to see him to greet him, but arrived at the time of the sunset prayer, and he had not recited the *Fātiḥa* beautifully. So I said to myself

29 Aḥmad al-Naqīb. I cannot identify him.

30 Al-Shiblī Abū Bakr (247–334/861–945), a famous Sunnī mystic; see *EI*, 4:360ff. *EI²*, 9:432.

31 Muʾnis al-Khādim (al-Muẓaffar), d. 321/933; a famous ʿAbbāsid general; see *EI*, 3:723ff. *EI²*, 7:575.

32 Ḥamza b. ʿAbdallāh al-ʿAlawī, a narrator of *ḥadīth*s. Muḥammad b. Jarīr al-Ṭabarī [*Tārīkh al-umam wa-l-muluk*], *Annales at-Tabari*, ed. M. J. de Goeje (Brill, 1870–1904), Series 3, 1:254, 1 4, p. 258, 1 12.

33 Abū al-Khayr al-Tinānī al-Aqṭaʿ (d. 349/960 or 961), a mystic noted for *karāmāt* and *firāsa*. Qushayrī, *al-Qushayri's Epistle*, trans. Knysh, p. 64; ʿAbd al-Wahhāb b. Aḥmad al-Shaʿrānī, *al-Ṭabaqāt al-kubrā* (Cairo: al-Maṭbaʿa al-ʿĀmira al-ʿUthmāniyya, 1316/1898), p. 87.

34 Abū Isḥāq Ibrāhīm b. Dāwūd al-Raqqī (d. 326/938), a leading shaykh among Damascus mystics. Qushayrī, *al-Qushayri's Epistle*, trans. Knysh, p. 59.

that my trip was in vain. When he had finished I went outside to perform my ablutions and a lion came at me, so I went back to Abū al-Khayr and told him that a lion had come at me. Then he went and shouted at it, 'Did I not tell you not to attack my guests?' Thereupon the lion turned aside and I performed my ablutions. When I returned he said to me, 'You have labored to make right that which is external (*al-ẓāhir*) and were afraid of the lion, while we have labored to make right that which is within (*al-bāṭin*) and the lion was afraid of us.'"

The stories of the insight of the shaykhs and their ability to know the thoughts and intents of men are numerous. Indeed the stories told of their seeing Khiḍr[35] ﷺ and asking questions of him, of hearing the voice of an unseen speaker (*hātif*),[36] and of various kinds of miraculous gifts are without number. A story is of no value to him who denies, as long as he does not see it with his own eyes, and he who denies the principle denies also the details.

The absolute proof that no one can deny consists of two things. One of them is in the wonders of the true dream-vision, for by it the unknown is unveiled. If this is permissible in sleep, it is also not impossible during waking hours; for sleep does not differ from waking, save that the senses are stilled and not busied in the things perceived by them. How many a waking man is there so deep in thought that he neither hears nor sees because of his preoccupation with himself!

The second is that the Messenger of God ﷺ was able to speak accurately about the unknown and things in the future, as is set forth in the Qurʾān. If that is permissible in the case of the Prophet ﷺ it is also permissible for others. For a prophet is merely a person to whom the true nature of things has been disclosed, and who works for the reformation of mankind. So it is not impossible that there should exist a person to whom the true nature of things has been disclosed, but who does not work for the reformation of mankind. Such a man is not called a prophet, but a saint (*walī*). So whoever believes in the prophets and considers true dream-visions as trustworthy must unquestionably assert that the heart has two doors: a

35 Khiḍr (al-Khaḍir), a popular figure of uncertain identity often referred to in legend and story; see *EI*, 2:861ff.; *EI*², 4:902. Massignon, *Essai*, pp. 111ff. Editor's note: he was a mystical figure mentioned in Sufi literature as one with *ʿilm ladunnī*. Cf. A. Yūsuf ʿAlī, trans., *The Meaning of the Holy Qurʾān* (Beltsville, MD: Amana, 2002), on *Sūra al-Kahf* 18:60–82 (pp. 725–31).

36 "Hātif," *EI*, 2:289. *EI*², 3:273.

door to the outer world, which is the external senses; and a door to the world of spirits from within the heart, which is the door of both general and prophetic inspiration and inbreathing within the heart. If he asserts his belief in both of these he cannot limit knowledge to what is gained by learning and the ordinary direct methods, but striving (*mujāhada*)[37] is also another way for him. This illustrates the fact that we have mentioned of the strange swaying back and forth of the heart between the material world and the world of spirits.

Now regarding the unveiling of a thing in sleep by means of an example that needs interpretation, and likewise the appearance of angels to prophets and saints in different forms, these are among the secrets of the wonders of the heart, and only that knowledge which comes through mystic unveiling befits them. So let us limit ourselves to what we have mentioned, for it is sufficient to encourage striving and seeking unveiling therein.

One of those to whom secrets are unveiled said,

"There appeared to me an angel who asked me to dictate to him something of what I had seen of unity (*tawḥīd*) in my secret devotions.

He said, 'What deed shall we write down to your account? We wish to take up [i.e., to God] for you a deed by which we shall draw near to God ﷻ.'

I said, 'Do you two not write down [the practice of] the prescribed duties (*farāʾiḍ*)?'

They answered, 'Surely.'

I said, 'That will suffice you.'"

This is an indication that the noble scribes (*al-kirām al-kātibīn*)[38] are not acquainted with the secrets of the heart, but only with deeds that are manifest.

One of the gnostics said,

"I asked one of the Substitutes (*abdāl*)[39] concerning the perception of certitude (*yaqīn*).

---

37 *Mujāhada*, struggle against the desires of the lower nature by compelling it to conform to the demands of the religious law. Jurjānī, *al-Taʿrīfāt*, pp. 216, 290.

38 Editor's note: the noble scribes (*al-kirām al-kātibīn*) are referred to in the Qurʾān, 82:11.

39 *Abdāl*, or Substitutes, are persons who are spiritual pillars by whom God continues the world in existence. No one can identify them. For the Sufi hierarchy and further definition see, Hughes, *Dictionary*; Lane, *Lexicon*; Edward Sell, *The Religious Orders of Islam* (London: Simpkin, Marshall, Hamilton, Kent, 1908), p. 24ff.; *EI*, *Supp.* p. 35; *EI*², 1:94. Massignon, *Essai*, pp. 112ff. The term here seems to be used non-technically for a Muslim saint. Editor's note: "According to Sufi tradition, the

He turned to his left and said, 'What do you say? God's mercy be upon you.' Then he turned to his right and said, 'What do you say? God's mercy be upon you.' Then he smote upon his breast and said, 'What do you say? God's mercy be upon you.' Thereupon he answered me with the strangest reply I have ever heard.

So I asked him about his turning and he replied, 'I did not have any ready answer in that matter; so I asked the angel on the left and he said, 'I do not know'; then I asked the angel on the right, who is more learned than he, and he also said, 'I do not know'; then I looked into my heart and asked it, and it told me the answer that I gave you, so therefore it is more learned than both of them.'"

This was the meaning of the saying of [the Prophet] ﷺ, "Verily there are in my nation recipients of discourse, and ʿUmar is one of them."

There is a tradition (*athar*) that God, the Exalted, says, "Whenever I examine the heart of a man and find persistent remembrance of me preponderant therein, I assume control over him and become his companion; I converse with him and become his familiar friend." Abū Sulaymān al-Dārānī,[40] may God's mercy be upon him, said, "The heart is like a pavilion that has been pitched, around which are closed doors, and whatever door is opened onto it influences it."

So it appears that the opening of one of the doors of the heart is toward the world of spirits and the highest beings. This door is opened by means of striving, scrupulous piety (*waraʿ*), and shunning the lusts of this present world. For this reason ʿUmar ؓ wrote to the commanders of the troops, "Remember what you hear from those who are obedient [to God] for they have inspirations that are true."

Some of the scholars have said, "The hand of God is on the mouth of the sages (*ḥukamāʾ*), and they only speak of that reality which God has

---

abdāl or *budalāʾ* (pl. of *badal* meaning literally 'substitute'), constitute one degree or rank in the spiritual hierarchy of saints or mystics after the time of the Prophet. They are said to be unknown to the generality of believers, but have a powerful influence in preserving the order of the universe. Sufi literature varies concerning both the different ranks that make up this hierarchy and the numbers within each of these ranks." Keeler, trans. *Tafsīr al-Tustarī*, note to 10:62.

40 Abū Sulaymān al-Dārānī (d. 205 or 215/820 or 830), a mystic who developed the doctrine of gnosis in Sufism. See Ibn Khallikān, *Wafayāt al-ʿayān*, trans. De Slane, 2:88; Philip Hitti, *History of the Arabs* (London: Macmillan, 1937), p. 434; Massignon, *Essai*, pp. 197ff.

prepared for them." Another said, "You can say, if you will, that God, the Exalted, acquaints the humble in worship (*khāshiʿūn*) with some of His secrets."

Chapter 11

An Exposition of the Domination of Satan over the Heart through Evil Promptings; the Meaning of such Suggestions, and the Means of Overcoming them

KNOW THAT THE HEART, as we have mentioned, is like a pavilion that has been pitched, to which there are doors, and influences, and their resultant effects pour into it from each door. It is also like a target into which arrows are shot from every direction. Or it is like a mirror that is set up, across which there pass various different images; so there appears in it one image after another, some image being always present. Or it is like a basin into which different streams of water empty from channels opening into it.

The entrances of these influences that are constantly being renewed in the heart are either from without, i.e., from the five external senses; or from within, i.e., imagination, appetence, anger, and characteristics that are made up from the temperament of man. For if he apprehends a thing by means of the senses it has an effect upon the heart. Likewise when passion is aroused, for example, that which is caused by hearty eating and a strong constitution, it leaves its mark upon the heart. Even if the effect upon the senses ceases, there remain the imaginative [images] that have been formed in the soul. The imagination shifts from one thing to another, and in accordance with the shifting of the imagination, the heart shifts from one state to another. We mean that the heart is constantly in a state of change and being influenced by these secondary causes. The most important of these influences that come into the heart are involuntary suggestions (*khawāṭir*). By involuntary suggestions I mean the ideas (*afkār*) and recollections (*adhkār*) that take place therein. By these I mean its perceptions of knowledge, either by way of renewal or recollection; for these are called involuntary suggestions since they come into the mind while the heart has been unmindful of them.

These involuntary suggestions are what move wills. Intention, resolution, and will are all unquestionably subsequent to the suggestion of the thing intended to the mind. Thus the basis of action is involuntary suggestion. Then the suggestion stirs up desire (*raghba*); desire stirs up resolution; resolution stirs up intention; and intention stirs up the members of the body.

The involuntary suggestions that stir up desire are divided into [two classes]: that which leads to evil, by which I mean what has a harmful result; and that which leads to good, by which I mean what is profitable in the next world. These are two different suggestions and need two different names. The praiseworthy suggestion is called 'general inspiration' (*ilhām*), and the blameworthy suggestion, by which I mean that leading to evil, is called 'prompting to evil' (*wiswās*).[1]

Moreover you know that these suggestions are created (*ḥāditha*), and also that every created thing must have a creator (*muḥdith*).[2] Whenever the created things differ, this indicates a difference in the secondary causes (*asbāb*). This is what is known from the laws (*sunna*) of God, the Exalted, regarding the relationship between effects and causes.

Whenever the walls of a house are lit by the light of the fire and its ceiling is blackened by the smoke, you know that the cause of the blackening differs from that of the lighting. Similarly the light of the heart and its darkness have two distinct secondary causes. The cause of the suggestion that leads to good is called an angel (*malak*), and the cause of the suggestion that leads to evil is called a demon (*shayṭān*).

The divine favor by which the heart is prepared to receive the inspiration of the angel of good is called 'divine succor' (*tawfīq*); while that by which it is prepared to receive the evil prompting of the demon is called 'deception' (*ighwāʾ*) and 'desertion' (*khidhlān*).[3] For these different meanings need different names.

'Angel' is a term for a creature whom God, the Exalted, has created, whose task it is to bestow benefits, to serve knowledge, to reveal the real,

1 *Wiswās*, cf. *al-khāṭir al-shayṭānī*, see page xxx.

2 MSS texts read, 'a secondary cause' (*sabab*).

3 *Khidhlān*, desertion. See Wensinck, *Muslim Creed*, pp. 143 and 213.

true and right, to promise good, and to command to good; and God has created him and compelled him to do these things.

'Demon' is a term for a creature whose task is the opposite of all this, namely, to promise evil, to command to excess, and to threaten with poverty whenever one intends to do good.[4] Thus prompting to evil stands in contrast with inspiration; the demon in contrast with the angel; and divine succor in contrast with desertion. To this, reference is made in the statement of the Exalted, *And of everything We have created pairs* (51:49). For all existing things have opposites, being in pairs, save only God, the Exalted, who is unique and has none in contrast to Him. Indeed He is the One, the Real, the Creator of all these pairs.

The heart, being between the demon and the angel, is attracted by each of them. [The Prophet] ﷺ said, "The heart has two calls (*lammatān*). The one is from the angel and it is a promise of good and belief in the divine Reality; and whoever finds this, let him know that it is from God, praise be to Him, and let him give thanks to God. The other call is from the enemy and it is a promise of evil, a denial of the divine Reality, and forbidding of good; and whoever finds it, let him take refuge with God from Satan the Accursed."[5] After that he repeated the statement of the Exalted, which begins, *Satan threatens you poverty and orders you to immorality [while God promises you forgiveness from Him and bounty. And God is All-Encompassing and All-Knowing.]* (2:268).

Ḥasan said, "There are two anxieties that revolve in the heart: an anxiety from God, the Exalted, and another from the enemy. God has mercy on the creature who pays attention to that which gives him concern, executing that which has its source in God, the Exalted, and struggling against that which has its source in His enemy." In regard to the attraction of the heart toward these two ruling forces,[6] the Messenger of God ﷺ said, "The heart of the believer is between two of the fingers of the Merciful." God is too highly-exalted to have a finger made up of flesh, bone, blood, nerve, and divided by joints. But the spirit (*ruḥ*) of a 'finger' is swiftness in turning and ability to move and change objects; for you do not want your finger for its own sake, but for what it will do in turning and replacing things, even as you ordinarily do your work with your fingers.

---

4 Cf. Qur'ān 2:271.

5 A *ḥadīth* from Ibn Masʿūd quoted by Tirmidhī and Nasā'ī, Wensinck, *Concordance*, 2:98a. Editor's note: lit., the "Stoned."

6 MSS texts read, 'two calls.'

God, the Exalted, does what He does by constraining the angel and the demon, the two of them being forced by His power to turn hearts, even as, for example, your fingers are compelled by you to turn objects. The heart in its original innate condition is fitted to receive the influences of angel and demon alike, with no preponderance of the one over the other. The preponderance of the one side over the other is, however, brought about by following desire (*hawā*) and giving one's self over to the appetites, or by turning from and opposing them.

When a man follows the dictates of anger and appetence, the domination of the demon through desire appears, and the heart becomes the nest of the demon and his seat. Desire is the pasture of the demon and his abundant provision. But when a man strives against the appetites and does not give them rule over him, and imitates the moral character of the angels عليهم السلام, then his heart becomes the habitation and resting place of the angels.

Since no heart is devoid of appetence, anger, miserliness, covetousness, hope of long life, and other similar human qualities that originate in desire, without doubt there is no heart in which a demon does not roam about prompting to evil. In regard to this [the Prophet] ﷺ said, "There is not one of you but has a demon."[7] They asked, "And you, O Messenger of God?" He answered, "And I also, save that God helped me to gain the victory over him and he became a Muslim, and commands only good." This is because the demon works only through appetence. So when God has given anyone the victory over appetence, so that it extends only in proper directions and within proper limits, then appetence does not invite to evil and the demon that is armed thereby commands naught but good.

Whenever the thought of this present world predominates in the heart because of the demands of desire, then the demon finds an opportunity and prompts to evil. But when the heart is devoted exclusively to the remembrance of God, the Exalted, the demon leaves it and his field is straitened, and the angel draws near and inspires.

In the battle of the heart there are constant attacks and counter-attacks between the forces of the angels and demons until it is conquered by one of them, which takes up its residence and abode therein. When the second enters, he takes it by a trick. Most hearts have been conquered and occupied by the troops of demons, and so [are] filled with promptings to evil, which call for the preference of the swiftly passing world and the casting

---

7 A *ḥadīth* given by Muslim. Zabīdī gives a number of variants of this *ḥadīth*. See "shayṭān," *EI*, 4:286ff. *EI*^{2}, 9:406.

aside of the world to come. The starting point of their occupation is the following of the appetites and desire. After this takes place, the heart cannot be reconquered except by emptying it of the demon's nourishment, which is desire and the appetites, and rebuilding it by means of remembrance of God, the Exalted, which is the place of angelic influence.

Jarīr b. ʿUbayda al-ʿAdawī[8] said, "I complained to al-ʿAlāʾ b. Ziyād,[9] 'I do not find any promptings to evil in my breast.' He said, 'This is like a house that thieves pass by; if there is anything in it they take it, otherwise they pass on and leave it.'" That is to say, the demon does not enter the heart that is devoid of desire. Regarding this God, the Exalted, said, *Indeed you have no authority over my servants* (17:65).

But whosoever follows desire is the servant of desire, not a servant of God; therefore God gives the demon power over him. The Exalted said, *Have you seen the one who takes his desire as his god?* (25:43). This indicates that his desire is his god and the object of his worship, and so he is a servant of his desire, not a servant of God.

ʿUthmān b. Abī al-ʿĀṣī[10] said to the Prophet ﷺ, "O Messenger of God, a demon has kept me from my prayer and reciting [the Qurʾān]." He replied, "That demon is called Khinzib,[11] so whenever you are conscious of his presence, take refuge from him with God, and spit three times to your left." He said, "I did so, and God sent him away from me." A narration says that ceremonial purification (*wuḍūʾ*) has a demon called Walhān,[12] so take refuge from him with God.

---

8 Jarīr b. ʿUbayda al-ʿAdawī (Cairo text has Jābir). I cannot identify him.

9 Al-ʿAlāʾ b. Ziyād b. Maṭar al-ʿAdawī al-Baṣrī (d. 194/810), a Follower and *ḥadīth* narrator. Shaʿrānī, *al-Ṭabaqāt*, p. 28; Nawawī, *Kitāb tahdhīb al-asmāʾ*, ed. Ferdinand Wüstenfeld (Götingen, 1842–7), p. 540.

10 ʿUthmān b. Abī al-ʿĀṣī al-Thaqafī (d. 51 or 55/671 or 675), one time governor of Ṭāʾif and Bahrain. See Ibn Ḥajar, *Biographical Dictionary*, 2:1098ff.; Ibn Qutayba, *Mukhtalaf al-ḥadīth*, p. 137. Following *Maḥajjat* MS and Zabīdī, *Itḥāf*. Cairo text and Zabīdī read ʿAmr b. al-ʿĀṣ in error.

11 Khinzib, according to Zabīdī. Hughes, *Dictionary*, and Buṭrus Bustānī, *Muḥīṭ al-muḥīṭ* (Beirut, 1867–70) give Khanzab; Murtaḍā al-Zabīdī, *Tāj al-ʿarūs* (Cairo, 1306/1888), and Ibn Manẓūr, *Lisān al-ʿArab* (Cairo, n.d.) give both vowellings and also Khunzub. The word means a piece of decayed meat, and is applied to the demon who interferes with the ritual prayer. Zabīdī (*Tāj al-ʿarūs*) says that Ibn al-Athīr quotes the *ḥadīth* about Khinzib among the *ḥadīth*s on ritual prayer.

12 Al-Walhān, also al-Walahān. The name signifies grief or distraction of mind. This demon deceives by calling for an abundance of water for the ritual ablution.

The evil prompting of Satan is not removed from the heart save by the remembrance of that which is other than what he suggests. For if there is suggested to the heart the thought of anything, what has been in it previously is annihilated. Everything other than God, the Exalted, and what is connected with Him may possibly become a field for Satan's activity. The remembrance of God is the safe side, for it is known that there is no room for Satan there. A thing is treated only by its opposite, and the opposite of all the evil promptings of Satan is the remembrance of God, by taking refuge with Him and disdaining strength and power. This is what you mean when you say, "I take refuge with God from Satan the accursed,"[13] and, "There is no strength nor power save in God the High, the Mighty."[14] This can be done only by the pious in whom the remembrance of God, the Exalted, predominates, and Satan only approaches them as by a sly trick at the times of their blunders (*falatāt*). God, the Exalted, said, *Indeed, those who fear God, when a thought touches them from Satan, they remember [God] and at once they have insight* (7:201). In regard to the meaning of the statement of God, the Exalted, *From the evil of the retreating whisperer* (114:4), Mujāhid[15] said, "He [i.e., Satan] stretches out his authority over the heart; if God, the Exalted, is remembered he [i.e. Satan] slinks away and crouches down, but if this is carelessly overlooked he stretches out his authority over the heart." The mutual hostility (*taṭārud*) existing between the remembrance of God, the Exalted, and the evil prompting of Satan is like the mutual hostility between light and darkness and night and day. Of their mutual opposition, God, the Exalted, said, *Satan has overcome them and made them forget the remembrance of God* (58:19).

Anas [☙] quotes the Messenger of God ﷺ as having said, "Satan places his snout on the heart of the son of Adam; if he remembers God, the Exalted, Satan slinks away, but if he forgets God, the Exalted, Satan gobbles up his heart."[16]

Bustānī, *Muḥīṭ*, p. 2287. This *ḥadīth* is quoted by Tirmidhī and Ibn Māja from Ubayy b. Kaʿb.

13   *Taʿawwudh*. Hughes, *Dictionary*, p. 624a.

14   See Wensinck, *Concordance*, 1:532a.

15   Mujāhid b. Jabr al-Makkī (d. between 101 and 104/719 and 722), a Successor. Ibn Khallikān, *Wafayāt al-ʿayān*, trans. De Slane, 1:568; Nawawī, *Tahdhīb al-asmāʾ*, p. 540; Massignon, *Essai*, pp. 142ff.

16   A weak *ḥadīth* given by Ibn Abī al-Dunyā and others.

Ibn Waḍḍāḥ,[17] in a *ḥadīth* that he narrated, said, "When a man becomes forty years old without repenting, Satan rubs his hand over the man's face and says, 'By my father, it is the face of one who will not succeed.'"[18]

Just as the appetites are mingled with the flesh and blood of the son of Adam, so the authority of Satan courses through his flesh and blood and surrounds the heart on all sides, Thus [the Prophet] ﷺ said, "Verily Satan courses through the son of Adam just like the circulation of his blood,[19] so make his coursings difficult by means of hunger." For hunger breaks down appetence, and Satan's course is in the appetites. Because of the fact that the appetites surround the heart on all sides, God, the Exalted, informed [us] about the words of Iblīs,[20] *I will lie in wait for them on your straight path; then I will surely come to them from before them and behind them, on their right and on their left* (7:16–7).

[The Prophet] ﷺ said, "Verily Satan lies in wait for the son of Adam in all his ways. He lay in wait in the path of Islam and said, 'Will you become a Muslim and leave your religion and the religion of your fathers?' But he [the son of Adam] disobeyed him and became a Muslim, then [Satan] lay in wait for him in the path of emigration (*hijra*)[21] and said, 'Will you emigrate; will you leave your land and your sky?' But he [the son of Adam] disobeyed him and emigrated. Then [Satan] lay in wait for him in the path of war (*jihād*)[22] saying, 'Will you engage in war, which is the destruction of self and property, and kill and be killed, and your wives be remarried and your property divided?' But he [the son of Adam] disobeyed him and struggled [in the war]." The Messenger of God ﷺ said, "Whoever does this and dies, it is [his] right from God to bring him into Paradise."[23]

---

17 Muḥammad b. Waḍḍāh (d. 287/900), a narrator of *ḥadīth* and ascetic, and a freedman of ʿAbd al-Raḥmān b. Muʿāwiya al-Umawī in Andalusia. Muḥammad b. Aḥmad al-Dhahabī, *Kitāb ṭabaqāt al-ḥuffāz*, ed. Wüstenfeld (Götingen, 1834), 2:61, no. 15; M. Amari, *Biblioteca Arabo-Sicula* (Turin: E. Loescher, 1880–1), 2:495, 702; Ibn Khallikān, *Wafayāt al-ʿayān*, trans. De Slane, 3:85.

18 ʿIrāqī says that he did not find a source for this *ḥadīth*.

19 An agreed upon *ḥadīth*, except for the last clause. See also *Iḥyāʾ*, 1:208; Wensinck, *Concordance*, 1:342a.

20 Editor's note: Iblīs is the proper name of Satan/the Devil.

21 "Hijra," *EI*, 2:302. *EI*², 3:366.

22 "Jihād," *EI*, 1:1041ff. *EI*², 2:538.

23 ʿIrāqī says that the chain of narrators for this *ḥadīth* is authentic (*ṣaḥiḥ*), given by Nasāʾī.

Thus the Messenger of God ﷺ mentioned the meaning of evil prompting, which is these involuntary suggestions that occur to the mind of the warrior (*mujāhid*): that he will be killed and his wives remarried, and similar thoughts that would keep him from the war. These suggestions are known, and so the evil prompting is known by observation. Every involuntary suggestion has a secondary cause that requires a name to define it, and the name of this cause is the demon. It is not to be imagined that any human being will be released from him. People differ only in that they disobey him or follow after him. Therefore the Prophet ﷺ said, "There is no one but has a demon."

From this sort of investigation there is made clear the meaning of 'prompting to evil,' 'general inspiration,' 'angel,' 'demon,' 'divine succor,' and 'desertion.'

In addition to this, some have speculated about the essence of Satan: whether he is a refined body, or incorporeal; and how, if he is a body, that which is a body can enter into the body of a man. But this is not now needed for the knowledge of proper conduct. He who seeks after this is like the man into whose clothing a snake has crawled. What he needs is to remove it and get rid of its harm; yet he occupies himself with investigating its color, form, length, and breadth, and this is absolute ignorance. The way in which these involuntary suggestions that incite to evil strike the soul is known. This indicates, undoubtedly, that a cause lies behind it. It is known that he who invites to forbidden evil in the future is an enemy. Undoubtedly also, man knows through experience who the enemy is, so he ought to busy himself in struggling against him. God, praise be to Him, has made known his enmity in many passages of His Book that men might believe in [his existence] and guard against him. The Exalted said, *Satan is a enemy to you, so take him as a enemy. But he only invites his party to be among the companions of the blaze* (35:6). Again, He, the Exalted, said *Did I not enjoin on you, O children of Adam, that you not serve Satan? Indeed he is to you a clear enemy* (36:60).

So the servant must work to ward off the enemy from himself, not by asking about his origin, his relationships, and his dwelling place. It is true that he must ask about his weapons, so that he may ward them off from himself. The weapons of Satan are desire and the appetites. This is sufficient for the intelligent. But in regard to the knowledge of the quality of his essence, his real nature—we seek refuge in God from him—and the real nature of the angels, this is the field of the gnostics who have penetrated deeply into the science of unveiling, and it is not required by the knowledge of proper conduct, such that one should know it. One must indeed know that involuntary suggestions are divided into the following: what is known certainly to invite to evil, which is manifestly evil prompting; what is known to invite to good, which is undoubtedly general inspiration; and what one is uncertain about, for he does not know whether it is from the call of the angel or the demon.

Indeed it is one of the tricks of Satan to set forth evil as though it were good. To make correct distinctions in this matter is a subtle problem and the majority of people perish therein. Satan cannot invite them to open evil, so he portrays evil in the form of good. Thus he will say to the man who is learned in the art of preaching:

"Will you not look at mankind, dead through ignorance, lost through heedlessness, and about to enter the Fire? Have you no mercy on the creatures of God, to rescue them from the dangerous places by your counsel and preaching? God has blessed you with a perspicacious heart, an eloquent tongue, and an acceptable manner of speaking; so how can you deny the grace of God, the Exalted, and expose yourself to His wrath by abstaining from spreading knowledge abroad and calling mankind unto the straight path?"

He continues to confirm this idea within the man's soul and to draw him on by agreeable tricks until he engages in preaching to the people for a time. After that [Satan] invites him to adorn himself for them, and to affect a more beautiful style of utterance and a show of good, saying to him:

"If you do not do this your discourse will make no impression upon their hearts, and they will not be guided to the Truth." [Satan] keeps confirming this to him, at the same time he ensures [that the preacher experiences] the stains of hypocrisy, popularity with the crowd, delight in high rank, pride in the power given by many followers and much learning, and a contemptuous attitude toward the people. Thus with his advice he leads the poor man gradually on to destruction, for he speaks, supposing that his purpose is good, whereas it is actually to attain high rank and popularity. By reason of this he perishes, supposing that he has a high standing in the sight of God.

He is one of those of whom the Messenger of God ﷺ said, "Verily, God aids this religion by a group for which there is no share of happiness,"[24] and again, "Verily, God establishes this religion by means of the impious man."[25]

It is related that the devil appeared to ʿĪsā b. Maryam[26] ﷺ and said to him, "Say, 'There is no god save God.'" He answered, "That is a true word, but I do not say it because of your saying." So, underneath the good, Satan has dissemblings, and his dissemblings of this sort are endless. By them are destroyed learned men, godly worshippers, ascetics, the poor and the rich, and all types of men who hate evident evil, and will not permit themselves to enter into open acts of disobedience.

We shall give a summary of the tricks of Satan in 'On the condemnation of self-delusion' in the latter part of this quarter.[27] It is our purpose, if time permits, to write a special book on the subject which we shall call 'The devil's deception' (*Talbīs Iblīs*).[28] His dissembling is now spread abroad among lands and peoples, especially among the sects and creeds, so that only a trace remains of good things. All of this is in submission to the dissemblings of Satan and his tricks. So it is the duty of man to pause at every intent that is suggested to him so that he may know whether it is from the call of the angel or of the demon, and to ponder it as he looks into it with true insight, not with the desire of nature. He should not consider it save in the light of piety, insight, and abundant knowledge, as the Exalted said, *Indeed, those who fear God, when a thought touches them from Satan, they remember Him* (7:201), i.e., return to the light of knowledge, *and lo they see,* i.e., the [resolution of] the difficulty is revealed to them.

---

24 ʿIrāqī says that the chain of narrators for this *ḥadīth* is good (*jayyid*), by Nasāʾī from Anas.

25 An agreed upon *ḥadīth*, from Abū Hurayra. See also *Iḥyāʾ*, 1:43; Wensinck, *Concordance*, 1:139a.

26 ʿĪsā, the Biblical Jesus; see *EI*, 2:524ff. *EI²*, 4:81. Editor's note: for more on ʿĪsā and other prophets, see Muḥammad al-Kisāʾī, *The Tales of the Prophets of al-Kisaʾi*, trans. W. M. Thackston (Boston: Twayne, 1978); Tarif Khalidi, ed. and trans., *The Muslim Jesus* (Boston: Harvard University Press, 2001). See also Qurʾān, 3:45–7, 4:157–9, 5: 111–8, 19:22–3.

27 Book 30 of the *Iḥyāʾ*, *Kitāb dham al-ghurūr* [On the condemnation of self-delusion], *Iḥyāʾ*, 3:367 of the Cairo edition.

28 Editor's note: a book by this title was written by Ibn al-Jawzī (d. 597/1200), who lived in the generation following Imam al-Ghazālī; see *Talbīs Iblīs* (Egypt: Idārat al-Ṭibāʿa al-Muniriyya, 1928).

But he who has not disciplined his soul through godly fear, and whose nature is inclined to submit to the dissembling [of Satan] by following desire, makes many mistakes thereby, and his destruction is, unknown to him, hastened through it. He, who is praised and exalted, said of such, *and there shall appear to them from God that which they had not taken into account* (39:47). It is said that this refers to deeds that they supposed to be good deeds, and behold they are evil deeds.

The most obscure type of the sciences of conduct to understand is the deceit of the soul and the wiles of Satan. This is the individual obligation (*farḍ ʿayn*) of every creature, but men have neglected it and busied themselves with sciences that bring evil promptings to them and give Satan authority over them, and cause them to forget his enmity and the way to guard against him. Nothing can deliver from an abundance of evil promptings save closing the doors of the involuntary suggestions. These doors are the five external senses, and the inner doors are the appetites and the ties to this present world. Solitude in a dark house will close the door of the senses, and disentangling one's self from kin and money lessens the entrances for evil promptings from within. There remain, however, inner entrances in the imaginings that flow through the heart, and these cannot be warded off save by busying the heart in the remembrance of God, the Exalted. But still [Satan] continues to contend and struggle with the heart, and to divert it from the remembrance of God, the Exalted. So there is no escape from struggling against him, and this struggle has no end but death, since no one, as long as he lives, is safe from Satan.[29]

It is true that one may become strong so that he is not led astray by him, and he may ward off his evil from himself by means of struggle (*jihād*), but he can never dispense with struggle and defense as long as the blood flows through his body. For as long as he is alive the gates [from whence] Satan [enters] are open to his heart and cannot be closed. They are appetence, anger, envy, covetousness, greed, and others, which will be explained later. So whenever the gate is open and the enemy not careless, he cannot be warded off except by watchfulness and struggle.

A man said to Ḥasan [al-Baṣrī], "O Abū Saʿīd, does Satan sleep?" He smiled and answered, "If he slept we should rest." Therefore the believer has

---

29 Zabīdī quotes a *ḥadīth* from Abū Saʿīd related by Aḥmad and others that Satan said, "By your power, O Lord, I shall not leave off leading your servants astray as long as their breath is in their bodies." The Lord answered, "By my power and majesty, I shall forgive them when they seek forgiveness of me." Cf. Qurʾān 38:83–4.

no escape from him. It is true that he does have a way of warding him off and weakening his power. [The Prophet] ﷺ said, "The believer can exhaust his demon just as one of you exhausts his camel on his journey."[30] Ibn Masʿūd[31] said, "The demon of the believer is emaciated." Qays b. al-Ḥajjāj[32] said, "My demon said to me, 'When I entered into you I was like a camel fit to be slaughtered, and now I am like a sparrow.' I asked him, 'Why is that?' He answered, 'You cause me to melt away by your remembrance of God, the Exalted.'"

Thus it is not impossible for pious people to close the doors of Satan and to keep them [closed] by being on guard; I mean the obvious doors and the clear paths that lead to overt acts of disobedience. But they stumble in his obscure paths, for they are not clearly guided to them so as to guard them, as we indicated in [the example above about] the self-delusion of the scholars and the preachers.

The difficulty is that the doors to the heart that are opened to Satan are many, while there is but a single door for the angels, and that one door is likely to be confused with all the others. Before them man is like a traveler in a desert that has many paths and obscure roads on a dark night, where he can hardly know the way except by the eye of insight or the rising of a shining sun. The eye of insight here is the heart that has been purified by piety; and the shining sun is that abundant knowledge derived from the Book of God, the Exalted, and the Sunna of His Messenger ﷺ. By these two he is rightly guided regarding [Satan's] obscure ways; otherwise, his paths are many and obscure.

ʿAbdallāh b. Masʿūd ﷺ said, "The Messenger of God ﷺ one day drew a line for us and said, 'This is the way of God.' Then he drew other lines to the right and left of that line and said, 'These are ways on every one of which there is a demon inviting [men] to him.' Then he repeated, *This is My straight path so follow it, follow not the other ways* (6:153) of those other lines."[33] Thus [the Prophet] ﷺ showed the abundance of [Satan's] ways.

We have mentioned an example of one of his obscure ways, namely that by which he deceives the scholars and the worshipful (*ʿubbād*) who have

---

30 Aḥmad quotes this *ḥadīth* from Abū Hurayra.

31 ʿAbdallāh b. Masʿūd b. Ghāfil (d. 32 or 33/652 or 653), a Companion; see *EI*, 2:403. *EI*², 3:873.

32 Qays b. al-Ḥajjāj al-Kalāʿī al-Miṣrī (d. 229/844), a narrator of *ḥadīth*.

33 ʿIrāqī says that the chain of narrators for this *ḥadīth* is authentic (*ṣaḥiḥ*), from Nasāʾī.

control over their appetites and abstain from overt acts of disobedience. Let us now mention an example of his plain ways, by which it is evident that the child of Adam must pass. This is contained in the following story, which is attributed to the Prophet ﷺ.

There was once an ascetic (*rāhib*)[34] of the children of Israel. Satan entered into a maid and caused her to have a fit, and put it into the hearts of her folk that she could be cured by the ascetic. So they brought her to him, but he refused to receive her. They continued asking him until he finally took her in. When she was with him for treatment, Satan came to him and made being near her seem very attractive; and he kept on tempting him until he ensnared her and she became pregnant by him. Then he whispered to him and said, "Now you will be disgraced openly. Her folk will come to you; so kill her, and if they ask you, say that she died." So he killed her and buried her. But Satan went to her folk and whispered to them, and put in their hearts the thought that he had seduced her and then killed and buried her. Her folk then came to him and asked him about her and he told them that she had died. They took him to kill him [in revenge for her]. Then Satan came to him and said, "I am he who caused her to have the fit, and I put the thought in the hearts of her folk. Now obey me and you will be rescued. Prostrate yourself before me twice." So he prostrated himself twice. It is he [Satan] of whom God, the Exalted, said, *Like the example of Satan when he said to man, "Disbelieve." But when he disbelieved, he said, "Indeed I am dissassociated from you"* (59:16).[35]

So look at his tricks and the way in which he compelled the ascetic to commit these great sins (*kabāʾir*),[36] and all of this because he obeyed him in taking in the maid for treatment. This in itself was an insignificant matter, and perhaps he who did it considered it a good and charitable act,

34 "Rāhib," *EI*, 3:1103b. *EI*², 8:397.

35 An accepted *ḥadīth*. Zabīdī gives several forms of it with their narrators. A much longer form is given in Ibn al-Jawzī, *Talbīs Iblīs*, pp. 26ff.

36 *Kabāʾir*. The great sins here referred to are adultery, murder, and worship of another beside God. Muslim theologians divide sins into two classes, greater sins (*kabīra*, pl. *kabāʾir*), and lesser sins (*ṣaghīra*, pl. *ṣaghāʾir*). This division is based on Qurʾān 53:33 and similar verses. The lesser sins are faults and imperfections inherent in human nature. The greater sins include the three here mentioned, and theft, etc. Great sins have a specific punishment. Wensinck, *Handbook*, p. 215b. Thus the twofold division corresponds in general with the Christian categories of mortal and venial sins. For discussion and bibliography, see Hastings, *Religion and Ethics*, 11:567ff.; and "khaṭīʾa," *EI*, 2:925ff. *EI*², 4:1106.

and he approved of it in his heart because of a hidden desire. So he went ahead with it as one desirous of doing good, and thereafter the matter went beyond the sphere of his choice, one thing leading him on to another, until he found no escape. We take refuge with God from the loss of the beginnings of things. To this is the reference in [the Prophet's] ﷺ saying, "He who hovers about a forbidden thing is in danger of falling into it."[37]

37 ʿIrāqī says this is an agreed upon *ḥadīth*, with the quoted wording from Bukhārī.

Chapter 12

A Detailed Exposition of the Ways by which Satan Enters the Heart

KNOW THAT THE HEART is like a fortress, and Satan is an enemy who wishes to enter the fortress, to take possession of it, and to rule over it. The fortress cannot be kept secure from the enemy except by guarding its doors and entrances, and the breaches in its walls. He who does not know its doors cannot guard them. The protection of the heart from the evil prompting of Satan is a prescribed duty and an individual obligation upon every morally responsible creature (*ʿabd mukallaf*).[1] That which is indispensably connected with fulfilling duty is itself also obligatory. The warding off of Satan cannot be achieved save by a knowledge of his ways of entering, and so the knowledge of his entrances becomes an obligation. The entrances of Satan and his doors are the qualities (*ṣifāt*) of the servant, and they are many. But we shall refer to the great doors, which are like the large street gates, which are not too narrow for the many troops of Satan.

One of his great gates is anger and appetence. Anger is the ogre of the intellect. If the troops of the intellect grow weak, the troops of Satan attack, and whenever man becomes angry, Satan plays with him just as a child plays with a ball.

---

1 *Mukallaf*; every sane human adult is responsible for his acts and will be judged for them in accordance with the provisions of the divine law. See *EI*, "taklīf," 4:631; *EI*², 10:138. Tahānawī, *Iṣṭilāḥāt al-funūn*, p. 1255; Reinhart Pieter Dozy, *Supplément aux Dictionnaires Arabes*, 2 vols. (Leiden, 1881), 2:485.

It is related that Iblīs found Mūsā[2] ﷺ and said,

"O Mūsā, you are he whom God chose to bring His message and to whom He spoke directly, and I am one of the creatures of God. I have sinned and desire to repent. So intercede with my Lord on my behalf that He may forgive me."

Mūsā said, "Very well." So Mūsā went up into the mountain and spoke with his Lord ﷻ, and wanted to descend, when his Lord said to him, "Be faithful in that which was entrusted to you."

Mūsā said, "O Lord, your servant Iblīs desires that you forgive him." Then God revealed to Mūsā, "O Mūsā, you have fulfilled your duty; order him to prostrate himself before the grave of Adam in order that he may be forgiven." Then Mūsā met Iblīs and said to him, "I have fulfilled your request. You are commanded to prostrate yourself before the grave of Adam in order to be forgiven." But he became angry and proud and said, "I would not prostrate myself to him when he was alive,[3] and shall I do it now that he is dead?"

Then he [Satan] said, "O Mūsā, you have made me indebted to you in that you have interceded with your Lord on my behalf. So remember me on these three occasions and I shall not destroy you: (1) Remember me when you are angry, for then my spirit is in your heart and my eye in yours, and I am coursing through you, even the circulation of your blood. Remember me when you are angry, for when a man is angry I breathe into his nose and he does not know what he is doing. (2) Remember me when you encounter the army of the enemy, for I come to a man who meets the army of the enemy and remind him of his wife, his children, and his people, so that he will turn back. (3) See to it that you do not sit by a woman who is unrelated to you,[4] for I am her messenger to you and yours to her, I keep on until I cause you to be enamored of her and her of you."

By this he referred to appetence and anger and greed. Fleeing from the army is greed for this present world. His refusal to prostrate himself to Adam after he was dead was envy, which is the greatest of his entrances.

It is related that one of the saints said to Iblīs, "Show me how you overcome a son of Adam."

---

2 Mūsā, the Biblical Moses; see *EI*, 3:738ff. *EI*², 7:638. Editor's note: also see al-Kisāʾī, *Tales of the Prophets,* trans. Thackston, pp. 226–59.

3 Cf. Qurʾān 2:32.

4 I.e., one who is not *dhāt maḥram*, or a woman so closely related that a man could not marry her. Lane, *Lexicon*, p. 556.

He replied, "I take him while in anger or desire."

The story is told that Iblīs appeared to an ascetic who asked him, "What characteristics of the sons of Adam are most helpful to you?"

He answered, "Hastiness of temper; for if a man is sharp-tempered we can turn him upside down even as youths toss a ball."

There is a reputed saying of Satan like this, "How can the son of Adam overcome me, for if he is content, I come so that I may be in his heart, and if he gets angry, I fly so that I may be in his head?"

Among the great doors for his entrance is that of envy (*ḥasad*) and greed (*ḥirṣ*). For whenever a man is greedy for anything, his greed makes him blind and deaf, as [the Prophet] ﷺ said, "Your love for the thing blinds and deafens."[5] The light of insight is that which makes known the entrances of Satan, but if envy and greed cover it up man cannot see and then Satan finds his opportunity. He makes everything that will help the attainment of his desire appear good to the greedy one, even though it be disapproved and immoral.

It is related that Nūḥ,[6] ﷺ when he entered the ark, took into it a pair of every sort as God, the Exalted, commanded him. He saw in the ark an old man whom he did not recognize.

So Nūḥ said to him, "What brought you here?"

He said, "I came to seize the hearts of your friends, so that their hearts would be with me and their bodies with you."

So Nūḥ said to him, "Go out from here, O enemy of God, for you are accursed."

Iblīs said to him, "By means of five things I destroy mankind, and I shall tell you about three of them, but I shall not tell you about the other two."

God, the Exalted, then revealed to Nūḥ, "You have no need of the three; let him tell you of the two."

Nūḥ said [to Iblīs], "What are the two?"

He replied, "They are the two that never deceive me nor disobey me, and by them I destroy man: they are greed and envy. Through envy I was cursed and became an accursed Satan; and as for greed, the whole garden was permitted to Adam, save only the tree, but I obtained my desire over him through greed."

---

5 A *ḥadīth*, the authenticity of which is discussed by Zabīdī at length. Wensinck, *Concordance*, 1:409a.

6 Nūḥ, the Biblical Noah; see *EI*, 3:948ff. *EI*², 8:108. Editor's note: also see al-Kisāʾī, *Tales of the Prophets*, trans. Thackston, pp. 91–105.

One of his great doors is a satiety (*shabaʿ*) of food, even though it be lawful and pure. Satiety strengthens the lusts, and lusts are weapons of Satan. It is related that Iblīs appeared to Yaḥyā b. Zakarīyā[7] عليه السلام who saw on him [i.e., Iblīs] hooks of every sort.

So he said to him, "O Iblīs, what are these hooks?"

He replied, these are the lusts by which I overcome the son of Adam."

He [Yaḥyā] عليه السلام asked, "Do I have any of these?"

[Iblīs] answered, "Perhaps you became surfeited with food and thus we made ritual prayer (*ṣalāh*)[8] and devotional exercises (*dhikr*) a burden to you."

He [Yaḥyā] asked, "Is there anything else?"

He answered, "No."

So he said, "By God I shall never fill my stomach with food again."

Iblīs replied, "And, by God, I shall never give advice to a Muslim again."

It is said that in eating abundantly there are six blameworthy qualities: First, it drives the fear of God from one's heart. Second, it drives from one's heart compassion toward mankind, for he supposes that they are all satiated. Third, it makes obedience a burden. Fourth, if one hears wise speech he finds nothing elegant in it. Fifth, if one speaks in admonition and wisdom it makes no impression on the hearts of men. Sixth, it stirs up disease within one.

Another of his great doors is the love of adornment in furnishings, apparel, and [one's] house. When Satan sees this quality dominant in the heart of man he lays eggs in that heart and hatches them,[9] and keeps on bidding him to make the house habitable, to adorn its ceiling and walls, and to enlarge its buildings. He invites him also to adorn his apparel and his riding animals, and seeks to enslave him therein his whole life long. If he overcomes him in this he has no need to return to him again. For one phase of this leads to another and continues to take him from one thing to another until his fixed term is brought to him, and he dies while he is in the way of Satan and of the followers of desire. Evil consequences are to be feared therefrom in unbelief; we take refuge with God from it.

---

7 Yaḥyā b. Zakarīyā, the Biblical John the Baptist; see *EI*, 4:1148ff. *EI*^{2}, 11:248. Editor's note: see Qurʾān, 3:39, 6:85, 19:12–5, 21:90.

8 "Ṣalāh," also "ṣalāt," see *EI*, 4:96ff.; *EI*^{2}, 8:925. Ghazālī, trans. Calverley, *Worship in Islam*, Introduction.

9 I.e., he stays there a long time, says Zabīdī.

Another of his great doors is covetous desire (*ṭamaʿ*) toward men. For if such desire predominates in the heart of a man, Satan constantly makes it seem good to him to use craftiness and flattery toward him on whom he has fixed his desire, using all sorts of hypocrisy and deception so that he who is the object of his desire becomes, as it were, the object of his worship. So [the man] keeps on thinking of a scheme to attract his love and affection, and tries every means possible to attain this end. The very least he does is to praise him for something he does not possess, and to treat him with flattery by not commanding him to do good (*al-amr bi-l-maʿrūf*) nor forbidding evil (*al-nahy ʿan al-munkar*).[10]

Ṣafwān b. Salīm[11] told how Satan appeared to ʿAbdallāh b. Ḥanẓala[12] and said to him, "O Ibn Ḥanẓala, learn from me a thing that I shall teach you." He answered, "I have no need of it." He said, "Look, and if it is good, take it, if bad, give it back. O Ibn Ḥanẓala, do not ask for anything you desire of any save God; and look how you will be if you become angry, for I take possession of you if you become angry."

Another of his great doors is haste, and giving up steadfastness in affairs. [The Prophet] ﷺ said, "Haste is from Satan and deliberate action from God, the Exalted."[13] [God] ﷻ said, *Man was created of haste* (21:37), and He, the Exalted, said, *And man is ever hasty* (17:11). He said to His Prophet ﷺ, *Do not hasten with [the recitation of] the Qurʾān before its revelation is completed to you* (20:114). This is because actions should follow clear understanding (*tabṣira*) and experiential knowledge. Clear understanding requires reflection (*taʾammul*) and measured action (*tamahhul*), but haste prevents this. For when a man seeks to make haste, Satan readily dispenses to him his own evil from whence the man knows not.

It is related that when ʿĪsā b. Maryam ﷺ was born the demons came to Iblīs and said, "All of the idols have bowed their heads this morning."

He answered, "This is some new event that has taken place; keep your places." So he [Iblīs] flew over the earth until he came from East to West, but he found nothing. Then he found that ʿĪsā ﷺ had been born, and

---

10 These are two oft-repeated phrases. Cf. Qurʾān 22:42; *Iḥyāʾ*, vol. 4, bk. 9.

11 Ṣafwān b. Salīm, Abū ʿAbdallāh al-Madanī (d. 132 or 133/749 or 750), a Follower, narrator of *ḥadīth*, and ascetic. Dhahabī, *Kitāb ṭabaqāt*, ed. Wüstenfeld, 1:24ff.; Shaʿrānī, *al-Ṭabaqāt*, p. 30.

12 ʿAbdallāh b. Ḥanẓala b. Abū ʿĀmir al-Rāhib al-Anṣārī (d. 173/789), a narrator of *ḥadīth*; see Ibn Ḥajar, *Biographical Dictionary*, 2:731.

13 A sound *ḥadīth* given by Tirmidhī. Wensinck, *Concordance*, 1:129a.

behold the angels were surrounding him. So Satan returned to them and said, "A prophet was born last night. No female ever conceived or brought forth [a child] except that I was present, save this one. So despair of idols being worshipped after this night, but approach the sons of Adam through haste and agility."[14]

Another of his great doors lies in dirhams and dinars, and other types of possessions, such as goods and beasts and estates; for whatsoever exceeds the bounds of daily sustenance and need is the abode of Satan. For he who has his daily provision supplied has an empty heart;[15] but if he found a hundred dinars, for example, on the road, ten desires would be stirred up in his heart, each one of which would require another hundred dinars. So what he found would not satisfy him, but he would need nine hundred more. Before he found the hundred he had been self-sufficient, and now, when he has found the hundred he thinks that through them he has become rich. But he has come to be in need of nine hundred in order to buy a house in which to dwell, to buy a servant girl, household effects, and fine clothing. Each one of these things calls for something else to go with it, and that for something else ad infinitum, until he falls into a pit the bottom of which is Jahannam,[16] for it has no other end.

Thābit al-Banānī[17] said that when the Messenger of God ﷺ was sent forth on his mission, Iblīs said to his demons,

"Something has happened, so go and see what it is."

They dispersed in their search until they were weary, and then they came back and said, "We do not know."

[Iblīs] said, "I shall bring you the news." So he went, and returned saying, "God has sent forth Muḥammad ﷺ"

---

14 Zabīdī says that parts of this *ḥadīth* are from Abū Hurayra and given in most of the large collections. Asín Palacios, in *Algazel*, p. 460n., says that this *ḥadīth* seems to have arisen from the following sources: (1) The story of the Apocryphal Gospels of the idols in Egypt falling down when Jesus went there. (2) Luke 2:13. (3) A very curious idea of St. Ignatius, quoted by St. Jerome (*In Evangelium secundum Mattheum*, Liber i, cap. 1).

15 I.e., a care-free heart, with no worries about a means of gaining a livelihood.

16 "Jahannam," or Hell; see *EI*, 1:908ff. *EI*², 2:381. Editor's note: see also Ghazālī, *Kitāb Dhikr al-mawt*, trans. Winter, pp. 219–31.

17 Thābit al-Banānī, Abū Muḥammad al-Baṣrī (d. between 21 and 29/642 and 650), a Qurayshī narrator of *ḥadīth*; Ibn Qutayba, *Mukhtalaf al-ḥadīth*, p. 241.

He [Thābit] went on to say, "So Iblīs began sending his demons to the Companions of the Prophet ﷺ, but they returned frustrated, saying. "We never associated with such folk as these. We no sooner smite some of them then they rise up for their prayers and it is all canceled."

Iblīs said to them, "Take your time with them; perhaps God will give them some of this present world's goods, and then we shall seize those of whom we have need."[18]

It is related that ʿĪsā ﷺ one day took a stone for a pillow and Iblīs passed by him and said, "O ʿĪsā, you have desired something in this present world." So ʿĪsā ﷺ took it and threw it away from beneath his head and said, "You may have this along with this present world." And in reality he who owns a stone to use as a pillow for sleeping possesses something of this world that Satan could possibly use as a tool against him. Take, for example, a man who rises by night for prayer. Whenever there is near him a stone that he can use for a pillow it keeps calling him to sleep, and to use it as a pillow. Were it not for this he would not think of doing such, nor would his desire for sleep be aroused. This being true for a stone, what is the state of one who possesses downy pillows and a soft bed and goodly recreation places? When will such a man rouse himself to the worship of God, the Exalted?

Another of his great entrances is stinginess and the fear of poverty. This is what prevents him from spending and giving alms, and [instead] summons [him] to store up goods, to lay up treasures, and to that painful punishment that is promised to those who vie with one another in possessions, even as the noble Qurʾān says.[19] Khaythama b. ʿAbd al-Raḥmān[20] quotes Satan as saying, "No son of Adam has overcome me, nor will any overcome me in three things when I command him: taking money wrongfully, spending it wrongfully, and withholding it from its proper use." Sufyān[21] said, "Satan has no weapon like the fear of poverty, and if man accepts this from him he undertakes vain deeds, withholding the right, talking passionately, and supposing evil of his Lord."

---

18 A fairly reliable *ḥadīth*. Zabīdī gives various readings and their authorities.

19 Cf. Qurʾān 9:34.

20 Khaythama b. ʿAbd al-Raḥmān (d. 86/705), a narrator of *ḥadīth*, the son and grandson of Companions; Dhahabī, *Kitāb ṭabaqāt*, ed. Wüstenfeld, 1:8.

21 Sufyān, Abū ʿAbdallāh Sufyān b. Saʿīd b. Masrūq al-Thawrī al-Kūfī (97–161), a celebrated theologian, ascetic, and reliable *ḥadīth* scholar; see *EI*, 4:500ff. *EI*², 9:770.

One of the evils of stinginess is a greedy frequenting of markets to gather money, for marketplaces are the nesting-places of demons. Abū Umāma[22] quoted the Messenger of God ﷺ as saying,

"When Iblīs descended to the earth he said, 'O Lord, You have cast me down to the earth and caused me to become accursed, so appoint for me a house.'

The Lord answered, 'The bath.'

Then he said, 'Appoint for me a place to sit.'

[God] answered, 'The marketplaces and the intersections of the streets.'

He said, 'Appoint food for me.'

He answered, 'That over which the name of God has not been mentioned.'

He said, 'Appoint drink for me.'

[God] answered, 'Everything intoxicating.'

He said, 'Appoint for me an announcer.'

[God] answered, 'Musical instruments.'

He said, 'Appoint a Qurʾān for me.'

[God] answered, 'Poetry.'

He said, 'Appoint for me a kind of writing.'

[God] answered, 'Tattooing.'

He said, 'Appoint speech for me.'

[God] answered, 'Falsehood.'

He said, 'Appoint snares for me.'

[God] answered, 'Women.'"[23]

Another of his great doors is sectarian and partisan prejudices (*al-taʿaṣṣub li-l-madhāhib wa-l-ahwāʾ*),[24] secret hatred of opponents, and looking upon them contemptuously and disdainfully. This is one of the things that destroy both pious and profligate together. For one of the savage characteristics in nature is an inborn disposition to calumniate, and to busy one's self with men's shortcomings. So when Satan makes this appear to a man as the truth and it is agreeable to his nature, its sweetness overcomes his heart, and he goes to work at it with all enthusiasm. He is glad and happy in it, and thinks that he is striving in the field of religion when he is really endeavoring to follow Satan. Thus you will see one who is a devoted partisan of Abū Bakr al-Ṣiddīq ﷺ, and at the same

22 Abū Umāma (Imāma) al-Bāhilī (d. 61 or 86/681 or 705), Companion. Ibn Qutayba, *Mukhtalaf al-ḥadīth*, p. 157ff.; Massignon, *Essai*, p. 127.

23 ʿIrāqī says this is a weak *ḥadīth*. See Madanī, *Aḥādīth qudsiyya*, pp. 636–7. *EI*, 4:266.

24 Cf. "ahl al-ahwāʾ," see *EI*, 1:183. *EI*², 1:257.

time a partaker of that which is unlawful, giving free rein to his tongue as a busybody and in falsehood, being addicted to all manner of corruption. Were it possible for Abū Bakr to see him, he would be his foremost enemy; for the follower of Abū Bakr is he who chooses his way and walks in his mode of life, and guards his mouth. It was a habit of [Abū Bakr] ﵁ to put pebbles in his mouth so that his tongue might be silent about what did not concern him. So how can such a busybody pretend loyalty to him and love for him while he does not follow his way of life?

Then you will see another individual who goes beyond all bounds in his partiality for ʿAlī ﵁. Now ʿAlī was such an ascetic in his manner of life that he wore, while he was caliph, a garment that he bought for three dirhams, and he cut off the end of the sleeve up to the back of the hand. But you see the profligate wearing silk garments and adorned with wealth gained unlawfully, while he quarrels over love of ʿAlī ﵁ and pretends such love, when in fact [ʿAlī] will be his foremost opponent on the day of resurrection. What would you say of a person who took a man's son, dear to him, his consolation and his heart's life, and began to beat him and tear him, to pluck out his hair and cut it off with shears, and at the same time pretend to love the boy's father and be loyal to him? What would the father think of such a man?

Now it is a known fact that religion and religious law were more loved by Abū Bakr, ʿUmar, ʿUthmān, and ʿAlī and the rest of the Companions ﵃ than family or son, nay rather, more than their own selves. Those who rush blindly into disobedience to the law are they who rend the law and cut it off with the shears of lusts, and thereby show their love for Iblīs, the enemy of God and of His saints. What then do you suppose will be their condition on the day of resurrection in the presence of the Companions [of the Prophet] and the saints of God? Nay rather, if the lid were removed so that these might know what the Companions desire in the people of God's Messenger ﷺ, they would be ashamed to mention them with their tongues because of the turpitude of their acts.

Satan also makes them imagine that if anyone dies devoted to Abū Bakr and ʿUmar the Fire will not come near him. He makes another imagine that if he dies devoted to ʿAlī there is no fear for him. This is what the

Messenger of God ﷺ also said to Fāṭima,[25] who was a part of himself,[26] "Do righteously, for I cannot take your place in anything God requires."[27]

We have cited this one as an example of all the partisan loyalties. Such also is the predicament of the partisans of Shāfiʿī[28] Abū Ḥanīfa,[29] Mālik,[30] and Aḥmad,[31] and other imams. For if anyone pretends to belong to the school of an imam and does not walk according to his manner of life, that imam will be his opponent on the day of resurrection, when he will say to him, "My belief is to do, and not merely to talk with the tongue; and talking with the tongue is to the end of doing, not raving. So why have you disobeyed me in the practice and manner of life which are my belief (*madhhab*), and my way, by which I advanced, and in which I departed to God, the Exalted, and then afterward pretended falsely to belong to my school?"

This is one of the great entrances of Satan and by it he has destroyed most of the world. The colleges[32] (*madāris*) have been given over to a group in which there is but little of the fear of God, whose insight into religion has grown weak, whose desire for this present world has become intense, and whose greed to gain followers has grown strong. They have not been able to gain a following and attain influence, save through their partisanship. So they have veiled this fact within their own breasts, and have not reminded their followers of the wiles of Satan therein, but indeed they have acted as the agents of Satan in carrying out his wiles against them. So men have continued in partisanship and have forgotten the principles

---

25 Fāṭima (d. 11/632), the daughter of Muḥammad and wife of ʿAlī; see *EI*, 2:85ff. *EI*², 2:841.

26 An agreed upon *ḥadīth*. Wensinck, *Concordance*, 1:187h.

27 An agreed upon *ḥadīth* from Abū Hurayra.

28 Al-Shāfiʿī, Abū ʿAbdallāh Muḥammad b. Idrīs (150–204/767–819), the founder of the school of law which bears his name; see *EI*, 4:252ff. *EI*², 9:181.

29 Abū Ḥanīfa (c. 80–150/699–767), Muslim jurist and founder of the Ḥanafī school; see *EI*, 1:90ff. and *Supp*. p. 6. *EI*², 1:123.

30 Abū ʿAbdallāh Mālik b. Anas (c. 94–179/713–795), jurist and founder of the Mālikī school; see *EI*, 3:205ff. *EI*², 6:262.

31 Aḥmad b. Muḥammad b. Ḥanbal (d. 241/855), a celebrated scholar for whom one of the four Sunnī schools of law is named; see *EI*, 1:188; *EI*², 1:272. Zabīdī, *Itḥāf*, 1:214ff.

32 MSS read, 'pulpits' (*manābir*).

(*ummahāt*)[33] of their religion. Thus they have perished and caused others to perish. May God, the Exalted, forgive us and them.

Ḥasan relates that Iblīs said, "I enticed the people of Muḥammad ﷺ to disobedience, but they overcame me by seeking forgiveness. Then I enticed them to sins for which they would not seek forgiveness from God, the Exalted: these are partisan prejudices." In this the accursed one told the truth, for they do not know that these are the causes that lead to acts of disobedience, so how should they seek forgiveness for them?

One of the great devices of Satan is to turn men's attention away from himself by causing them to become busied with the disputes and contentions that arise between people in the matter of sects. ʿAbdallāh b. Masʿūd said,

> A group of people were seated at a *dhikr* of God, the Exalted, and Satan came to cause them to abandon their assembly and to cause divisions among them, but he could not. So he came to another company who were conversing on worldly affairs, and stirred up strife among them so that they began to fight with one another. But it was not they on whom he had set his purpose. Then they who were engaged in the *dhikr* of God, the Exalted, rose up and busied themselves in deciding between those who were fighting, and so were scattered from their assembly, and this was the thing that Satan was aiming to accomplish with them.

Another of his great doors is to induce the common people,[34] who are not experienced in the science of theology and have not gone deeply into

33 Cf. Qurʾān 3:5 *umm al-kitāb*, with Bayḍāwī's comment.

34 Cf. Ghazālī's book, *Iljām al ʿawāmm*, of which a brief abstract is here given. This tract was written to show that the common people should not study theology because of the danger of a wrong idea of God and His attributes through literal interpretation of terms applied to Him, such as: form, hand, foot, descent, movement, sitting on the throne, etc. Those who hold these literal interpretations think that they are following the belief of the Predecessors (*salaf*). So Ghazālī writes first to explain the true doctrines of the Predecessors, i.e., the Companions and the Followers. Whenever one of the common people hears any such statements he is obligated to do seven things: (1) To believe that God is far above a corporeal nature or any of its concomitants. (2) To believe that what the Prophet taught was true in the way he said it and intended it. (3) To confess his inability to grasp the subject and that it is not his province. (4) Not to seek its meaning, which would be innovation, nor to delve into that which would be dangerous for his faith and likely to lead to unbelief. (5) To quote such language only as it is revealed without grammatical variation or change. (6) To honestly cease investigating

it, to set themselves to thinking about the essential nature and attributes of God, the Exalted, and about subjects to which their limited intelligence cannot attain, until he causes them to doubt the principles of their religion or to indulge in vain imaginings unworthy of God, the Exalted. By this, a man becomes an unbeliever (*kāfir*)[35] or an innovator (*mubtadiʿ*),[36] while at the same time he is happy, joyful, and rejoicing at that which has come into his heart. He supposes it to be gnosis and insight, and that this has been revealed to him because of his own perspicacity and greater intelligence. The most foolish of men are those who believe most strongly in their own intelligence; and the men of the most stable intelligence are those most suspicious of themselves and most ready to ask of the scholars.

ʿĀʾisha ﵂ quoted the Messenger of God ﷺ as having said,

"Verily Satan will come to one of you and say, 'Who created you?'

He will reply, 'God, who is blessed and exalted.'

Then Satan will say, 'But who created God?'

Therefore if one of you has this experience, let him say, 'I believe in God and His Messenger,' and Satan will go away from him."[37]

The Prophet ﷺ did not order any investigation of a way of treating this evil prompting because it affects the common people rather than the scholars. The common people should content themselves with believing, submission, and occupying themselves with their worship and their means of gaining a living, and leave learning to the scholars. Were the common man to commit adultery and steal, it would be better for him than to talk about the science of theology. For he who speaks about God and His religion without the mastery of knowledge falls into unbelief in

---

it and pondering over it. (7) Not to think that because it is hidden from him that it is hidden from the Messenger of God, or the prophets, the trustworthy (*al-ṣiddiqūn*), and the saints. Ghazālī then goes on, in the second part, to prove that this doctrine of the Predecessors is the only true teaching, and that whoever diverges from it is an innovator. In the third part of the book he answers objections raised against his position and questions regarding it. He concludes that the happiness of mankind lies in a fixed belief in things as they are: in God, His attributes, His books, His messengers, and the last day, even though this belief is not by means of a formulated proof. God does not require more than this of them. Editor's note: for a detailed exposition of Muslim creed, see Imam al-Ṭaḥāwī, *Creed of Imam al-Ṭaḥāwī*, trans. H. Yusuf.

35 "Kāfir," *EI*, 2:618ff. *EI*², 4:407.

36 "Mubtadiʿ," see "bidʿa," *EI*, 1:712ff. *EI*², 1:1199.

37 An agreed upon *ḥadīth*. Zabīdī mentions some slight variations.

a way which he knows not, and is like one who embarks on the fathomless sea without knowing how to swim. The devices of Satan that relate to creeds and sects are countless, and we have only mentioned these by way of example.

Another of the doors by which Satan enters the heart is thinking evil of Muslims (*sūʾ al-ẓann bi-l-muslimīn*). God, the Exalted, has said, *O you who believe, avoid suspicion as much [as possible], for suspicion in some cases is a sin* (49:12). For if anyone passes an evil judgment on another through conjecture, he is sent by Satan to slander him by means of backbiting, and he shall perish. Satan may induce him to give the other less than his just rights, or to be remiss in honoring him, or to look at him with the eye of disdain, considering himself much better than the other. These are all among the things that destroy.[38] Divine law has therefore forbidden man to indulge in accusations.

[The Prophet] ﷺ said, "Beware of places of accusations."[39] He himself ﷺ guarded against exposure to accusation. It is related in a narration from ʿAlī b. Ḥusayn[40] that Ṣafiyya bint Ḥuyayy[41] told him,

"The Prophet ﷺ was spending a time of retreat in the mosque, and I came to him and began to converse with him. When I bade him good evening and was leaving, he arose and walked with me. There passed by him two of the Helpers (Anṣār)[42] who greeted him and withdrew. But he called to them and said, 'She is Ṣafiyya bint Ḥayy.'

They replied, 'O Messenger of God, we suppose naught but good concerning you.'

He said, 'Satan flows through the son of Adam even as the circulation of the blood in his body, and I feared lest he might enter into you.'"[43]

Observe how [the Prophet] ﷺ was concerned about their religion and guarded them, and how he felt concern for his nation and taught them how to guard themselves against accusation. Thus the scrupulously pious

---

38 Editor's note: lit., *muhlikāt*, mortal vices or acts that lead to perdition.

39 ʿIrāqī says that he did not find a source for this *ḥadīth*. Zabīdī gives two variations of it with sources. Editor's note: things that lead one to accusations.

40 ʿAlī b. Ḥusayn b. ʿAlī b. Abū Ṭalib al-Ḥashimī, Zayn al-ʿĀbidīn (d. 93 or 94/712 or 713), one of the twelve Shīʿī imams; see *EI*, 1:288. *EI*², 11:481.

41 Ṣafiyya bint Ḥuyayy b. Akhṭab (d. 50 or 52/670 or 672), a Jewish woman who became the eleventh wife of Muḥammad after Khaybar; see *EI*, 4:57. *EI*², 8:817.

42 "Anṣār," *EI*, 1:357ff. *EI*², 1:514.

43 An agreed upon *ḥadīth*. Wensinck, *Handbook*, p. 211a.

scholar, who is known for his religion, should not think lightly about his affairs and say in self-admiration, "No one would suppose aught but good of a man like me." For all men do not look at even the most godly and pious and benevolent people in the same way. Some look upon them with the eye of approval, but others with the eye of displeasure. "The eye of approbation is dulled to every fault, but the eye of disapproval reveals the defects."[44]

So one must guard against supposing evil of another, and against accusing evil men. Wicked men think naught but evil of all men; so whenever you see a person thinking evil of men and looking for faults, know that he is a corrupt person in his own heart. His wickedness is his thinking evil of others, and this fairly oozes out of him. He thinks of others only from his own standpoint. The believer looks for excuses; the hypocrite for faults. The believer is sound-hearted in his attitude toward all creatures.

These are some of the entrances of Satan into the heart. If I desired to encompass all of them I should be unable to do so. But this number will point to others. There is no blameworthy characteristic in man that is not an instrument of Satan, and one of his entrances into the heart.

Now you may ask, "What then is the remedy and the way to ward off Satan?" And, "Is it not enough to remember God, the Exalted, and for a man to say, 'There is no might nor power save with God'?" Know that the remedy for the heart in this matter is to close these entrances by purifying the heart of these blameworthy characteristics. This is something that would take a long time to mention. Our aim in this quarter of the book is to set forth the remedy for the characteristics that destroy, and every characteristic needs a separate book, as will be explained later.

It is true that if you were to cut out of the heart the roots of these characteristics, Satan would still be able to pass through it and make suggestions to it, but it would not be an abode for him. Remembrance of God, the Exalted, prevents him from passing through it. The true nature of remembrance does not dominate the heart until after it has been built up in piety and cleansed of all blameworthy qualities. Otherwise remembrance is merely a suggestion of the self that has no power over the heart and does not ward off the power of Satan. Therefore God, the Exalted, said, *Indeed, those who fear God, when a thought touches them from Satan, they*

---

44 A quotation from a poem which might be rendered: "Favor's eye to every fault is dull / But anger's eye is quick to set forth ill."

remember [God] and at once they have insight (7:201). He thereby made this a special characteristic of the godfearing person.

Satan is like a hungry dog that comes to you. If you have neither bread nor meat in your hands, it is driven back by your saying 'go away,' the voice alone sufficing to ward it off. But if you have some meat in your hands and the dog is hungry, it will rush at the meat and will not be driven away by mere talk. Thus Satan can be driven away from the heart that is devoid of his food by merely remembering [God]. But if appetence overcomes the heart it drives the true nature of remembrance [of God] to the marginal regions of the heart so that it does not gain the mastery over its core. This core is thus the abode of Satan.

But Satan tempts the hearts of those who fear God (*muttaqīn*), which are devoid of passion and blameworthy characteristics, not to lusts, but to emptiness through neglect of remembrance; when one begins the exercise of remembrance, again Satan draws back. The proof of this is the statement of the Exalted, *Seek refuge in God from Satan the accursed one* (16:98), and also the other narrations (*akhbār*) and verses on the subject of remembrance.

Abū Hurayra[45] related that the demon of the believer met the demon of the unbeliever. The demon of the unbeliever was sleek, fat, and well clothed, while the demon of the believer was emaciated, dishevelled, dust-colored, and naked.

The unbeliever's demon asked that of the believer, "What is the matter with you that you are so emaciated?"

He replied, "I am with a man who names the name of God when he eats, and so I remain hungry. He repeats the name of God when he drinks, so I stay thirsty. He says the name of God when he dresses, and I continue naked; and when he perfumes himself he repeats the name of God and I remain dishevelled.'

The other said, 'I dwell with a man who does nothing of all this, so I share with him in his food, his drink, and his clothing."[46]

Muḥammad b. Wāsiʿ[47] used to say every day after the morning prayer,

45 Abū Hurayra (d. 57 or 58/677 or 678), a Companion and the most prolific narrator of *ḥadīth*; see *EI*, 1:93ff. *EI*², 1:129.

46 Zabīdī quotes a number of *ḥadīth*s that parallel this story at certain points.

47 Muḥammad b. Wāsiʿ b. Jābir al-Baṣrī (d. 120/738), a pious ascetic; see Ibn al-Nadīm, *Kitāb al-fihrist*, p. 183; Ṭabarī, ed. De Goeje, *Annales at-Tabari*, 2:1326.

"O God, you have given power over us to an enemy who has insight into our faults, and who with his cohorts sees us from where we cannot see them. O God, cause him to despair of us even as you have caused him to despair of Your mercy. Make him abandon hope of us as you have made him abandon hope of Your pardon. Remove him far from us as you have removed him far from Your mercy, for You are able to do all things."

One day as he was on his way to the mosque, Iblīs appeared to him and said, "O Ibn Wāsiʿ, do you recognize me?"

He replied, "Who are you?"

He said, "I am Iblīs."

He asked, "What do you want?"

He said, "I desire that you will not teach anyone this formula for seeking protection and I shall never oppose you."

He answered, "By God, I shall not keep it from anyone who desires it, and you may do what you will."

ʿAbd al-Raḥman b. Abī Laylā[48] said, "There was a demon who used to come to the Prophet ﷺ with a firebrand in his hand and stand before him as he prayed. [The Prophet] would recite and take refuge [in God], but the demon would not go away. Then Jibrīl,[49] عليه السلام, came and said to the Prophet, "Say, 'I take refuge in the complete words of God, which neither pious nor impious creature may cross, from the evil which persists in the earth and from what goes forth from it; from what comes down from heaven and what ascends up into it; from the temptations of the night and the misfortunes of the day, except that which brings good, O Merciful One.'" So he said this and the demon's firebrand was extinguished and he fell on his face.[50]

Ḥasan said, "I was informed that Jibrīl عليه السلام came to the Prophet ﷺ and said, 'Verily an *ʿifrīt*[51] of the *jinn*[52] is plotting against you, so when you retire to your bed recite the Throne Verse.'"[53]

---

48 ʿAbd al-Raḥmān b. Abū Laylā al-Anṣārī (d. 81 or 83/700 or 702), a Follower; see Ibn Khallikān, *Wafayāt al-ʿayān*, trans. De Slane, 2:84; Ibn Ḥajar, *Biographical Dictionary,* 2:1008.

49 "Jibrīl," see *EI*, 1:990ff. *EI*[2], 2:362.

50 ʿIrāqī says that this *ḥadīth* was given by Ibn Abī al-Dunyā.

51 "ʿIfrīt," *EI*, 2:455a. *EI*[2], 3:1050.

52 "Jinn," *EI*, 1:1045ff. *EI*[2], 2:546.

53 ʿIrāqī says that this *ḥadīth* was given by Ibn Abī al-Dunyā. Editor's note: the verse of the throne (*ayāt al-kursī*) is in the Qurʾān, 2:255.

[The Prophet] ﷺ said, "A demon came to me and contended with me and contended with me again, so I seized him by the throat. By Him who sent me forth as a messenger of truth, I did not release the demon until I found the cold saliva from his tongue on my hand, and had it not been for the supplication of my brother Sulaymān,[54] عليه السلام he [i.e., the demon] would have been left prostrate in the mosque."[55] [The Prophet] ﷺ also said, "ʿUmar never traveled a path but that Satan took a different course from his."[56]

This is because the hearts of these [prophets and saints] had been cleansed of that on which Satan pastures and feeds, namely the appetites. So however much you desire that Satan be warded off from you by mere remembrance of God, as he was warded off from ʿUmar رضي الله عنه, you will find it is impossible. You will be like a man who takes medicine before he abstains from food, whose stomach is burdened with heavy foods, and yet he hopes that the medicine will benefit him, even as it benefits one who has taken it after abstinence and emptying his stomach.[57] Remembrance [of God] is the medicine, and piety is abstinence that frees the heart from the appetites. So when remembrance comes into a heart empty of all else save the thought of God, Satan is warded off, even as illness is repelled when the medicine enters a stomach empty of all foods.

God, the Exalted, said, *Indeed this is a Message for any that has a heart* (50:37). He, the Exalted, also said, *it is decreed that whosoever takes him for a friend, indeed, he will lead him astray, and will guide him to the punishment of the blaze* (22:4).

Whoever helps Satan by his work is his follower, even though he makes mention of God with his tongue. If you say that the *ḥadīth* is absolute, that remembrance [of God] drives out Satan, and [you] do not understand that most general statements of the divine law are limited in their particular application by conditions laid down by those learned in religion, then

---

54 Sulaymān, the Biblical Solomon; see *EI*, 4:519ff. *EI*², 9:822. Editor's note: also see al-Kisāʾī, *Tales of the Prophets*, trans. Thackston, pp. 300–21, and Qurʾān, 27:15–44, 34:12–4, 38:30–40.

55 ʿIrāqī says that there is a weakness (*ḍaʿf*) in the chain of narrators of this *ḥadīth*. It is quoted with variations by various authorities. Wensinck, *Concordance*, 2:87a, gives it from Aḥmad.

56 One form of this *ḥadīth* that shows how Satan avoided ʿUmar is noted in Wensinck, *Handbook*, p. 234b. ʿIrāqī says that it is agreed upon.

57 Editor's note: at the time of Imam al-Ghazālī, it was thought that medicinal remedies should be taken on an empty stomach, in order to be effective.

look to your own self, for hearing a statement is not like seeing with the eye. Consider that the highest point of your remembrance [of God] and of your worship is the ritual prayer. So watch your heart when you are at prayer and see how Satan attracts it to the markets, to the reckoning of dealers, and to answering those [with whom you] contend. Observe how he causes you to pass through the valleys of this present world and its places of destruction, so that you do not recall the unnecessary things of this world that you had forgotten, except during your prayer. Satan does not press upon your heart save while you pray. Thus prayer is the touchstone of hearts, by which its good qualities and vile qualities both are made manifest. Ritual prayer that comes from hearts laden with lusts is not accepted. It is no wonder then that Satan is not driven away from you; nay rather, his evil promptings to you may increase, just as the medicine taken before abstaining from food may increase the harm to you. So, if you seek deliverance from demons, begin with abstinence through piety, and then follow it with the medicine of remembrance and Satan will flee from you as he fled from [the shadow of] ʿUmar ﷺ.

Regarding this Wahb b. Munabbih[58] said, "Fear God, and do not curse Satan openly while in secret you are his friend," that is, while you are obedient to him. Another said, "How strange it is that a man, knowing the Benefactor's goodness, will disobey him; and knowing likewise the Accursed One's rebellion, will yet obey him." As God, the Exalted, said, *Call on me, I will answer your [prayer]* (40:60), and you call and He does not answer; so also you practice remembrance of God, and Satan does not flee from you because of your failure to observe the conditions of remembrance and supplication (*duʿāʾ*).[59]

Ibrāhīm b. Adham[60] was asked, "Why is it that we supplicate and [our petitions] are not granted, although the Exalted has said, *Call upon me, I will answer you*"?

He answered, "Because your hearts are dead."

---

58 Wahb b. Munabbih (d. 110/728), a Follower and famous South Arabian narrator of *ḥadīth* and ascetic; see *EI*, 4:1084ff. *EI*², 11:34. See also article by J. Horovitz, "The Earliest Biographies of the Prophet and their Authors," *Islamic Culture* 1, no. 4 (Oct. 1927), pp. 553–9; and article by F. Krenkow, "The Two Oldest Books on Arabic Folklore," *Islamic Culture* 2, no. 1 (Jan. 1928), pp. 55ff.

59 "Duʿāʾ," *EI*, 1:1077b. *EI*², 2:617.

60 Ibrāhīm b. Adham b. Manṣūr b. Yazīd b. Jābir al-ʿIjlī (d. 161/778), a famous ascetic of Balkh; see *EI*, 2:432ff. *EI*², 3:985.

He was asked, "What killed them?"

He answered, "Eight bad habits:

[1] You have known God's right [over you] but have not done your duty toward Him.

[2] You have read the Qurʾān but have not acted according to the limitations it has imposed.

[3] You have said, 'We love the Messenger of God' ﷺ but you have not followed his law (Sunna).

[4] You have said, 'We fear death' but you have not prepared for it.

[5] The Exalted has said, *Indeed Satan is an enemy to you, so take him as an enemy* (35:6), but you have agreed with him upon acts of disobedience.

[6] You have said, 'We fear the Fire,' and constrained your bodies to enter it.

[7] You have said 'We love Paradise,' but have not labored to gain it.

[8] When you have risen from your beds you have cast your faults behind your backs and spread the faults of other men before your faces. You have angered your Lord, so how can He answer your prayers?"

If you ask whether he who invites to the different acts of disobedience is a single demon or different demons, know that in practice you have no need to know about this matter. Busy yourself in warding off the enemy, and do not ask about his characteristics. "Eat the vegetable wherever it comes from, and do not ask where the garden is."[61] However in the light of investigation and the testimony of narrations it appears evident that the demons are "troops set in array," and that every type of disobedient act has its own demon, appointed to it and inviting to it.[62] But the path of

---

61 Zabīdī says that this is a proverb. The MSS indicate that it is in poetic form.

62 For the names of these demons see Zabīdī, *Tāj al-ʿarūs*; Ibn Manẓūr, *Lisān al-ʿArab*; Bustānī, *Muḥīṭ*; Ibn al-Jawzī, *Talbīs Iblīs*, pp. 32ff.; Muḥammad b. Mūsā al-Damīrī, *Ḥayāt al-ḥayawān al-kubrā*, trans. A. S. G. Jayakar (Bombay, 1906), p. 465. The following information may be added to that given here by Ghazālī. Thabr is also written *thubar* (Princeton MS), *bathr* (Damīrī, *Ḥayāt al-ḥayawān*), and *al-abtar* (Zabīdī, *Tāj al-ʿarūs*, 3:24; Ibn Manẓūr, *Lisān al-ʿArab*, 5:99). This latter is described as a short-tailed snake called *al-shayṭān*. Whoever sees it flees from it, and if a pregnant woman sees it she miscarries. Miswaṭ, so named from the stick used to

investigation is a long one, and what we have mentioned will suffice you, namely, that different effects indicate different causes. This is what we have mentioned regarding the light of the fire and the blackness of smoke.

As for narrations, Mujāhid said,

> Iblīs has five sons and has appointed to each one of them the charge over a certain matter. They are Thabr, al-Aʿwar, Miswaṭ, Dāsim, and Zalanbūr. Thabr is the master of afflictions who commands destruction, rending of clothes, smiting of cheeks, and the claim of the days of ignorance (*al-jāhiliyya*).[63] Al-Aʿwar is the master of adultery who commands thereto and makes it appear beautiful. Miswaṭ is the master of lying. Dāsim enters into the relations between a man and his family, accusing them of faults, and making him angry at them. Zalanbūr is the master of the marketplace, and by reason of him those in the market continue to be unjust to one another.

The demon of the ritual prayer is called Khinzib, and the demon of ablution is al-Walhān. Many narrations have been handed down on this subject.

Even as the demons are a host so also there are a host of angels. In the *Book of Patience and Thankfulness*[64] we have mentioned the secret of the multitude of angels, and that each one of them is appointed for a special work uniquely his own.

Abū Umāma al-Bāhilī quoted the Messenger of God as saying,

> One hundred and sixty angels have been given charge over the believer to drive away from him that which he cannot ward off. Of these, seven are for sight and they drive away [evil] from it, even as flies are driven away from a plate of honey on a summer day. They also drive away those whom, were they to appear to you, you would see on every plain and mountain, each one with outstretched hand and open mouth; and that which, if the believer were given charge of himself therein for a single instant, the demons would snatch him away.[65]

---

stir up the contents of a cooking pot, and thus he stirs up trouble (Ibn Manẓūr, *Lisān al-ʿArab*, 9:198). Damīrī gives other names of sons of Satan: *lākīs*, *al-haffāf*, *muṭawwas*, *al-aḥnas*. Cf. also reference to Satan's progeny, Qurʾān 18:48.

63 The 'call' of the *jāhiliyya* was prohibited. See Bukhārī in Wensinck, *Handbook*, p. 41a.

64 See *Iḥyāʾ*, 4:104ff.

65 ʿIrāqī says that there is a weakness (*ḍaʿf*) in the chain of narrators of this *ḥadīth*.

Ayyūb b. Yazīd[66] said that the report had come to him that there are born children to the *jinn* along with the children of mankind, and these grow up together.

Jābir b. ʿAbdallāh[67] said that when Adam ﷺ was cast down to the earth, he said, "O Lord, You have placed enmity between this creature and myself, so will You not help me against him so that I shall be able to overcome him?"

God answered, "There shall not be a child born to you but he will be given into the charge of an angel."

He said, "O my Lord, give me more."

[God] answered, "I shall recompense an evil deed with an evil deed and a good deed with ten."[68]

He said, "O Lord, give me more,"

[God] answered, "The door of repentance is open as long as the spirit is in the body."

Then Iblīs said, "O Lord, will You not help me against this creature who You have honored above me, so that I may be able to overcome him?"

[God] answered, "No son shall be born to him but there shall be one born to you also."

He said "O Lord, give me more."

[God] answered "You shall flow through them as the circulation of their blood, and you shall take their breasts as dwelling-places."

He said, "O Lord, give me more."

[God] answered, *bear down upon them with your horse and with your foot, and share with them in their wealth and their children; and make them promises, but Satan promises them nothing but deceit.* (17:64).

A [*ḥadīth*] from Abū al-Dārdāʾ ﷺ relates that the Prophet ﷺ said,

> God has created the *jinn* of three sorts. One sort is snakes, scorpions, and creeping insects of the earth. Another is like the wind blowing through the sky. The third sort is subject to reward and punishment. God, the Exalted, has also created three kinds of

---

66 Ayyūb b. Yazīd, an unknown man who related *ḥadīth*s from the Followers, says Zabīdī.

67 Jābir b. ʿAbdallāh b. ʿAmr (d. 74 or 78/693 or 697), a Helper. Ibn Qutayba, *Mukhtalaf al-ḥadīth*, p. 156; Ḥājjī Khalīfa, *Kashf al-ẓunūn*, ed. and trans. Gustavus Flügel as *Lexicon Bibliographicum et Encyclopaedicum*, 7 vols (Leipzig and London, 1835–58), 2:332, 334.

68 Zabīdī has 'or as many more as I please' (7:289).

> humans. One kind is like the beasts, as the Exalted said, *They have hearts with which they do not understand, they have eyes with which they do not see, and they have ears with which they do not hear. Those are like livestock; rather, they are more astray* (7:179). Another kind has bodies that are those of human beings and spirits that are those of demons. A third sort are those who will be in the shade of God, the Exalted, on the day of resurrection, the day when there is no shade save His shade alone.[69]

Wahīb b. al-Ward[70] relates the following [narration]:

"Iblīs appeared to Yaḥyā b. Zakarīyā ﷺ, and said, 'I want to give you some advice.'

He answered, 'I do not need your advice, but tell me about the sons of Adam.'

He said, 'From our point of view they are of three sorts. The first sort, which is the strongest of them all against us, is such that, when we come to one of them to tempt him and gain control over him, in fear he hastens to seek forgiveness and repentance. Thus he destroys every advantage we may have gained over him. We return to him again and he repeats the same thing. Thus we neither despair of him, nor do we achieve our purpose in him, so we are in distress regarding him. Another kind consists of those who are in our hands just like a ball in the hands of your children, and we turn them as we will, for we can cope with their souls. The other kind are those who, like yourself, are preserved from sin (*maʿṣūmūn*),[71] and we can do nothing with them.'"

You may say, "But how can Satan appear to some men and not to others? If one sees his form, is it his real form, or is it an image in which [Satan] appears to him? If it is his real form, how is it that he is seen in different forms? How can he be seen in two places and in two forms at the same time in such a way that two people see him in two different forms?" Know that the angel and demon each have two forms which are their real forms. These are not perceived by natural sight, save only by the illumination of the prophetic office. The Prophet ﷺ only saw Jibrīl, may the best blessings and peace be upon him, in his true form on two

---

69 A weak *ḥadīth* quoted in varying forms by Tirmidhī and others.

70 Wahīb b. al-Ward al-Makkī (also Wuhayb; ʿAbd al-Wahhāb), (d. 53/763), a pious narrator of *ḥadīth*; Nawawī, *Tahdhib al-asmāʾ*, p. 620; Massignon, *Essai*, p. 146.

71 "Maʿṣūmūn," see "ʿiṣma," *EI*, 2:543. *EI*², 4:182.

occasions.[72] Once [the Prophet] asked him to show himself to him in his real form, and[73] [Jibrīl] appointed for him a place, Baqīʿ.[74] He appeared to him at Ḥirāʾ and filled the whole horizon from East to West. He saw him again in his true form the night of the Heavenly Journey (*al-miʿrāj*) at the lote tree of the boundary.[75] But for the most part he saw him in the form of a man. He used to see him in the form of Diḥya al-Kalbī[76] who was a man of a goodly countenance.[77]

For the most part he [the spiritual being: angel or demon] unveils an image of his form to the people of unveiling (*ahl al-mukāshafa*) and possessors of hearts (*arbāb al-qulūb*);[78] and thus he appears to one of them while he is awake, and this man will see him with his eye and hear his speech with his ear. This will take the place of his real form. In like manner he is revealed to a majority of good men during sleep. Revelation during waking hours is made only to one who has attained such a high rank that the occupation of his senses with the things of this world does not prevent the revelation which comes in sleep, so he sees while awake what another sees during sleep.

It is also related on the authority of ʿUmar b. ʿAbd al-ʿAzīz,[79] may God have mercy on him, that a man asked his Lord to show him the place Satan occupies in relation to the heart of a man. He saw in his sleep a man's body, which was like crystal, and the inside of it was visible from

---

72 An agreed upon *ḥadīth* related by Bukhārī and Muslim from ʿĀʾisha. Wensinck, *Handbook*, p. 59a.

73 MSS texts read, '… he promised this to him at Ḥirāʾ.' And Jibrīl appeared to him and filled … .' Ḥirāʾ; in a cave in this place the Prophet used to spend considerable time prior to receiving revelation. "Ḥirāʾ," *EI*, 2:315. *EI²*, 3:462.

74 Editor's note: this is a cemetery in Medina where many of the Companions are buried.

75 Cf. Qurʾān 53:1–13.

76 Diḥya b. Khalīfa b. Farwa b. Fuḍāla al-Kalbī, a Companion, died during the caliphate of Muʿāwiya; see *EI*, 1:973, 4:57. *EI²*, 2:274.

77 An agreed upon *ḥadīth* quoted by Bukhārī and Muslim. Wensinck, *Handbook*, p. 59a.

78 Possessors of hearts. Macdonald, "Emotional Religion in Islam as Affected by Music and Singing," *JRAS* (1901–2), p. 725n., says that Ghazālī means by this expression "those who are of an emotional nature and can be affected through the heart."

79 ʿUmar b. ʿAbd al-ʿAzīz (63–101/683–702), the eighth Umayyad caliph (r. 99–101/717–20); see *EI*, 3:977ff. *EI²*, 10:821.

without. He saw Satan in the form of a frog sitting on the left shoulder, between the shoulder and the ear, and he had a long and thin proboscis which he had put in through the left shoulder into the heart in order to make evil promptings to it. Whenever [the man] made mention of God, the Exalted, Satan withdrew. This very same thing is sometimes seen in waking hours, for some of the [people of] unveiling have seen Satan in the form of a dog reclining on a carcass and inviting men to it. The carcass represents this lower world.

This is like observing his real form. For, of necessity, reality must appear in the heart from that side of it which is turned toward the world of spirits. Then its influence shines upon the side which is turned toward the visible material world, for the two sides are connected, the one with the other. We have already explained that the heart has two sides. One of them is turned toward the world of the unseen, which is the place of entrance of inspiration, both general (*ilhām*) and prophetic (*waḥy*). Another side is turned toward the world of sense; and that which appears of this world in the side turned toward the world of sense is only an imagined form, for the world of sense is entirely subject to imaginative reproduction. Sometimes the image comes from looking by means of the sense [of sight] at the exterior of the visible world. Thus it is possible that the form may not correspond to the ideal reality. You may see a person with a beautiful external appearance, while he is abominable in his heart and hideous in his inner life, because the world of sense abounds in deception (*talbīs*).

But the form produced in the imagination by the illuminating effect of the world of spirits upon the inner secret hearts cannot but reflect accurately their qualities and correspond to them. For the form in the world of spirits follows the true characteristic and corresponds to it. So it is not strange that the hideous reality is not seen, save in a hideous form. Thus Satan is seen in the form of a dog, a frog, a pig, and so on. The angel is seen in a beautiful form, and this form is an indication of the ideal realities and a true reflection of them. Therefore the monkey or pig seen in sleep indicates some hideous likeness, while a sheep indicates a man of integrity.

Thus it is with all the categories of dreams and their interpretetion. These are strange mysteries, and they belong to the wonders of the heart. It is not fitting to mention them in [this book on] the knowledge of proper conduct. But the intent is that you shall believe that Satan is revealed to possessors of hearts, and so also the angel, sometimes by means of a representation and reflection, such as takes place in sleep, and sometimes in reality. For the most part revelation is representation by a form that reflects the ideal reality, not the ideal reality itself. The latter is, however, seen by the eye in genuine eyewitnessing. Only the [person of] unveiling has this direct sight, not others around him, as for instance a man asleep.

Chapter 13

An Exposition of that for which Man is Held Accountable and that for which he is Pardoned and not Punished for Evil Promptings of Hearts, their Decisions, Involuntary Suggestions, and Purposes

KNOW THAT THIS IS an obscure matter and that there have appeared narrations and verses regarding it which conflict with each other. It is confusing for all save discriminating scholars of the law (*sharʿ*) to find a way of harmonizing these statements.

It is related that the Prophet ﷺ said, "My people are pardoned the suggestions of the self."[1] Abū Hurayra said the Messenger of God ﷺ said, "Verily God, the Exalted, says to the recording angels (*al-ḥafaẓa*), 'If a servant of mine intends to do an evil deed, do not write it down; but if he does it, then write it down as an evil deed. If he intends to do a good deed, record it as a good deed, and if he does it, write it as ten.'" Both Muslim and Bukhārī included this *ḥadīth* in their collections (*Ṣaḥīḥayn*).[2] This points to pardon for the action of the heart and its intention to do an evil deed.

Another wording is, "He who intends to do a good deed but does not do it has the intent reckoned to him as a good deed; and he who intends a good deed and does it has it reckoned to him up to seven hundred fold. He who intends an evil deed but does not do it does not have it reckoned

1 An agreed upon *ḥadīth*, quoted by all from Abū Hurayra. Cairo text and Zabīdī add the rest of the *ḥadīth*, 'so long as they do not utter them nor do them.'

2 For this *ḥadīth* see Wensinck, *Handbook*, p. 111; Madanī, *Aḥādīth qudsiyya*, nos. 120, 127, 202.

against him, but if he does it, it is written down." Another wording is, "If he contemplates doing an evil deed, I will forgive him this, so long as he does not do it." All of this points to pardon.

Regarding that which indicates punishment, we have the statement of [God] praise be to Him, *If you show what is within yourselves, or conceal it, God will bring you to account for it, then He will forgive whom He wills, and punish whom He wills* (2:284). And the saying of the Exalted, *And do not pursue that of which you have no knowledge; Indeed the hearing, the sight, and the heart, about all of these [one] will be questioned* (17:36). This indicates that the deed of the heart is like that of the hearing or sight and is not pardoned. And the saying of the Exalted, *And do not conceal testimony, for whoever conceals it, his heart is indeed sinful* (2:283). And the saying of the Exalted, *God will not hold you accountable for what is unintentional in your oaths, but He will hold you accountable for that which your hearts have earned* (2:225).[3]

One cannot become well acquainted with the true nature of this matter, as it seems to us, until he comprehends the details of the heart's actions, from the time they begin to appear until the act is committed by the members of the body.[4] Thus we say that the first thing that comes to the heart is the involuntary suggestion (*khāṭir*). For example, the thought of the form of a woman may be suggested to a man, and that she may be behind him on the road, so that if he were to turn around he would see her.

The second is the stirring up of his desire to look, which is the moving of appetence that is in human nature. This is generated by the first involuntary suggestion and we call it natural inclination (*mayl al-ṭabʿ*), while the first is called the suggestion of the self (*ḥadīth al-nafs*).

The third is the judgment of the heart that the thing must be done, that is, that he must look at her. For when there exists a natural inclination, there is still no decision (*himma*) nor intention (*niyya*)[5] until the inhibitions (*ṣawārif*) are suppressed. Thus modesty or fear may prevent him from looking. The nullification of these inhibitions may come through reflection (*taʾammul*), but in any case it is a judgment of the reason and

3 Cf. Qurʾān 24:18 and 49:12.

4 For a parallel to the development that follows here, and a probable contributing source, see Smith, "Forerunner," p. 67 with references there given.

5 "Niyya," intention, an important principle in all religious life and activity in Islam; see *EI*, 3:930. *EI*², 8:66.

is called a conviction (*iʿtiqād*). This is subsequent to the involuntary suggestion and natural inclination.

The fourth [stage] is to fix his determination (*ʿazm*) upon looking, and to make it his definite intent. This we call a decision (*hamm*) to act, intent, and purpose (*qaṣd*). This decision may have a weak beginning, but if the heart gives heed to the first involuntary suggestion, until its attraction to the self is prolonged, this decision becomes inevitable, and it becomes a determination of the will. Then when the will is determined, [the man] may repent after determination and give up the action. Perhaps he may neglect it, because of some[thing] happening and neither do it nor give heed to it. Or again, perhaps some hindrance may come along to prevent him from the action.

Here then are four states of the heart before the bodily member acts: involuntary suggestion, which is the suggestion of the self; then inclination; then conviction; then decision.

Now regarding the involuntary suggestion [the first stage], we say that one is not held accountable for it because it is not included in voluntary choices. Such also is the case with inclination [the second stage] and the stirring up of appetence, for they too are involuntary. These are what [the Prophet] ﷺ intended in his statement, "My people are pardoned the suggestions of the self." The suggestion of the self is thus an expression to denote the involuntary suggestion that suddenly comes into the mind, but is not followed by any determination to carry it out.

Determination and decision [the fourth stage] are not, however, called suggestions of the self. The narration regarding ʿUthmān b. Maẓʿūn[6] illustrates the suggestion of the self.

He said to the Prophet, ﷺ "O Messenger of God, my heart tells me that I ought to divorce Khawla."[7]

[The Prophet] answered, "Go slowly; my Sunna includes marriage."[8]

He said again, "My heart tells me to emasculate myself."

6 ʿUthmān b. Maẓʿūn b. Ḥabīb b. Wahb al-Jumaḥī (d. 3 or 4/624 or 625), one of the earliest Companions and the thirteenth man to adopt Islam, he showed the ascetic tendency in early Islam; see *EI*, 3:1011. *EI*², 10:951.

7 Khawla bint Ḥakīm b. Umayya al-Silmī was the wife of ʿUthmān b. Maẓʿūn, and disagreed with his ascetic practices. Wensinck, *Handbook*, p. 159a.

8 ʿIrāqī analyzes this *ḥadīth* and discusses its various parts and their degrees of authenticity.

[The Prophet] answered, "Go slowly; castration in my nation is persistent fasting."[9]

He said, "My heart tells me to become a celibate."

[The Prophet] answered, "Go slowly; the asceticism[10] of my people is warfare (*jihād*) and the pilgrimage (*ḥajj*)."[11]

He said, "My heart tells me to give up meat."

[The Prophet] answered, "Go slowly, for I like it. When it is available, I eat it; and if I were to ask God for it, He would feed me therewith."

These were involuntary suggestions, unaccompanied by a determination to carry them out, and they were the suggestions of the self. Therefore he consulted with the Messenger of God ﷺ since he had made no determination or decision to act.

The third [stage] is conviction (*iʿtiqād*), and the judgment of the heart that the thing must be done. There is an element of uncertainty in this, in that it may be compulsory or voluntary, and the states differ accordingly. One is held accountable for that which is voluntary, but not for that which is compulsory.

The fourth [of these stages] is a decision to act, and one is held accountable for it, but if it is not carried out, the case is to be considered. If the man has given it up through fear of God, the Exalted, and contrition for his decision, then this is reckoned to him as a good deed. His decision was evil, but his abstaining from it and struggle with himself against it were good. A decision in accord with nature does not indicate a complete heedlessness of God, the Exalted, but abstinence through struggle against the nature requires great power. So his effort in acting contrary to nature, which is a work done for God, the Exalted, is stronger than his effort to agree with Satan by agreeing with his own nature. Thus it is reckoned to him as a good deed, because his effort in abstaining and his decision thereto outweighed his decision to do the deed. But if the act is stopped by some hindrance, or if he gave it up for any reason other than the fear of God, the Exalted, it is reckoned to him as an evil deed. His decision is a voluntary act of the heart.

The proof of this detailed analysis [mentioned above] is related in the well-attested (*ṣaḥīḥ*) [texts] that are explained in the wording of the

9 Muslim quotes this *ḥadīth*.

10 "Rahbāniyya," asceticism; see *EI*, 3:1103; *EI*², 8:396. Lane, *Lexicon*, p. 1168; Massignon, *Essai*, p. 124; Wensinck, *Concordance*, 1:388ff.

11 "Ḥajj," *EI*, 2:196ff. *EI*², 3:31.

ḥadīth: The Messenger of God ﷺ said, "The angels ﷺ said, 'O Lord, that servant of yours desires to do an evil deed,[12] although He perceived [that] better [than they]. He said, 'Keep watch of him, and if he does it, write it down as it is; but if gives it up, write it down for him as a good deed, for he has given it up only for My sake.'" When He said, 'If he does not do it,' He meant the forsaking of it for God's sake.

But if a man has determined on an act of turpitude, which is then made impossible for him by some cause or neglect, how can this be reckoned to him as a good deed? [The Prophet] ﷺ said, "People will be judged according to their intentions alone."[13] We know that he who determines at night to get up the next morning and kill a Muslim or commit adultery with a woman, and then dies that night, dies with his mind made up and will be judged according to his intention, having decided upon an evil deed and not carried it out.

The decisive proof of this is in what has been related of the Prophet ﷺ, "If two Muslims meet in a sword fight, both the slayer and the slain will be in the Fire."[14] Someone said to him, "O Messenger of God, 'This one was a murderer, but why include the slain man also?'" He replied, "Because he desired to slay his fellow." This is an authoritative statement which shows that by mere desire he became one of the people of the Fire even though he himself was unjustly slain.

How can anyone suppose that God will not punish for intention and decision, when man is punished for everything that comes within the scope of voluntary action, save what he atones for by a good deed? Destroying the determination by contrition is a good deed, and it is therefore reckoned to him as a good deed. But to miss the thing desired because of some hindrance is not a good deed.

But involuntary suggestion, the suggestion of the self, and the stirring up of desire are all outside the realm of voluntary acts. So to consider them as worthy of punishment would be to make man responsible for what is beyond his power. So when there was revealed the statement of the Exalted, *and if you show what is in yourselves or conceal it, God will bring you to account for it* (2:284), some of the Companions came to the Messenger of God ﷺ and said,

---

12 A *ḥadīth* from Abū Hurayra given by Muslim. Wensinck, *Handbook*, p. 111.

13 ʿIrāqī gives several versions of this agreed upon *ḥadīth* which is quoted by Muslim and others. Wensinck, *Concordance*, 1:194b.

14 An agreed upon *ḥadīth* given by many authorities. Wensinck, *Handbook*, p. 172a.

"A responsibility has been put upon us that we cannot bear. One of us experiences a suggestion of the self about something that he does not like to have remain in his heart, and then he is judged for it!"

[The Prophet] ﷺ said, "Perhaps you will say, as the Jews said, 'We hear and disobey.' Say [instead], 'We hear and obey.'"

Then they said, "We hear and obey."

So God sent down that which dispelled their anxiety[15] in His statement, *On no soul does God place a burden greater than it can bear* (2:286).[16] From this it appears that man is not held accountable for the deeds of the heart that are not within his power.[17]

Here then is an uncovering (*kashf al-ghiṭāʾ*) of this ambiguity. Whoever supposes that every action of the heart is called a suggestion of the self and does not differentiate between these three classes must inevitably err. For how could it be that man would go unpunished for the acts of his heart, such as pride, conceit, hypocrisy, dissimulation, envy, and all the malicious acts of the heart? Nay rather, *the hearing, the sight, and the heart, about all of these [one] will be questioned* (17:36), that is, as much as is included in voluntary action. If the eye of a man were to fall involuntarily upon [a woman] other than a near relative whom he could not lawfully marry, he would not be blameworthy for it, but if he followed it with a second look, it would be punishable, for it would be done voluntarily. In like manner, the involuntary suggestions of the heart follow the same course. Indeed the heart is more deserving of blame since it is the source (*aṣl*).

The Messenger of God ﷺ said, "Piety is here,"[18] pointing toward his heart. God, the Exalted, said, *Their meat will not reach God, nor will their blood; but what reaches Him is piety from you* (22:37).[19]

[The Prophet] ﷺ said, "Sin is the allurement (*ḥawwāz*)[20] of the heart."[21]

He also said, "Righteousness (*birr*) is that in which the heart quietly trusts, even though men may give you legal decision after legal decision."[22]

---

15 Editor's note: this is following Zabīdī's text. The Cairo text adds, 'after a year.'

16 A *ḥadīth* given by Muslim from Abū Hurayra.

17 Cf. note on *mukallaf*, page 91.

18 A *ḥadīth* given by Muslim from Abū Hurayra.

19 MSS add, 'and piety is in the heart.'

20 Other readings: *ḥazzāz*, grief; *ḥawāzz*, perplexity; *jawāz*, permission. True reading uncertain.

21 Zabīdī gives various readings of this *ḥadīth* and discusses it at length (*Itḥāf*, 1:159).

22 ʿIrāqī says that this *ḥadīth* was given by Ṭabarānī. Aḥmad gives a very similar

So we can say that if the heart of a *muftī* gives a decision making anything obligatory, even though it errs therein, this becomes a meritorious act. Indeed, if a man thinks that he is purified and must pray, and then prays, but afterwards remembers that he had not performed the necessary ablutions, he still has the reward for doing it. But if he remembers and then neglects it, he is punished.[23] If a man finds a woman in his bed and supposes her to be his wife, he commits no act of disobedience by lying with her, even though she is a stranger. But if he thinks that she is a stranger and then lies with her, he becomes disobedient even though she is his wife. All of this is so because the heart is what is considered, not the bodily members.

ḥadīth. Wensinck, *Concordance*, 1:163b; *Iḥyā*ʾ, 2:93. Editor's note: A version of this *ḥadīth*, which is sound, is narrated in Nawawī, *Forty Ḥadīth*, p. 90–1.

23 Cf. the *ḥadīth* given by Ibn Māja and Aḥmad. Wensinck, *Handbook*, p. 192b.

Chapter 14

An Exposition of whether or not Evil Promptings Can be Conceived of as Entirely Cut Off during Remembrance [of God]

KNOW THAT THE SCHOLARS, who have observed the heart of man and investigated its characteristics and its wonders, disagree on this question, and [are in] five groups [holding different opinions].

One group says that evil suggestion is cut off by the remembrance of God ﷻ. They [refer to] the saying of [the Prophet] ﷺ, "Whenever God is remembered, he [i.e., Satan] hides himself."[1] To hide oneself is to keep still, so it is as though he keeps silent.

Another group says that the source of evil suggestion does not entirely cease to exist, but continues to flow in the heart. It has no effect, however, for the heart, since it is entirely immersed in remembrance, is veiled from the effect of the evil suggestion. The heart is like a man so engrossed in his chief concern that, if he were spoken to, he would not understand, even though the voice reaches his hearing.

Another group says that neither the evil suggestion nor its effects are cut off entirely, but its domination over the heart is cut off. It is as though [Satan] whispered from a distance and weakly.

A group says that the evil suggestion ceases to exist for a moment at the remembrance [of God], and that remembrance is also annihilated for a moment. These two states follow each other at such close intervals that they seem, because of their closeness, to be pressing against each other.

---

1 A weak *ḥadīth* given by Ibn Abī al-Dunyā, also referred to in Chapter 11.

They are like a ball that has several separate dots on it, for if you roll it rapidly you will see the dots as though they were circles, because of the speed with which the motion brings them together. This group says that [Satan's] hiding is mentioned, while we observe the evil suggestion along with remembrance, and that there is no other explanation for it than this.

A group says that the evil suggestion and remembrance crowd upon each other constantly within the heart, in a struggle which is unending. Just as a man may see two things at the same time, so also the heart may be the channel for two things. The [Messenger of God] ﷺ said, "Every man has four eyes. Two are in his head and through them he sees what pertains to his relationships to this present world. The other two are in his heart, and through them he sees what pertains to his religion."[2] Muḥāsibī[3] held this view.

But in fact, as we see it, all of these groups are correct. Each one fails to include all the species of evil suggestions, and looks only at one species of evil suggestion and tells of it.

Evil suggestions are of different sorts. The first is clothed with truth to a degree, for Satan may be garbed with truth. Thus he will say to a man, "Do not give up the enjoyment of pleasures; life is long and resisting your desires throughout your whole life causes great suffering." But if the man remembers at this time the greatness of the right of God, the Exalted, [over him] and His great rewards and punishments, he will say to himself, "Resisting the desires is hard, but it is still more difficult to endure the Fire, and one of the two is inevitable." So if the man remembers the promise and threat of God, the Exalted, and renews his faith and certainty, then Satan hides himself and flees. For he cannot say that the Fire is easier to bear than resisting acts of disobedience, nor can he say that disobedience does not lead to the Fire, because his faith in the Book of God ﷻ prevents him from that, and thus his evil whisperings are cut off. So also he will suggest that one should be proud of his own deeds, saying, "What creature knows God, the Exalted, as you know Him, or serves Him as you serve [Him]? How great then is your place with God." But then the man remembers that his knowledge, his heart, and his members, with which he works, and his

---

2 A *ḥadīth* that ʿIrāqī says is not authentic.

3 Al-Muḥāsibī, Abū ʿAbdallāh al-Ḥārith b. Asad (d. 243/857), a highly-trained Sunnī mystic and a prolific writer. His chief work, *al-Riʿāya li-ḥuquq Allāh* held a high place in Islamic mysticism and was one of Ghazālī's source-books. See *EI*, 3:699. *EI*², 7:466. See also Smith, "Forerunner," p. 67.

work itself are all of them created by God, the Exalted, so how can he be proud of them? Then Satan hides himself, for he cannot say, "This is not from God," because his knowledge and faith compel him. This is a sort of whispering that can be cut off entirely from those who have mystical knowledge (*ʿārifīn*) and are enlightened by the light of faith and gnosis.

The second species of evil suggestion is that which moves and stirs up appetence. This is divided into that which man knows assuredly to be an act of disobedience, and that of which he is strongly suspicious. If he knows it assuredly, Satan withdraws from the stirring-up, which results in moving appetence, but does not withdraw from stirring-up per se. But if it is of the suspicious sort, it may continue to exert its influence in such a way as to call for a struggle in warding it off. Thus the evil suggestion exists, but is warded off and does not gain the victory.

The third type of evil suggestion is that which comes only from involuntary thoughts and recollecting past states; for example, thinking about something other than prayer.[4] So when [the man] begins [the practice of] remembrance (*dhikr*), conceivably it is warded off and returns again and again. Remembrance and evil suggestion thus keep alternating. It is conceivable that they press so closely upon one another that the understanding will include an understanding of the meaning of the thing recited, and also of those involuntary suggestions, as though the two were in two different places in the heart. That this sort of evil suggestion should be entirely warded off so as not to recur is very unlikely but it is not impossible, since [the Prophet] ﷺ said, "Whoever prays a two-cycle prayer without experiencing any suggestions of the self about this present world during the prayer will have all his former sins forgiven."[5] If this were not conceivable he would not have mentioned it. This cannot be conceived, however, save of a heart over which love has so gained the mastery that it has become as one [utterly] devoted. Thus we sometimes see a man whose heart is so wholly occupied with an enemy who has injured him that he may think about contending with his enemy for the space of two prayers and many more, and no other thought save that of his enemy will cross his mind. So, too, one deeply in love may think in his heart about conversing with his beloved and be so deeply submerged in this thought that nothing else save conversing with his beloved ever occurs to him. If

---

4 *Maḥajjat* MS adds, 'while praying.'

5 An agreed upon *ḥadīth* given by Bukhārī and Muslim. Wensinck, *Concordance*, 1:434a; *Iḥyāʾ*, 1:134.

someone else were to speak to him he would not hear, and if one should pass in front of him he would be as one unseeing. If this is conceivable in the case of fearing an enemy and coveting reputation and money, why should it be inconceivable in the case of fearing the Fire and coveting Paradise? But this is rare because of the weakness of faith in God, the Exalted, and the last day.

If you consider all of these classifications and types of evil suggestions you will understand that each one of these groups has its own point which applies under particular circumstances. To summarize: Salvation (*khalāṣ*) from Satan for a moment or for an hour is not an unlikely thing, but safety from him for a long lifetime is very remote indeed and impossible to attain. If anyone could have escaped from the evil suggestions that Satan makes by means of involuntary thoughts and the rousing of desire, the Messenger of God ﷺ surely would have escaped.

It is related of him "that he looked at the ornamented border of his robe during prayer, and when he had finished the prayer he cast the robe away, saying, 'It distracted me from prayer.'[6] He[7] said, 'Take it to Abū Jahm[8] and bring me his coarse garment (*anbijāniyya*).'" Another time he had a gold ring on his finger, and he looked at it while he was at the minbar. Then he flung it away, saying, "One look at it and one at you."[9] This was due to the evil suggestion of Satan by arousing the pleasure of looking at the gold ring and the ornamented border of the garment. This took place before gold was forbidden, and therefore he wore it and then cast it aside.

The evil suggestions of the adornments of this world and its money are cut off only by casting them away, and separating one's self from them. For as long as a man owns anything beyond his actual need, be it but a single dinar, Satan will not allow him during prayer to be completely free from the thought of his dinar. How will he keep it? For what will he spend it? How can he hide it so that no one will know about it? How shall he show it so as to boast of it, and so on. Whoever fixes his clutches on this present world and then desires to get rid of Satan is like a man dipped in

6 An agreed upon *ḥadīth* from ʿĀʾisha. *Iḥyāʾ*, 1:59; Wensinck, *Handbook*, p. 189.

7 Zabīdī and Princeton MS omit the sentence.

8 Abū Jahm. Ibn Ḥajar, *Biographical Dictionary*, 4:62ff.; Nawawī, *Tahdhīb al-asmāʾ*, pp. 686ff. Bukhārī quotes this *ḥadīth* in *Kitāb al-libās*.

9 Editor's note: ʿIrāqī says that this *ḥadīth* has an authentic chain of transmission, found in Nisāʾī on the authority of Ibn ʿAbbās, without mention of the ring being of gold or silver. Previously mentioned in *Iḥyāʾ*, 1:165 of the Cairo edition.

honey who thinks that the bees will not alight on him. This is impossible, for this present world is a great entrance for the evil suggestions of Satan. Indeed there is not one entrance only, but many.

One of the wise men said, "Satan approaches the son of Adam from the direction of his acts of disobedience. If he abstains from them, Satan comes to him by way of giving advice, in order to cause him to fall into some innovation (*bidʿa*). If he refuses this, he commands a life of narrowness and abstinence so that he considers as unlawful that which is lawful. If he refuses this, [Satan] makes him doubt regarding his ablution and prayer so that he may not have certain knowledge [about the performance of them]. If he abstains from this, [Satan] makes righteous acts easy for him so that men may see him as patient and pure, and their hearts be turned to him. Then he becomes proud of himself, and by this he [i.e., Satan] destroys him." At this point man is in great need, for this is the extreme degree of temptation, and Satan knows that if man passes by it he has escaped from him into Paradise.

Chapter 15

An Exposition of the Rapidity of the Heart's Changes; and of the Way Hearts are Classified in Respect to Change and Stability

KNOW THAT THE HEART, as we have mentioned, is surrounded by the qualities that we have spoken of, and that various effects and states are poured into it from the entrances we have described. So it is, as it were, a target that is being hit constantly from every direction. Whenever a thing hits the heart, it influences it, and it is also hit from another direction by an opposing influence, so that its character is changed. If a demon comes to the heart and calls it to desire, there comes also an angel to drive it away. If a demon entices it to one evil, another demon entices it to another. If an angel attracts it to one sort of good, another angel attracts it to some other good. So at one time it is torn between two angels, at another between two demons, and at another between an angel and a demon. It is never left alone at all.

To this is the reference of the statement of the Exalted, *We will turn away their hearts and their eyes* (6:110). The Messenger of God ﷺ, because of his wide observation of the wondrous acts of God in the wonders of the heart and its constant changes, used to swear by it and say, "No, by Him who overturns hearts."[1]

He [the Prophet] often used to say, "O You who overturn hearts, establish my heart firmly upon Your religion."[2]

---

1 A *ḥadīth* quoted from Ibn ʿUmar by Bukhārī.

2 A *ḥadīth* quoted by Tirmidhī and Ibn Māja. Wensinck, *Concordance*, 1:287b.

They said, "Do you fear, O Messenger of God?"

He answered, "What is there to make me sure, since the heart is between two of the fingers of the Merciful, who turns them about as He wills?" Or, according to another wording, "if He wills to establish it He causes it to stand, and if He wills it to go astray He does so."[3]

[The Prophet] ﷺ used three similes of the heart: "The heart is like a sparrow, turning about every hour."[4] And he ﷺ said, "The heart in its constant changes is like a pot when it reaches boiling."[5] And he said, "The heart is like a feather in an empty land, which the winds blow along over and over."[6] These changes and the wonders of the acts of God, the Exalted, in causing them, which cannot be sought out, are known only by those who watch and ponder over their own condition in relation to God, the Exalted.

Hearts are divided into three classes from the standpoint of being fixed on good, on evil, or alternating beween the two of them.

There is a heart that is built up by means of piety, purified by means of discipline and cleared of all evil characteristics. Into it are poured involuntary suggestions of good from the storehouses of the unseen and the entrances to the [world of] spirits. The intellect is then wholly occupied with thinking about that which has been suggested to it, so as to know the minute details of good therein and understand the secrets of its benefits. Thus its purpose is revealed to the intellect by the light of insight, and so it decides that this thing must be done. It then urges [the heart] and calls it to undertake the act. The angel looks to this heart and finds it good in its substance (*jawhar*), pure because of its piety, enlightened by the light of reason, furnished with the light of gnosis, and he sees that it is worthy to be his place of abode and alighting. Thereupon he supplies it with unseen troops, and guides it into other blessings, so that good is thus led on to greater good unceasingly. His help in causing it to desire good and making it easy of attainment does not cease. To such [a heart] is reference made in the statement of the Exalted, *But as for him who gives [in charity] and fears God and believes in goodness, we will ease his path to happiness* (92:5–7). In such a heart there shines the light of the lamp from the niche of lordship,

3 An authentic *ḥadīth*. Wensinck, *Concordance*, 1:287b.

4 A *ḥadīth* quoted by Muslim and others.

5 A *ḥadīth* quoted by Bukhārī and others.

6 A *ḥadīth* quoted by Ibn Māja and others. Wensinck, *Handbook*, p. 95a.

so that there is no secret polytheism (*shirk*)[7] concealed therein, for such is more hidden than the creeping of a black ant on a dark night. No hidden thing is concealed from this light, nor do any of the wiles of Satan spread in a heart like this. Indeed Satan stands and speaks alluring words, striving to deceive, but the heart will not turn to him. This heart, after being purified from the things that destroy (*al-muhlikāt*), soon becomes filled with the things that save (*al-munjiyāt*). We shall mention these: thanksgiving, patience, fear, hope, poverty, asceticism, love, satisfaction, longing, trust, meditation, examination of conscience, and others.[8] This is the heart to which God ﷻ turns His face. It is the heart at rest referred to the statement of the Exalted, *Verily in remembrance of God do hearts find rest!* (13:28); and His statement ﷻ, *O reassured soul* (89:27).

The second heart is forsaken, burdened by passion, corrupted by foul actions, stained by blameworthy characteristics. Its doors for demons are open, and its doors to angels closed. The starting point of evil in it is an involuntary suggestion of passion that is cast into it and speaks therein. Then the heart turns to the intellect as judge, to take its decision and learn the right course therein. But the intellect has become accustomed to serve passion, and familiar with it, and continues to invent tricks to agree with passion and assist it until they entice the soul and help the passion. Thus the breast rejoices in passion whose darkness covers it because of the withdrawal of the forces of the intellect from the defense of the heart. Accordingly the power of Satan grows because of the breadth of his field due to the spread of passion. [Satan] then approaches the heart with allurement and seduction and anticipations, speaking alluring words to deceive. The power of faith in [God's] promise and threat grows weak and the light of certainty regarding fear of the world to come is extinguished. For there rises up from passion a dark smoke over the heart that fills it entirely so that its lights are extinguished. Then the intellect becomes like an eye whose lids are full of smoke so that it is not able to see. This is what the victory of appetence does to the heart, so that there is no possibility left for the heart to stop and look. If a warner should try to make it see and hear what the truth is, it would blind itself to understanding and close its ears against hearing. Appetence is roused up in it and Satan overpowers it. The bodily members move in accordance with the desires of passion,

---

7 "Shirk," *EI*, 4:378ff. *EI*^{2}, 9:484.

8 Editor's note: these are other books of volume 4, the fourth quarter of the *Iḥyāʾ ʿulūm al-dīn*.

and the act of disobedience appears in the physical material world from the world of the unseen, in accordance with the general and particular decree (*qaḍāʾ wa qadar*)[9] of God, the Exalted. To such a heart is reference made in the statement of the Exalted, *Have you seen the one who takes his desire as his god? Then would you be responsible for him? Or do you think that most of them will hear or reason? They are but like livestock; rather, they are more astray* (25:43–4). And in His statement, ﷻ *Already has the judgement proved true of most of them, for they believe not* (36:7). And in the statement of the Exalted, *It is all the same for them whether you warn them or do not warn them—they will not believe* (36:10).

Many[10] a heart is in this state with regard to certain desires, like a man who abstains from some things, but if he sees a pretty face he cannot control his eye and heart. Or it may be like [a man] who cannot control himself in anything having to do with high rank, leadership, and pride. He has no grip to hold himself firm when the occasion appears. It may be like one who cannot control himself in anger, no matter how much he may despise it and recall its faults. Or it may be like [a man] who cannot control himself when he is able to get a dirham or a dinar, but he covets it as one bereft and disordered, forgetting therein chivalry and piety. All of this is because of the rising of the smoke of passion over the heart so that the light of modesty, chivalry, and faith is extinguished, and he strives to secure what Satan desires.

The third heart is that in which there appear suggestions of passion that summon it to evil. But there follows then a suggestion of faith that summons it to good. The soul with its lusts hastens to the aid of the evil suggestion, the lust grows stronger, and enjoyment and delight seem good. But the intellect hastens to the aid of the good suggestion, repels the idea of the lust, and makes doing it appear abominable, attributing it to ignorance and likening it to a beast or a lion in rushing blindly into evil and showing little concern for consequences. The soul then inclines toward the advice of the intellect. The demon in turn attacks the intellect and makes the call of passion louder, saying,

"What is this cold narrow aloofness? Why do you abstain from your passions and torment yourself? Do you see any of your contemporaries going contrary to his passions, or giving up his aim? Will you thus leave

9 "Qaḍāʾ" and "qadar," *EI*, 2:603–5. *EI*², "al- qaḍā; wa-l-qadar," 4:365.

10 MSS adds this statement to the beginning of this paragraph: 'Many a heart is in this condition with regard to all desires'; Zabīdī omits the whole paragraph.

the pleasures of this present world for them to enjoy, and deprive yourself of them until you are avoided, miserable, and worn out, and become the laughing-stock of modern folk? Do you want to attain a higher rank than so-and-so and so-and-so? They have done what you have longed to do and have not abstained. Do you not see the learned man, so-and-so? He does not guard against doing this, and if it were evil he would abstain from it."

Thus the soul inclines to the demon and is turned to him. Then the angel attacks the demon and says,

"Has anyone ever perished save he who followed the pleasure of the moment, forgetting the consequences? Will you be contented with a trifling pleasure and forsake the pleasure of Paradise and its blessedness forever? Or do you think that the pain of resisting your lust is too great a burden, but do not think the pain of the Fire grievous? Will you be deceived by men's neglect of themselves, their following their own passions, and their taking sides with Satan, in spite of the fact that the torment of the Fire will not be made easier for you to bear because of the disobedience of another? Now if it were a very hot summer day and all the people were standing in the sun, but you had a cool house, would you stay with the people, or would you seek safety for yourself? How could you disagree with men through the fear of the sun's heat and not disagree with them through fear of the Fire?"

Thereupon the soul inclines to the saying of the angel. The heart continues to sway between the two forces, being attracted by each of the two parties, until there overcomes it that which is dominant therein. For if the characteristics of the heart are predominantly the satanic qualities that we have mentioned, then Satan is victorious and the heart inclines to its own sort among the parties of demons, turning away from the party of God, the Exalted, and His saints, and taking sides with the party of Satan and enemies [of good]. Because of predestination (*sābiq al-qadar*) its members have done that which is the reason for its remoteness from God, the Exalted.

If the angelic characteristics are the dominant element in the heart it will not give heed to the allurement of Satan, nor his urging the claim of the swiftly passing [world], nor his making light of the world to come. But it inclines to the party of God, the Exalted, and its obedience appears in its members in accordance with what has previously been decreed.

"The heart of the believer is between two of the fingers of the Merciful," that is, between the attraction of these two parties. This is the case with most men; I mean the turning and shifting from one party to another. But perpetual constancy in the party of the angels or that of the demons is rare in both cases.

These acts of obedience and of disobedience appear, coming from the storehouses of the unseen into the material world, by means of the storehouse of the heart; for it is one of the storehouses of the [world of the] spirit. When these appear they are signs that teach possessors of hearts (*arbāb al-qulūb*) the fact of the predetermined decree (*sābiq al-qaḍāʾ*). For one who is created for Paradise, the means of obedience are made easy, and for one who is created for the Fire, the means of disobedience are made easy. Evil companions have been empowered over him, and the rule of Satan has been cast into his heart. For by varieties of sayings he [i.e., Satan] deceives the foolish. Examples of these sayings are: "Truly God is [forgiving and] merciful, so do not worry. Men do not all fear God, so do not differ from them. Life is long, so wait and repent tomorrow."

Satan promises them and arouses desire in them. But Satan does not promise them except delusion (4:120). He promises them repentance and stirs up within them a desire for forgiveness, but he destroys them, by the permission of God, the Exalted, through these tricks and the like. He opens a man's heart to receive the deception, but contracts it against the reception of truth. All of this is because of the general and particular decrees of God. *Whoever God wants to guide, He expands his breast to [accept] Islam and whoever He wishes to misguide, He makes his breast tight and constricted, as though he were climbing into the sky* (6:125). *If God should aid you, no one can overcome you; but if He should forsake you, who is there that can aid you after Him?* (3:160).

He is the One who guides aright and leads astray. He does as He wills and judges as He desires. There is none to avert His judgment, nor is there any who can avert His decree. He has created Paradise and created a people for it, and He engages them in obedience. He has also created the Fire and created a people for it, and He engages them in disobedience. He has taught mankind the sign of the people of Paradise and of the people of the Fire. He said, *As for the righteous they will be in bliss, and the wicked they will be in the Fire* (82:13–4). Then He, the Exalted, said, as related by His Prophet ﷺ, "These are in Paradise and I care not, and these are in the Fire and I care not."[11] So God, the King, the Real, is exalted; *He will not be questioned about what He does, but they shall be questioned* (21:23).

---

11 A *ḥadīth* from Aḥmad and others. Cf. Madanī, *Aḥādīth qudsiyya*, nos. 259–61.

Let us then limit ourselves to this brief mention of the wonders of the heart, for to undertake it in complete detail is not appropriate for [a discussion of] the knowledge of proper conduct (*muʿāmala*). But we have mentioned what is needed in order to know the depths and secrets of the knowledge of proper conduct, in order to benefit the one who is not satisfied with the external, nor content to take the shell instead of the kernel, but longs to have a detailed knowledge of the true nature of causes. In what we have mentioned he will find that which, if God wills, will both suffice and convince. God is Lord of success.[12]

The *Book of the Marvels of the Heart* is complete, and to God be praise and gratitude. It is followed by the *Book of Disciplining the Soul and Refining the Character*.

Praise be to God alone, and may
His blessing be upon
every chosen
servant.

12 Zabīdī omits all that follows; MSS have slightly varying endings.

تم بحمد الله

Bibliography

ʿAlī, A. Yūsuf, trans. *The Meaning of the Holy Qurʾān*. Beltsville, MD: Amana, 2002.

Amari, M. *Biblioteca Arabo-Sicula*. 2 vols. Turin: E. Loescher, 1880–1.

Arberry, Arthur J., trans. *The Koran Interpreted*. New York, 1955.

Aristotle. *De Anima*. Translated by W. S. Hett. London: W. Heinemann, 1935.

Aristotle. *Aristotle*. W. D. Ross. London, 1923.

Aristotle. *Aristotle*. G. R. G. Mure. New York, 1932.

Asín Palacios, M. *Algazel, Dogmática, Moral, Ascética*. Zaragoza, 1901.

Badawi, Elsaid M. and Muhammad Abdel Haleem. *Arabic–English Dictionary of Qur'anic Usage*. Leiden: Brill, 2008.

Bayḍāwī, ʿAbdallāh b. ʿUmar. *Anwār al-tanzīl wa asrār al-taʾwīl*. Edited by F. O. Fleischer. 2 vols. Leipzig, 1846–8.

Brett, George Sidney. *A History of Psychology*. 3 vols. London: Allen & Unwin, 1912–21.

Brockelmann, Carl. *Geschichte der Arabischer Litteratur*. 2 vols. Weimar: E. Felber, 1898–1902; *Supplementband*. 3 vols. 1936–7.

Browne, Edward G. *Arabian Medicine*. Cambridge, 1921.

Bustānī, Buṭrus. *Muḥīṭ al-muḥīṭ*. Beirut, 1867–70.

Chittick, William. *The Sufi Path of Knowledge*. Albany: State University of New York Press, 1989.

Damīrī, Muḥammad b. Mūsā. *Ḥayāt al-ḥayawān al-kubrā*. Edited and translated by A. S. G. Jayakar. Bombay, 1906.

Dhahabī, Muḥammad b. Aḥmad al-. *Kitāb ṭabaqāt al-ḥuffāz*. Edited by Wüstenfeld. Götingen, 1834.

Dozy, Reinhart Pieter. *Supplément aux Dictionnaires Arabes*. 2 vols. Leiden, 1881.

Encyclopaedia of Islam. Edited by M. Th. Houtsma, et al. 9 vols. Leiden, Brill, 1913–37.

Encyclopaedia of Islam. Second Edition. Edited by P. Bearman, Th. Bianquis, C. E. Bosworth, E. van Donzel, and W.P. Heinrichs. 13 vols. Leiden: Brill, 1954–2009.

Encyclopaedia of Religion and Ethics. Edited by James Hastings. 13 vols. New York: C. Scribner's Sons, 1908–27.

Freytag, G. W. *Arabum Proverbia*. [*Amthāl al-ʿArab*]. 3 vols. Bonn, 1839.

Gairdner, W. H. T. "Al-Ghazālī's Mishkāt al-Anwār and the Ghazālī Problem." *Der Islam* 5, no. 2 (1914), pp. 121–53.

Ghazālī, Abū Ḥāmid al-. *Ayyuhā al-walad*. Translated by George H. Scherer as *O youth!* Beirut: American Press, 1933.

———. *Iḥyāʾ ʿulūm al-dīn*. 4 vols. Cairo: Muṣṭafā al-Bābī al-Ḥalabī, 1346/1927.

———. *Iḥyāʾ ʿulūm al-dīn: Kitāb asrār al-ṣalāt wa-muhimmātihā*. Translated by Edwin Calverley as *Worship in Islam*. Madras, 1925.

———. *Iḥyāʾ ʿulūm al-dīn: Kitāb al-ʿilm*. Translated by Nabih Amin Faris as *The Book of Knowledge*. Lahore: Sh. Muhammad Ashraf, 1966.

———. *Iḥyāʾ ʿulūm al-dīn: Kitāb al-tawḥīd wa'l-tawakkul*. Translated by David Burrell as *Faith in Divine Unity and Trust in Divine Providence*. Louisville, KY: Fons Vitae, 2001.

———. *Iḥyāʾ ʿulūm al-dīn: Kitāb Dhikr al-mawt wa-mā baʿdahu*. Translated by Timothy J. Winter, as *The Remembrance of Death and the Afterlife*. Cambridge: Islamic Texts Society, 1989.

———. *Iljām al-ʿawāmm ʿan ʿilm al-kalām*. Cairo, 1309/1891.

———. *Kīmiyāʾ al-saʿāda* and *al-Risāla al-ladunniyya*. Cairo: Saʿāda Press, 1343/1924.

———. *Kīmiyāʾ al-saʿāda*. Translated by Henry Homes as *The Alchemy of Happiness*. Albany, NY: J. Munsell, 1873.

———. *Maʿārij al-quds fī madārij maʿrifat al-nafs*. Cairo, 1346/1927.

———. *Maqāṣid al-falāsifa*. Cairo, 1936.

———. *Mishkāt al-anwār*. Cairo, 1322/1904.

———. *Mīzān al-ʿamal*. Cairo: Muḥyī al-Dīn Ṣabrī al-Kurdī, 1342/1923–4.

———. *al-Munqidh min al-ḍalāl*. Translated by Claud Field as *The Confessions of Al-Ghazzali*. New York: E. P. Dutton and Company, 1909.

———. *Tahafot al-falasifat*. Edited by Maurice Bouyges. Beirut: Imprimerie Catholique, 1927.

Griffel, Frank. *Al-Ghazālī's Philosophical Theology*. New York: Oxford University Press, 2009

Ḥājjī Khalīfa. *Kashf al-ẓunūn ʿan asāmī al-kutub wa-l-funūn*. Edited and translated by Gustav Flügel as *Lexicon Bibliographicum et Encyclopaedicum*. 7 vols. Leipzig and London, 1835–58.

Hava, J. G. *Arabic–English Dictionary*. Beirut, 1921.

Hitti, Philip. *History of the Arabs*. London: Macmillan, 1937.

Horovitz, J. "The Earliest Biographies of the Prophet and their Authors." *Islamic Culture* 1, no. 4 (October 1927).

Horten, Max. *Theologie des Islam*. Leipzig, 1912.

Hughes, Thomas P. *Dictionary of Islam: Being a Cyclopædia of the Doctrines, Rites, Ceremonies, and Customs, together with the Technical and Theological terms, of the Muhammadan religion*. London: W. H. Allen, 1885.

Ibn Ḥajar al-ʿAsqalānī. [*al-Iṣāba fī tamyīz al-ṣaḥāba*] *A Biograhical Dictionary of Persons who knew Mohammed*. 4 vols. Calcutta, 1856.

Ibn al-Jawzī. *Talbīs Iblīs*. Egypt: Idārat al-Ṭibāʿa al-Muniriyya, 1928.
Ibn Khallikān. *Kitāb wafayāt al-ʿayān*. Translated by MacGuckin de Slane as *Ibn Khallikan's Biographical Dictionary.* 4 vols. Paris, 1842–71.
Ibn Manẓūr, Muḥammad b. Mukarram. *Lisān al-ʿArab*. 20 vols. in 10. Cairo, n.d.
Ibn al-Nadīm, Muḥammad b. Isḥāq. *Kitāb al-fihrist*. Edited by Gustav Flügel. Leipzig: F. C. W. Vogel, 1871–2.
Ibn Qutayba, ʿAbdallāh b. Muslim. *Ibn Coteiba's Handbuch der Geschiehte*. Edited by Ferdinand Wüstenfeld. Götingen: bei Vandenhoeck und Ruprecht, 1850.
———. *Taʾwīl mukhtalaf al-ḥadīth*. Cairo: Maṭbaʿa Kurdistān al-ʿIlmiyya, 1326/1908.
Ibn Taghrībirdī, Abū al-Maḥāsin Yūsuf. *Abū l-Maḥāsin Ibn Ṭagri Bardii Annales* [Nujūm al-zāhira fī mulūk Miṣr wa-l-Qāhira]. Edited by T. W. J. Juynboll and B. F. Matthes. 2 vols. Leiden: E. J. Brill, 1851–5.
Iskandarī, Aḥmad al-, and Muṣṭafā ʿInānī. *al-Wasīṭ fī-l-ādāb al-ʿarabī wa-tārīkhihi*. Cairo, 1925.
Jeffery, Arthur. "Abū ʿUbaid on the Verses Missing from the Qurʾān." *Moslem World* 28, no. 1 (January 1938), pp. 61–5.
Jibrān, Jibrān Khalīl, *al-Badāʾiʿ wa-l-ṭarāʾif.* Cairo, 1923.
Jurjānī, ʿAlī b. Muḥammad al-. *Kitāb al-taʿrīfāt*. Edited by Gustav Flügel. Leipzig: Sumptibus F. C. G. Vogelii, 1845.
Khalidi, Tarif. *The Muslim Jesus: Sayings and Stories in Islamic Literature.* Boston: Harvard University Press, 2001.
Kisāʾī, Muḥammad b. ʿAbdallāh al-. *The Tales of the Prophets of al-Kisaʾi.* Translated by W. M. Thackston. Boston: Twayne, 1978.
Krenkow, F. "The Two Oldest Books on Arabic Folklore." *Islamic Culture* 2, no. 1 (January 1928).
Kumushkhānawī, Aḥmad b. Muṣṭafā. *Jāmiʿ al-uṣūl fī al-awliyāʾ*. Egypt: Maṭbaʿat al-Jamāliyya, 1328/1910.
Lane, E. W. *Arabic–English Lexicon*. London, 1863–93.
Macdonald, Duncan B. *Development of Muslim Theology, Jurisprudence, and Constitutional Theory*. New York: C. Scribner's Sons, 1926.
———. "The Development of the Idea of Spirit in Islam." *Acta Orientalia* 9 (1931); reprinted in *The Moslem World* 22 (1932), pp. 25–42.
———. "Emotional Religion in Islam as Affected by Music and Singing." *Journal of the Royal Asiatic Society*, pts 1 and 2 (1901–2), pp. 195–252, 705–48, 1–22.
———. "The Life of al-Ghazālī." *Journal of the American Oriental Society* 20 (1899), pp. 71–132.
———. "The Meanings of the Philosophers by al-Ghazzali." *Isis* 25, no. 1 (1936), pp. 9–15.
———. "Note on 'The Meanings of the Philosophers by al-Ghazzali.'" *Isis* 27, no. 1 (1937), pp. 9–10.
———. *The Religious Life and Attitude in Islam*. Chicago: University of Chicago Press, 1912.

Madanī, Muḥammad al-. *al-Ithḥāfāt al-saniyya fi-l-aḥādīth al-qudsiyya*. Hyderabad, 1323.

Makkī, Abū Ṭālib al-. *Qūt al-qulūb*. Cairo, 1310/1892.

Massignon. *Essai sur les Origines du Lexique Technique de la Mystique Musulmane*. Paris: P. Geuthner, 1922.

Maydanī, Aḥmad b. Muḥammad al-. *Majmaᶜ al-amthāl*. Egypt: al-Maṭbaᶜa al-Bahiyya al-Miṣriyya, 1342/1923.

Moosa, Ebrahim. *Ghazālī and the Poetics of Imagination*. Chapel Hill: University of North Carolina Press, 2005.

Nawawī, Abū Zakariya Yaḥyā al-. *Kitāb tahdhīb al-asmāʾ*. Edited and translated by Ferdinand Wüstenfeld as *The Biographical Dictionary of Illustrious Men, Chiefly at the Beginning of Islamism*. Götingen: London Society for the Publication of Oriental Texts, 1842–7.

Nicholson, Reynold A. *The Mystics of Islam*. London: G. Bell and Sons, 1914.

———. *Studies in Islamic Mysticism*. Cambridge: Cambridge University Press, 1921.

Ormsby, Eric. *Ghazali: The Revival of Islam*. Oxford, UK: Oneworld, 2008.

Pickthall, Marmaduke, trans. *The Glorious Koran*. London: 1976.

Plato. *Timaeus*. Translated by R. G. Bury. London: Loeb Classical Library, 1929.

Plotinus. *The Essence of Plotinus*. Based on the translation of Stephen Mackenna; annotated by Grace H. Turnbull. New York: Oxford University Press, 1934.

Qurʾān: Arabic Text with Corresponding English Meanings. Jeddah: Saheeh International, 1997.

Qushayrī, ᶜAbd al-Karīm b. Hawāzin al-. *al-Risāla al-Qushayriyya*. Egypt: Maṭbᶜat Muṣṭafā al-Bābī al-Ḥalabī, 1940.

———. *al-Qushayri's Epistle on Sufism*. Translated by Alexander Knysh. Reading, UK: Garnet Publishing, 2007.

Rahman, S. M. "Al-Ghazzālī." *Islamic Culture* 1 (July 1927).

Sell, Edward. *The Religious Orders of Islam*. London: Simpkin, Marshall, Hamilton, Kent, 1908.

Shaᶜrānī, ᶜAbd al-Wahhāb b. Aḥmad al-. *al-Ṭabaqāt al-kubrā*. Cairo: al-Maṭbaᶜa al-ᶜĀmira al-ᶜUthmāniyya, 1316/1898.

Smith, Margaret. *Al-Ghazali, The Mystic*. London: Luzac and Co., 1944.

———. "The Forerunner of al-Ghazālī." *Journal of tbe Royal Asiatic Society*, no. 1 (January 1936), pp. 65–78.

———. *Studies in Early Mysticism*. New York: Macmillan, 1931.

Ṭabarī, Muḥammad b. Jarīr al-. [*Tārīkh al-umam wa-muluk*] *Annales at-Tabari*. Edited by M. J. De Goeje. Brill, 1870–1904.

Tahānawī, Muḥammad Aᶜlā b. ᶜAlī. *Kitāb kashshāf iṣṭilāḥāt al-funūn*. Edited by Muḥammad Wajih, ᶜAbd al-Ḥaqq, and Ghulam Qādir, under the superintendence of Aloys Sprenger and W. Nassau Lees; translated as *Dictionary of the Technical Terms used in the Sciences of the Musulmans*. 2 vols. Calcutta, 1862.

Ṭaḥāwī, Abū Jaʿfar al-. *The Creed of Imam al-Ṭaḥāwī*. Translated, introduced, and annotated by Hamza Yusuf. Zaytuna Institute, 2007.

Ueberweg, Friedrich. *A History of Philosophy*. 2 vols. New York: C. Scribner's and Sons, 1901.

Warren, Howard C., ed. *Dictionary of Psychology*. Cambridge, MA, 1934.

Watt, W. Montgomery. *Muslim Intellectual: A Study of al-Ghazali*. Edinburgh: Edinburgh University Press, 1963.

Weliur-Rahman, Muʿtazid. "The Psychology of Ibn-i-Sina." *Islamic Culture* 9, no. 2 (April 1935).

Wensinck, A. J. *Concordance et Indices de la Tradition Musulmane*. Leiden: E. J. Brill, 1933–7.

———. *A Handbook of Early Muḥammadan Tradition*. Leiden: E. J. Brill, 1927.

———. *The Muslim Creed*. Cambridge: Cambridge University Press, 1932.

———. *On the Relation between Ghazālī's Cosmology and his Mysticism*. Amsterdam, 1933.

Windelband, Wilhelm. *A History of Philosophy*. Translated by James Tufts. New York: Macmillan, 1907.

Wolfson, Harry A. "The Internal Senses in Latin, Arabic, and Hebrew Philosophic Texts." *The Harvard Theological Review* 28, no. 2 (April 1935).

———. *The Philosophy of Spinoza*. 2 vols. Cambridge, MA: Harvard University Press, 1934.

Yusuf, Hamza, trans. *Purification of the Heart*. Starlatch, 2004.

Zabīdī, Murtaḍā al-. *Itḥāf al-sāda al-muttaqīn*. 10 vols. Cairo: Būlāq, 1311/1893.

———. *Tāj al-ʿarūs*. Cairo, 1306.

Index

G

H

I

J

K

T

Translator's Biography

WALTER JAMES SKELLIE was born in Argyle, New York, on Dec. 20, 1899, the son of Archibald Gow and Elizabeth Hersha Skellie. He attended country school, and graduated from Argyle High School in 1916. His college was Westminster College, New Wilmington, Pa., where he graduated with honor in 1921. He entered Pittsburgh Theological Seminary that fall and received the degree of Th. B. with honor in 1924 and was awarded the Jamieson Scholarship for that year.

In the Church in which he had been reared he was ordained to the ministry of the Gospel for Foreign Missionary service by the Argyle Presbytery of the United Presbyterian Church in May 1924. He served the Egyptian Mission under the Board of Foreign Missions of that Church. From 1924 until 1926 he was located in Cairo for language study, and then he was sent to Alexandria to assist in the work of that city and district.

His first furlough in America was spent at the Kennedy School of Missions in Hartford, where he received the B.A. degree in Islamics in 1930.

Returning to Egypt in September 1930, he was located in Luxor for evangelistic work in that district, with supervision of some schools in the district. This service was rendered in close cooperation with the Egyptian Evangelical Church.

Colophon

Marvels of the Heart is set in Minion Pro, an Adobe typeface designed by Robert Slimbach and released in 2000. Minion Pro is inspired by classical, old style typefaces of the late Renaissance, a period of elegant and highly readable type designs. It combines the aesthetic and functional qualities that make text type highly readable for computerized typesetting needs.

Printed on acid-free, Glatfelter offset 50 # extra bulk off-white paper made by the Glatfelter corporation of York, PA. It provides superior opacity, print clarity, and meets the requirements of ANSI/NISO Z39.48-1992 (Permanence of Paper). It was printed by the Friesens Corporation of Altona, Manitoba, Canada and perfect bound in 10 point full-color cover stock.